Reindustrialization and Technology

Roy Rothwell

Walter Zegveld

M. E. SHARPE, INC.
Armonk, New York

First published in the United States of America in 1985 by
M. E. Sharpe, Inc., 80 Business Park Drive, Armonk, New York 10504

This edition of *Reindustrialization and Technology* is published by
arrangement with Longman Group Limited, London

Library of Congress Cataloging in Publication Data

Rothwell, Roy.
    Reindustrialization and technology.

    Includes bibliographies.
    Includes index.
    1. Technological innovations. 2. Technology.
3. Industrialization. 4. High technology industries.
I. Zegveld, Walter. II. Title.
HD45.R75   1985   338'.06   85-2064
ISBN 0-87332-330-0
ISBN 0-87332-331-9 (pbk.)

Printed in the United States of America

Reindustrialization and Technology

Contents

Acknowledgments

First and foremost, Roy Rothwell would like to thank the Leverhulme Trust Fund for their financial support during the preparation of this book, and Walter Zegveld would like to acknowledge the contribution of the Ministry of Economic Affairs for allowing access to information gathered as part of the Netherlands Technology Policy Project.

Thanks are due to Christopher Freeman of SPRU for his informed comments on several chapters and to all those authors who kindly gave permission for the use of their work in this book.

Thanks are also due to Sally Marjoram and Jeanine van der Voort for their patience and help in preparing the manuscript.

We would like to thank in particular Jan Wielemaker for his significant contribution in bringing together a great deal of useful information and for his informed and critical comments on various chapters.

We are indebted to Brand Bros. & Co. London for permission to reproduce an extract from p.3 *Academic Enterprise, Industrial Innovation and the Development of High Technology Financing in the United States* by Matthew Bullock, 1983.

Finally we would like to thank our wives for their patience and encouragement during the many weekend hours we spent working on the manuscript.

Roy Rothwell
and
Walter Zegveld

CHAPTER ONE

Technology, Industry, Trade and Cycles

It would, perhaps, be sensible to begin this book by posing the question: 'Why are we interested in the combination of reindustrializ- ation and technology?' Implicit in the title is the assumption – and one that we shall attempt to justify in the book – that reindustrialization (and subsequent economic growth) are in some way linked to the emergence of new technological possibilities; that existing industries can in some way be regenerated through radical technological change and that new industries can be created in a similar way. Of course, the formulation and adoption of technology policies to these ends implies in the first case the desirability of reindustrialization, and there are those who would dispute this. A phrase often used during the past decade is 'post-industrial society', and some would argue that the advanced industrial societies should move towards the provision of services, leaving the provision of goods to the newly industrializing nations. We reject this argument, largely on the grounds that services and the goods used in their provision are closely related; that the development of goods and services go hand in hand; that they are complementary, rather than separate, functions; and that future competitiveness will depend largely on the provision of both. Even where services are provided outside the formal economy (in the home) – which, increasingly, appears to be the case – a process defined by Gershuny (1982;1983) as 'social innovation', the (self) provision of such services depends on the availability of a range of manufactured goods.

A second sensible question to ask at the outset is 'What do we mean by reindustrialization?' We would define reindustrialization as 'the structural transformation of industry into higher added value, more knowledge-intensive sectors and product groups, and the creation of major new technology-based industries and products serving new markets'. A good example of the former can be found in the structural shifts in Japanese industry during the past thirty years; an example of the latter is the emergence in the United States in the 1950s and 1960s of a group of new, high-technology industries.

Further we would contend – at least as far as manufacturing industry is concerned – that 'higher added value' is generally synonymous with 'greater technological intensity'. The data in Figure 1.1, which plots the added value ratio against the R&D/sales ratio for twenty-eight industrial sectors in Japan (fiscal year 1978), indicate a positive relationship between the two. If we can take the ratio of R&D to sales as indicating technological intensity, at least to a first approximation, then we can see that value added and technology do indeed go hand in hand.

Finally, this chapter consists of three basic themes. The first of these

Fig 1.1   R&D Investments and Added Value Ratio

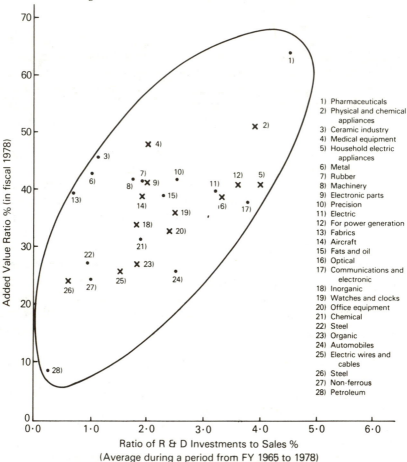

Ratio of R & D Investments to Sales %
(Average during a period from FY 1965 to 1978)

1) Pharmaceuticals
2) Physical and chemical appliances
3) Ceramic industry
4) Medical equipment
5) Household electric appliances
6) Metal
7) Rubber
8) Machinery
9) Electronic parts
10) Precision
11) Electric
12) For power generation
13) Fabrics
14) Aircraft
15) Fats and oil
16) Optical
17) Communications and electronic
18) Inorganic
19) Watches and clocks
20) Office equipment
21) Chemical
22) Steel
23) Organic
24) Automobiles
25) Electric wires and cables
26) Steel
27) Non-ferrous
28) Petroleum

Added value ratio = Added value /shipped product value × 100% (Added value and shipped product value based on industrial statistics)

(Data Sources: Science and Technology Agency Survey Report. Industrial Statistic Table (1978 Industrial Issue); taken from: *Towards New Research and Development*, Agency of Industrial Science and Technology, Ministry of International Trade and Industry, Tokyo, Japan, 9 October 1981) is the issue of technology and international competitiveness, in which we make a number of dynamic comparisons between the US, Japan and Western Europe. The second theme develops the technology/trade argument further with respect to product cycle theories. The third theme concerns economic cycles and new technology systems. In the concluding section we attempt briefly to identify the policy implications of technology-dependent trade, product and economic cycles.

TECHNOLOGY AND THE CURRENT ECONOMIC CRISIS

There are a number of interpretations of the factors underlying the current world economic and unemployment crisis, but perhaps the most widely accepted explanation is the one concerned with the 'oil shock' of 1974 and the subsequent dramatic increases in energy costs. According to this interpretation, because of the considerable increase in the national energy bill in the oil-importing economies, real national disposable incomes have been reduced resulting in a drop in demand for goods and services with accompanying increases in unemployment. Inflation induced by the cost of oil has further reduced effective demand, in turn further increasing unemployment. At the same time wage increases outstripped productivity growth as workers fought to maintain their standards of living, further fuelling both the upward inflationary spiral and the rate at which businesses shed labour. Finally, faced with large and growing budget deficits, many governments began to cut back on public expenditure thereby further reducing the effective level of national demand with accompanying negative employment effects. We thus see the establishment of a series of negative feedback loops creating a downward economic spiral.

Turning now to prescriptions for recovery, there appear to be two dominant contenders: the monetarist prescription and the Keynesian prescription. The first sees the problem as one primarily of inflation caused by too much money in the system chasing too few goods (demand growth outstripping productivity growth). If inflation can be reduced to 'normal' levels, the economy will somehow recover. The second sees the problem essentially as one of demand deficiency. If the level of demand for goods and services is increased, output and employment will both follow suit and, once again, the economy will recover. Clearly both prescriptions cannot simultaneously be correct.

Whilst we would accept that the oil shocks of the 1970s undoubtedly did have a marked and deleterious influence on the world economy in a number of ways, we would contend that they acted mainly to exacerbate an already established trend; that the current recession is part of a longer-term cycle of industrial structural change characterized by the maturing of the 'new' industries of the post-World War II era; and that the products of these industries, now generally rather mature and

3

standardized in form, are suffering from demand saturation. (Rothwell and Zegveld, 1981, Chapters 2 and 3. See our discussion later in this chapter on the Kondratiev waves). Indeed, there are those who would claim that the recessionary trend of the past decade or so is the direct result of a paucity of radical innovations (Mensch, 1979). In short, while 'traditional' macroeconomic policies have their role to play in the economic recovery, a particularly crucial role exists for technology policies. In practice the two should be closely linked. These are essential not only to the regeneration of existing industries and to the creation of new industries but also, as we shall see below, to ensure the international competitiveness of individual nations.

DIFFERENCES BETWEEN THE UNITED STATES, JAPAN, AND WESTERN EUROPE*

One useful way of approaching the question of the relationship between industrial development and technology is to consider some of the significant differences between the United States, Japan and Western Europe concerning their technological and industrial development during the past thirty years or so. In terms of the introduction of new technologies, the overriding impression is that in the United States the new postwar, technology-based leading sectors come into being sooner and grew more rapidly than elsewhere. In Western European industry, with some exceptions, the strategy mostly seems to be that of a 'follower', at least as far as commercialization is concerned. In Japan, the strategy clearly has been one of rapid 'catching-up' based on the adoption and adaption of foreign technology, coupled to highly efficient and quality-orientated mass production.

In order to support this impression, a number of economic and technological indicators will be used below to illustrate the differences between these countries. Among other things, substantial shifts in international trade have taken place during the past twenty years or so, particularly in the area of high-technology goods. In general economic development since World War II has shown rapid growth in Japan and a number of Western European countries, while the development within the United States has been much slower, although still at a relatively high level. An initial illustration of trade shifts between a number of economic blocs is given in Table 1.1, which shows the shares of total exports in international trade between 1963 and 1980 of six major trading blocs or countries.

The figures demonstrate that, after rising from 41.5 per cent to 45.0 per cent in the period 1963–73, Western Europe's share in international

*Based on J. Hagerdoon, *Technology and Economics*, paper presented at the Conference on Technology and Economic Development, The Hague, 1983.

Table 1.1 Shares in world exports, 1963–1980 (in % of total)

	1963	1968	1973	1980
Total world trade (in milliards of $)	155	238	574	1973
Total, of which	100	100	100	100
EC (9 countries	33.8	34.6	36.6	33.3
(of which intra-EC trade)	(15.2)	(16.4)	(19.3)	(17.6)
Other West European countries	7.7	8.0	8.4	7.7
United States	13.4	14.6	11.9	10.6
Japan	3.4	5.6	6.4	6.6
Comecon	12.1	11.3	10.0	9.0
Developing countries	20.6	18.4	19.2	27.5
including newly industrialized countries.				

(*Source*: GATT, International Trade)

trade subsequently dropped to 41 per cent in 1980. The United States' share dropped to 10.6 per cent in 1980, after a slight increase in the 1960s. Striking features of these data are the gradual rise in Japan's share from 3.4 per cent in 1963 to 6.6 per cent in 1980 and the increasing share gained by the newly industrializing countries.

The differences between the United States, Japan and Western Europe (EEC) become clearer, moreover, if we look on a lower level of aggregation, in other words at the export figures for each product group separately. While it can be seen from Table 1.2 that the EEC is the largest exporter in the OECD, Japan nevertheless proves to have achieved a greater increase in its share in the period 1973–1980. The figures show, furthermore, that while Japan occupies a relatively weak position in the product groups (grouping I) relating to agricultural products and raw materials, in other product groups where there is greater emphasis on industrial articles and goods, Japan's position shifts considerably towards greater export shares.

In the manufactured products group the respective OECD export shares of the EEC, the US and Japan are 38.6 per cent, 22.3 per cent and 19 per cent. However, in the period 1973-80, Japan achieved a considerable improvement of 2.6 per cent, while during the same period the EEC's share dropped 0.4 per cent. This improvement in Japan's position is even more pronounced in the machinery, equipment and transportation grouping of manufactured products (grouping III, by far the largest of the manufacturing groupings). While it is true that the US and the EEC account for the greater part of total exports in most of these product groups, Japan has been able to improve its share considerably in almost all the product groups in this category. The US share, and to an even larger degree that of the EEC, fell in a number of product groups over the period 1973–80. In the last category of product groups (grouping IV), which are primarily basic consumer goods, eg textiles, leather, etc, the EEC's position is dominant. The decline in Japan's share in the period 1973–80 in OECD trade in these 'traditional', low-technology groups is marked. It can also be seen that in the 1970s Japan

Table 1.2 Changes in shares of OECD exports 1973–80

	OECD exports* in 1980 billion US $	%	Shares of OECD exports* in 1980			Changes 1973–80		
			Japan	USA %	EEC*	Japan percentage	USA points	EEC* difference
Total Products	852		15.3	25.1	37.2	2.25	0.09	1.82
I Food, beverages, tobacco	75		2.3	42.8	33.3	−0.6	−1.1	7.6
Agricultural products	27	21.5	0.7	55.8	9.4	−0.1	6.5	−0.8
Mineral fuels	41		1.2	19.4	47.5	0.3	−1.4	11.2
Metals unworked	18		4.1	33.1	13.1	2.5	13.1	2.6
Other raw materials	22		1.0	16.3	40.0	−0.5	0.9	5.7
Manufactured products of which:	668		19.0	22.3	38.6	2.6	0.8	−0.4
II Non-met. min. products	31		13.0	18.2	44.4	0.9	2.9	−2.1
Iron and steel	46		34.2	7.5	38.0	2.2	−0.4	−3.6
Metal products	22	20.8	15.7	16.1	44.5	−0.0	−0.9	2.8
Basic materials	45		9.0	28.8	44.4	0.9	3.3	−1.8
Chemical products	24		4.8	25.1	47.5	0.5	2.2	−1.2
III Agricultural machinery	9		10.3	34.8	39.7	3.4	−2.7	−0.5
Electrical machinery	40		22.3	23.0	40.1	7.7	−3.8	−2.0
Power gen. machinery	20		17.1	27.5	40.9	3.8	−0.1	−4.4
Other machinery	90	42.0	13.3	23.9	45.4	4.2	0.2	−4.0
Office and telecom. equipment	42		34.6	27.2	25.7	2.1	2.6	−1.4
Optical, clock, photo	31		24.4	26.6	30.8	7.5	0.2	−3.6
Road vehicles	89		32.5	16.4	32.7	14.8	−5.0	−4.7
Other transport equipment	37		14.6	43.2	33.8	−9.5	11.8	−9.0
IV Textiles	24		22.0	15.2	39.9	−1.2	4.2	−3.2
Clothing	9		3.7	12.1	48.1	−7.0	4.5	3.7
Leather, shoes	8		4.9	9.7	51.3	−1.8	3.3	−0.0
Paper	32	16.7	3.5	19.0	16.3	0.5	2.9	0.9
Wood furniture	9		3.3	12.7	41.3	−2.8	−1.3	11.8
Plastic, rubber	31		15.1	20.7	47.5	−0.9	−0.4	0.2
Other manuf. products	30		14.7	29.4	45.1	−1.4	−3.8	6.1

* Not including intra-Community trade
(*Source: EEC, The Competitiveness of European Community Industry*, March 1982, p 10)

Table 1.3 Specialization coefficients EEC, US and Japan, 1963, 1973, 1980

	Community*			USA			Japan		
	1963	1973	1980	1963	1973	1980	1963	1973	1980
Iron and steel	0.99	1.01	0.96	0.42	0.35	0.3	1.72	1.85	1.75
Metal products	1.08	0.99	1.11	0.84	0.74	0.70	1.06	0.89	0.80
Basic chemicals	0.99	1.12	1.08	1.05	1.13	1.22	0.60	1.57	0.44
Chemical products	1.21	1.25	1.23	1.14	1.07	1.14	0.38	0.26	0.25
Agricultural machinery	0.80	1.03	1.10	1.83	1.74	1.69	0.07	0.42	0.58
Electrical machinery	1.16	1.06	1.06	1.03	1.24	1.07	0.75	0.88	1.20
Power generating machinery	1.15	1.03	1.15	1.20	1.43	1.35	0.52	0.89	0.98
Other machinery	1.07	1.32	1.27	1.24	1.16	1.17	0.39	0.57	0.75
Office, telecommunications equipment	0.95	0.74	0.71	1.31	1.23	1.32	1.55	2.12	1.96
Optical clock, photo	0.78	0.93	0.84	1.11	1.30	1.27	0.95	1.09	1.36
Road vehicles	1.31	0.96	0.84	1.00	1.00	0.73	0.47	1.08	1.69
Other transport equipment	0.78	0.77	1.04	1.43	1.79	2.33	1.32	1.78	0.91
Textiles	0.94	0.95	0.87	0.43	0.44	0.58	2.47	1.22	0.98
Clothing	0.99	0.79	0.83	0.27	0.25	0.37	2.05	0.45	0.13
Shoes	1.05	1.16	1.06	0.38	0.27	0.35	1.22	0.36	0.21
Paper	0.51	0.55	0.56	0.80	0.79	0.76	0.35	0.25	0.24
Wood, furniture	0.65	0.62	0.84	0.45	0.54	0.45	1.64	0.30	0.14
Plastic, rubber	0.98	1.01	1.03	1.11	0.82	0.79	0.90	0.81	0.67
Other manufactured goods	0.86	1.03	1.22	1.82	1.68	1.39	1.07	1.06	0.81
Total manufacturers	1.00	1.00	1.00	1.00	1.00	1.00	1.00	1.00	1.00

* Extra-EC trade
(*Source*: EEC, 1982, p 18)

improved its position in the technically more advanced groups of machinery and equipment manufacturing and, most notably, in road vehicles. Indeed, while between 1962 and 1977 the US share in OECD exports in technologically intensive manufactured goods declined from 28.3 per cent to 18.9 per cent, the share enjoyed by Japan increased from 4.2 per cent to 16.1 per cent (Aho and Rosen, 1980).

Another way of approaching the differences in trading patterns, and one which has become generally accepted, is by using the so-called 'export specialization coefficient'. This has some methodological shortcomings, in particular if it is used for a comparison between large economic blocs, but nevertheless gives some indication of changes in specialization. The export specialization coefficient refers to the relationship between the export share of a given sector in the total exports of a country or group of countries and the corresponding figure for a control group. The formula is:

$$S_{jk} = \frac{X_{jk}}{X_{jt}} : \frac{X_{nk}}{X_{nt}}$$

where X = exports
j = the exporting country
n = the control group
k = the sector or the product category
t = the total products of the industry

(See:EEC, The Development of Industrial Sector Structures in Europe Since the Oil Crisis, Brussels 1979.) Table 1.3 shows the export specialization coefficients for the EEC, the USA and Japan in the years 1963, 1973 and 1980; the control group is made up of the combined OECD countries. The figures therefore indicate the extent to which the exports of the three separate blocs depart from the trend in the OECD as a whole.

Since the figures in Table 1.3 largely speak for themselves, we shall only remark that the EEC has apparently only been partially successful in increasing its specialization in trade in products in grouping III. This would also seem to be true of the United States, although to a lesser extent. Japan has been able dramatically to improve its position in the equipment sector in the past few years. The table also shows that as early as the 1960s Japan had reduced its specialization in traditional product groups like textiles and clothing. Patterns of trade specialization today for Japan, the US and West Germany are shown graphically in Figure 1.2, which confirms the pattern suggested in Table 1.3 (*Economist*, 9 July 1983).

In the foregoing, trends in international trade have been outlined and the degree to which Japan, the US and the EEC have developed in this respect has been explored. We will now take a closer look at the role which technology and the production of high-technology goods have played in the development of the three blocs. In Table 1.4 we again give specialization coefficients, but this time for the category, high-tech-

Figure 1.2   Trade Specialization: Japan, US and West Germany

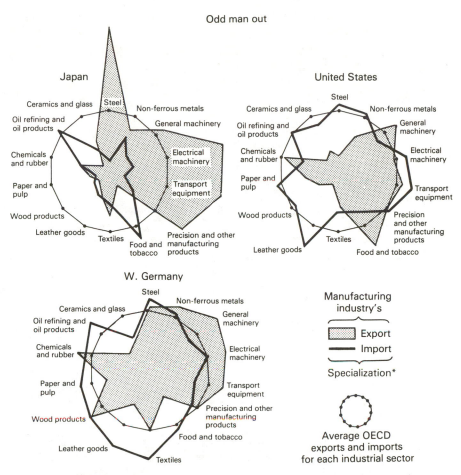

*Export (import) specialization (i.e. relative share) = share of product group in country's exports (imports) relative to product group's share in total OECD exports (imports)

(*Source*: OECD, MITI. Taken from: *The Economist* 8 July 1983)

nology products. From this it can clearly be seen that the EEC's position worsened in the years 1963–80. Next to the EEC the US also shows a decline, but to a lesser extent. Japan, on the other hand, dramatically improved its position with respect to high-technology products; this resulted in a rise in the specialization coefficient from 0.56 in 1963 to 1.41 in 1980.

A further indication of changes in patterns of trade is the ratio of exports to imports in a particular commodity class (assuming, of course, that there are no differences in trade barriers between nations), and Figure 1.3 plots this ratio for the US, Japan and three major 'technology-rich' countries of the EEC, for technology-intensive goods.

Table 1.4   Specialization coefficients for high-technology goods

	1963	1970	1980
EEC	1.02	0.94	0.88
USA	1.29	1.27	1.20
Japan	0.56	0.87	1.41

Control group: Total world trade in industrial products.

(*Source*: EEC, 1982, p 19)

Figure 1.3:   Exports relative to imports for technology-intensive goods for selected OECD countries

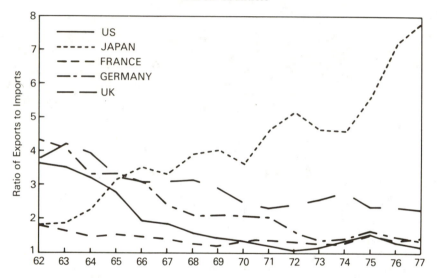

Prepared by ILAB/OFER with OECD Trade Series C data
(*Source*: AHO AND ROSEN, 1980)

The most significant finding displayed in Figure 1.3 is the large increase in the ratio for Japan from less than two in 1962 to almost eight in 1977. On the other hand, the other four 'technology-rich' countries exhibited a faster growth of imports than exports of technology-intensive products over the same period.

The US ratio of exports to imports in the technology-intensive commodities declined precipitously during the 1960s, falling from 3.63 in 1962 to 1.34 in 1970. In 1977 the ratio was 1.18. The depreciation of the dollar appears to have halted this rapid deterioration, but it has not reversed the decline. The United Kingdom's ratio continued to deteriorate after 1970 even though the pound depreciated. France's and Germany's ratios remained largely unchanged between 1970 and 1977 (Aho and Rosen, 1980, pp.40 and 43).

The data presented in Figure 1.3 and in Tables 1.2, 1.3 and 1.4 might be taken to indicate a significant shift in patterns of international trade during the past twenty or so years. That is, the dominant position of the US in technology-intensive trade has eroded significantly, while that of

Japan has undergone marked improvement. In the case of the EEC there has been some erosion, but not so great as with the US.

Table 1.5 Receipts and Expenditures on patents, invention, processes, copyrights, and related items by selected industrial countries (Millions DM)

Country		1972	1976	1978	1980
Austria	Receipts	23	50	57	66
	Payments	122	217	238	279
	Balance	−99	−167	−1801	−213
Belgium and	Receipts	483	261	292	336
Luxembourg[a]	Payments	682	491	578	826
	Balance	−199	−227	−286	−490
France	Receipts	277	492	698	902
	Payments	904	1472	1364	1866
	Balance	−627	−980	−666	−964
Germany, Federal	Receipts	674	765	922	1101
Republic of	Payments	1574	2029	2387	2624
	Balance	−900	−1264	−1465	−1523
Italy[b]	Receipts	291	201	206	1565[a]
	Payments	1295	808	1001	2365[a]
	Balance	−1004	−607	−795	−800[a]
Japan[b]	Receipts	223	441	564	643
	Payments	1741	2014	2348	2411
	Balance	−1518	−1573	−1784	−1768
Netherlands	Receipts	329	526	585	760
	Payments	490	892	894	1166
	Balance	−161	−366	−309	−406
Sweden	Receipts	66	145	143	168
	Payments	199	346	289	400
	Balance	−133	−201	−146	−232
Switzerland[c]	Receipts	3024	4876	5511	
	Payments	794	1370	1536	
	Balance	2230	3506	3975	
United Kingdom[b]	Receipts	1079	1515	1772	2185
	Payments	978	1203	1402	1681
	Balance	101	312	370	504
United States[d]	Receipts	8833	10,991	11,791	12,698
	Payments	938	1213	1225	1375
	Balance	7895	9778	10,566	11,323

(*Source*: Monthly Reports of the Deutsche Bundesbank; taken from Horn, 1983)

a = including film business; b = excluding film business and copyrights; c = including working expenses, bank commissions, film business, etc; d = including film business, management fees, etc.

It is not, of course, technology per se that affords a nation its competitive advantage in world markets, but rather the ability of companies in that nation effectively to translate national technological advantages into marketable goods. The data we have presented so far relate more to the embodiment of technology in goods rather than to the technology itself. There does exist, however, a set of data which concerns trade in technological know-how rather than in technology-embodying goods: these are the statistics on international flows of patents, inventions, processes and copyrights, and Table 1.5 presents data on receipts and expenditures on technical know-how for eleven advanced market economies during the period 1972 to 1980 (Horn, 1983). (A different time series, 1965 to 1967, is presented by Peck and Goto (1981) for Japan, West Germany, France, the UK and the US.)

The data in Table 1.5 shows some interesting differences between countries. As we might expect, most of the smaller countries (Austria, Belgium, Luxembourg, the Netherlands and Sweden) have a consistently negative balance of know-how trade. The United States, in contrast, has a consistently positive trade balance as does the UK, but at a very much lower level than the US. Italy and France, but much more notably West Germany and Japan, have negative know-how trade balances throughout the period.

It is striking that West Germany and Japan, the two most economically advanced nations after the US, both show a considerable deficit on the technology trade balance. According to Peck and Goto (1981), Japan's deficit appears to result solely from its trade with the US. While statistical data of this kind provide an indication of technological and scientific dominance, most notably in the case of the United States, the fact that a country is a net importer of technology does not mean necessarily that there is a restraining effect on its economic development. This is, of course, best exemplified in the case of Japan, but also with West Germany:

Furthermore, and contrary to expectations based on misguided interpretations of the technology balance of payments, the West German economy has so far performed reasonably well in trade in technology intensive products (Kronstein, 1967). In itself, the deficit in payments on patents, inventions and processes hardly gives rise to worry about international competitiveness. Other industrial countries, for which the patents and licences account seems to look more favourable, do not necessarily exhibit superior performance in international competition, be it in trade in general or in 'high technology' products trade (Horn, 1983, p 103).

Figure 1.4 shows a variety of indicators of the technological potential of a number of countries. This figure strikingly demonstrates that both the US and the UK show a decline in the second half of the 1970s, compared with the latter half of the 1960s, on all the indicators presented. France, on the other hand, shows an increase on indicators like the export of technology, trade in technology and the export of technology-intensive products. In West Germany there appears to have been only a moderate change in the 1970s, in comparison with the 1960s, with the exception of expenditure on research, which has doubled. Japan shows a remarkable increase, a doubling on almost all indicators.

Figure 1.4   Indicators of technological potential in the 1960s and 1970s

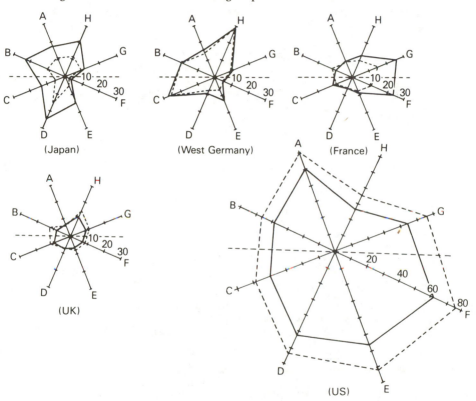

Notes: 1) ----- in latter half of 1960s; ——— in latter half of 1970s
2) A: Total added value in manufacturing
B: Number of patents registered
C: Number of patents registered overseas
D: Number of researchers
E: Research expenditure
F: Exports of technology
G: Trade in technology
H: Exports of technology-intensive products

(*Source*: Science and Technology Agency, White Paper on Science and Technology in Japan, Tokyo, July 1981)

These data might be taken to support our contention earlier that the dominant technological position of the US has eroded during the past decade or so. Indeed, this was one of the messages emerging from the results of a recent OECD workshop on Patent and Innovation Statistics (Paris, 28–30 June 1982) and Figure 1.5, which shows external patent applications by US and Japanese firms during the period 1956 to 1977, was taken to confirm this view. It can be seen that while US firms' external patent applications peaked in 1968 and declined thereafter, Japan's external applications show strong growth through most of the period (OECD, 1983).

Figure 1.5   External Patent applications: selected OECD member countries

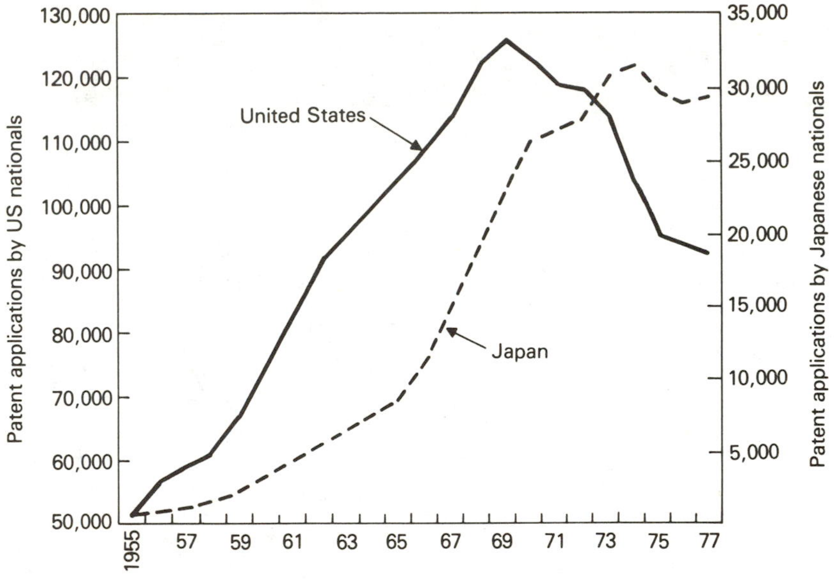

(Taken from: OECD, 1983)

This more recent strong growth by Japan has been highlighted by Vickery (1980). While the data in Table 1.5 are cumulative, Vickery has analysed new technology agreements and shown that, in these areas, Japan has become a net exporter of technology:

Japan regularly publishes data in which 'new programmes' for technology export and import are distinguished from 'continued programmes' both by number and value. This allows a detailed comparison between production of new technology in Japan and the total technological requirements of Japanese industry.

It is clear . . . that by 1972 Japan already had a positive overall balance on new agreements (exports/imports greater than 1) even though the balance on con-

14

tinued agreements was, and remains, negative. This situation applied to the total of all manufacturing industry, and the new agreements were in surplus for the chemical industry and temporarily for electrical machinery. By 1977 the chemical, iron and steel, and non-electrical machinery industries were in surplus on new agreements and the iron and steel industry had been in overall surplus since 1974. The total balance was still in deficit because of the accumulated effects of past agreements. However, the deficit was improving rapidly as the surpluses of recent years accumulated.

The data clearly suggest the strength of Japan as a net producer of new, commercially valued technology by the early 1970s, despite an *overall* deficit of technological payments that has continued to the present (Vickery, 1980 p 8 and 9).

It is worth adding here that during the 1960s the number of patents granted in the US to residents in Japan increased more than tenfold from 232 to 2720; by 1976 Japan was being granted twice as many patents in the US as was the UK.

Although the differences between Japan, the United States and Western Europe can be illustrated fairly simply on the basis of statistical material, this does not mean that these differences in technological and economic development are easy to explain. Too many factors – cultural, social, managerial and economic – are involved. Moreover, a factor which appears to have a positive influence on technological develop-ment within the social context of one economic bloc or country may have a negative effect in another bloc or country. For example, the lack of worker-mobility in Western Europe may be contrasted with the large mobility in the United States which, again in contrast with Europe, has resulted in a great deal of 'spin-off' entrepreneurship in the USA. One of the most striking characteristics of the social structure in Japan, on the other hand, is the great immobility of the labour force in large firms. This fact does not seem to have any negative effects on the acceptance of new technologies in that country. On the contrary, Japanese workers in larger firms, with life-employment expectations, have little to fear and much to gain from the acceptance of new technology. Any explanations of the differences between Japan, the United States and Western Europe must therefore be highly speculative. Possible or partial explanations of the differences that have developed between Japan, the United States and Western Europe will now briefly be summed up.

In their attempt to analyse differences in technological developments in Japan and the United States, Peck and Goto point to difference in R&D efforts in the 1960s. During this period the policy of the Japanese government was aimed at discouraging direct investment by (American) multinationals and stimulating technological agreements between these corporations and Japanese firms. This created a situation in Japan of a growing R&D effort and large-scale import of technological knowledge. Research work in Japan in the 1960s was consciously direc-ted towards cost cutting and product improvement. In America much more emphasis was placed on the development of 'major new products'. By the 1970s, however, a certain degree of convergence had taken place (Peck and Goto, 1981). Referring to the general background to this problem area, Colombo (1977) has pointed out in a number of publications the major differences between Japan, the United States and Western Europe. Paraphrased and reproduced in tabular form, these differences can be expressed as follows in Table 1.6.

Table 1.6   Differences between Japan, United States and Western Europe

Japan	United States	Western Europe
strictly coordinated export policy	'market-pulled' innovation	long tradition of scientific research
politico-economic infrastructure with interweaving of state, banks and industry	great personal mobility and competitiveness. Many new technology based firms formed	lack of entrepreneurship and the formation of new technology based firms
aggressive industrial policy, long-term public and private sector strategies	legislation and education directed towards entrepreneurship	emphasis on supporting traditional sectors
coordinated policy towards the acquisition of technology	support for strategic sectors in connection with position as a superpower (defence, aerospace)	relative weakness in product development and marketing. Lag in the commercial exploitation of new technologies
strong emphasis on efficient massproduction and on total quality control	rapid growth of new industrial sectors based on radical technologies	
home market which demands innovation	high availability of venture capital	paucity of venture capital
	large home market which demands innovation	

Colombo stresses that:

In Europe, laws and public attitudes have not favoured lively and diffused competition, but rather permitted the formation of monopolistic or oligopolistic situations in several industrial sectors. Similarly, industrial cartels of a defensive character and therefore substantially non-innovative have been formed contrary to what takes place in the Japanese industrial and trading concentrations, whose function is, instead, directed towards attack abroad (Colombo, 1977, p 515).

Among the other factors which may have led to a 'follower' strategy in European industry are: the segmented and regionalized market structure in Europe; the defensive nature of industrial policy, which has meant that major emphasis has been placed on supporting unprofitable companies; the relative failure to direct research in the universities to industrial development.

It can be concluded that the problems in the relationship between industrial development and technology in industrialized countries can usefully be viewed against the background of the differences we have highlighted between the US, Western Europe and Japan.

TECHNOLOGY POLICY AND THE THEORY OF CYCLES

Perhaps a useful way of tackling the issue of technology policy is through consideration of cycles in economic and industrial activity and in particular of the role that technological change is seen to play in the formation of such cycles. Much of the discussion in modern economics has centred around explaining fluctuations in economic activity, and empirical data on such measures as GNP, industrial output and investment suggest that economic activity does not progress smoothly; that economic growth is not a unidirectional process, but rather one characterized by 'upturns' and 'downturns' of varying lengths and amplitudes. Perhaps the best known, and least contentious, of these cycles is the normal business or investment cycle (sometimes known as the Jugular – average length, seven to eleven years). Other economists have also distinguished the Kitchin, or inventory cycle (average length, three to five years) (van Duijn, 1983).

The product cycle

A concept often utilized by both economists and businessmen is that of the product life cycle. This is illustrated in Figure 1.6(a) which shows the conceptualized variation over time in the volume of sales of a single new product. Initially, during the period of introduction, the level of sales is low and increases only slowly. The product itself, initially imperfectly adapted to users' needs, passes through a period of adaptation and improvement. At the same time users are themselves gaining greater expertise in its use and so confidence in the performance of the product increases. As information concerning the benefits conferred by the product spreads, levels of production increase and the product undergoes further design improvements, the number of users begins to increase rapidly and the product enters its growth phase. Eventually, during the maturity phase, demand levels off and the market becomes progressively more saturated. This eventually leads to a fall in demand and sales begin to decline.

There is no reason, of course, for companies to accept the inevitability of this pattern and positive action can be taken to stave off the decline. For example, major subsequent innovations might act to regenerate demand. The electric light industry, for instance, achieved a series of such partial reversals from a state of saturation with the introduction of

17

Figure 1.6(a)   The product life cycle: four-phase model

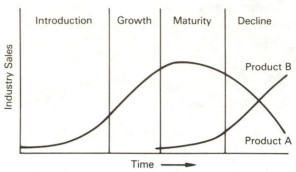

Figure 1.6(b)   Variations to the simple life-cycle pattern

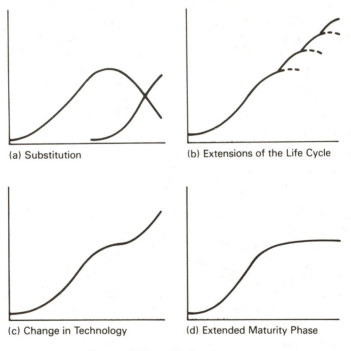

(a) Substitution

(b) Extensions of the Life Cycle

(c) Change in Technology

(d) Extended Maturity Phase

(*Source*: J. J. van Duijn, 1983)

the fluorescent lamp in 1938 and the halogen lamp in 1959 (Haustein, 1980). Alternatively, the firm might initiate a programme of product improvements or extensions to stretch the product cycle or to create a 'family' of products having a range of characteristics, in order to broaden the product's appeal. Ford UK, for example, achieved this with their Cortina model, producing a family of cars of varying performance, enabling it to maintain a relatively high market share for something like twenty years. This contrasted sharply with British Leyland's 1100/1300 series which failed to develop sufficiently to prevent a declining market share and shorter product life (Rothwell and Gardiner, 1982). Finally, innovations in manufacturing procedures and processes might considerably reduce the unit cost of the product, thus making it accessible to a progressively wider range of customers and thereby effectively lengthening its life. This occurred in the case of black and white television which, although superseded by colour television, became progressively cheaper, thus reaching greater numbers of low-income consumers (Figure 1.6(b)).

An alternative – or perhaps even a parallel – strategy to the extension of product life is the phased introduction of new products such that when the original product enters saturation and decline the new product is beginning its growth phase. This would imply the need for rational and carefully planned product development strategies in order to avoid problems of over- or undercapacity, cash flow problems and so on.

A second cyclical model that relates to the product life cycle, but which is more technologically specific, has been developed by Abernathy and Utterback (1978); this is illustrated in Figure 1.7. Here, rather than dealing necessarily with a single product, the authors' unit of analysis is a 'productive unit'.

For a simple firm or a firm devoted to a single product, the productive unit and the firm would be the same thing. In the case of a diversified firm, a productive unit would usually report to a single operating manager and normally be a separate operating division. The extreme of a highly fragmented production process would mean that several separate firms taken together would be a productive unit (Abernathy and Utterback, 1978).

According to this model, as a major new class of product emerges, the emphasis of technological development shifts from one of major product innovation to one of process innovation and minor product improvement. In the early stages, production is associated with small, dynamic and flexible units, often new small firms. As the technology matures and the unit shifts towards large-scale production, the production system becomes increasingly 'specific', ie geared towards the efficient production of a well-defined product, and, as a consequence, it becomes increasingly 'rigid', ie less flexible and able to accommodate product changes. The dominant ethos of the firm is centred on the manufacturing process, and management skills are predominantly suited to the efficient production of the now 'dominant design' rather than the creation of major new products that might form the basis of a new productive unit.

The product cycle and the product/process cycle of Abernathy and Utterback do, of course, have clear implications for the competitive strategies of industrial companies. Both imply that competitiveness is linked, in the first instance, to market-oriented product innovation, and that continued competitiveness and sales are linked to continuous innovations affecting both product performance and manufacturing pro-

19

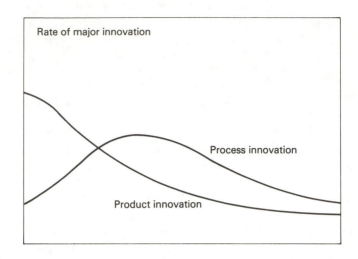

	Fluid pattern	Transitional pattern	Specific pattern
Competitive emphasis on	Functional product performance	Product variation	Cost reduction
Innovation stimulated by	Information on users' needs and users' technical inputs	Opportunities created by expanding internal technical capability	Pressure to reduce cost and improve quality
Predominant type of innovation	Frequent major changes in products	Major process changes required by rising volume	Incremental for product and process, with cumulative improvement in productivity and quality
Product line	Diverse, often including custom designs	Includes at least one product design stable enough to have significant production volume	Mostly undifferentiated standard products
Production processes	Flexible and inefficient; major changes easily accommodated	Becoming more rigid, with changes occurring in major steps	Efficient, capital-intensive, and rigid; cost of change is high
Equipment	General-purpose, requiring highly skilled labour	Some subprocesses automated, creating "islands of automation"	Special-purpose, mostly automatic with labour tasks mainly monitoring and control
Materials	Inputs are limited to generally-available materials	Specialized materials may be demanded from some suppliers	Specialized materials will be demanded; if not available, vertical integration will be extensive
Plant	Small-scale, located near user or source of technology	General-purpose with specialized sections	Large-scale, highly specific to particular products
Organizational control is	Informal and entrepreneurial	Through liaison relationships, project and task groups	Through emphasis on structure, goals, and rules

Figure 1.7   The changing character of innovation, and its changing role in corporate advance. Seeking to understand the variables that determine successful strategies for innovation, the authors focus on three stages in the evolution of a successful enterprise: its period of flexibility, in which the enterprise seeks to capitalize on its advantages where they offer greatest advantages, its intermediate years, in which major products are used more widely: and its full maturity, when prosperity is assured by leadership in several principal products and technologies.
(*Source*: Abernathy and Utterback, 1978)

cess efficiency. Eventually, of course, all products exhibit a tendency towards obsolescence and competitiveness will then depend on the introduction of wholly new products or on *major* shifts in the characteristics and performance of existing products through radical innovation. Sooner or later the firm might be compelled to shift to the use of different technologies (technological diversification), or to new market areas, or both. The available evidence suggests that successful 'endogenous' product diversification by firms is generally into areas that relate to the firm's core technological expertise, although firms might move to completely new areas through acquisition (Peters and Waterman, 1982).

Process technologies developed by firms in-house will also generally follow a cyclical pattern of development, with the initial major innovation-analogous to a new product – being followed by a series of improvement innovations. For both products and processes, of course, 'reversals' can occur in which the rate and/or direction of technological change alters rapidly in response to changing technological or economic needs, threats and opportunities. A good illustrative example is the recent spate of product-oriented innovations currently taking place in the automobile (a 'mature' product) yielding a safer, more energy efficient and less pollutive car. In this instance, the rate of manufacturing process innovations has also increased. Finally, it is possible to visualize situations where product innovations increase while process innovations decrease, which would yield a 'butterfly' shaped product/ process innovation curve.

Technology and trade cycles

Another aspect of economics that incorporates both a role for technological change and a measure of cyclicity, and one that we can relate to our discussion of product cycles, is trade theory. In this respect we can point to the so-called 'neo-technology' theories of trade in manufactured goods. The first of these, the Technology-Gap model, was proposed by Posner (1961). According to this theory, comparative advantage is determined by product innovation in response to perceived market demand. This leads to sales at home and abroad and to the rapid exploitation of both static and dynamic scale economies. Imitators enter at a disadvantage because of teething problems and the time involved in production learning and achieving scale economies. In the meantime, scale economies-enjoyed by the innovator offer him a continued price advantage and generally prolong the life and increase the volume of technology-gap exports.

The second neo-technology theory (an extension of the first) was developed by Hirsch (1965) and Vernon (1966) in an attempt to explain US trading behaviour. This is the Product Cycle theory. Essentially it argues that the location of production depends more on the characteristics of production at different stages of the product's lifetime rather than on the degree to which competitors succeed in imitating new products. The product cycle, according to Hirsch, is summarized in Table 1.7. Briefly, this theory argues that in the early phases of the product cycle a great deal of product and production process innovation takes place which requires risk capital, entrepreneurship and the presence of high level scientific, engineering and marketing skills. Product performance is the dominant factor determining competitiveness. Eventually, product characteristics become quite standardized, albeit with some product differentiation, economies of scale increase in importance and, as competition increases, price becomes a key factor in competitiveness. The advantages of meeting export demand for mature

Table 1.7 Characteristics of product cycle

Characteristics	Product-Cycle Phase		
	Early	*Growth*	*Mature*
Technology	Short runs Rapidly changing techniques Dependence on external economies	Mass production methods gradually introduced Variations in techniques still frequent	Long runs and stable technology Few innovations of importance
Capital density	Low	High, due to high obsolescence rate	High, due to large quantity of specialized equipment
Industry structure	Entry is know-how determined Numerous firms providing specialized services	Growing number of firms Many casualties and mergers. Growing vertical integration	Financial resources for entry, high Number of firms, small
Critical human inputs	Scientific and engineering	Management	Unskilled and semi-skilled labour
Demand structure	Seller's market Performance and price of substitute determine buyers' expectations	Individual producers face growing price elasticity Intra-industry competition reduces prices Product information spreading	Buyers' market Information easily available

(*Source*: Hirsch, 1965)

products from the home industry decrease and production is shifted abroad. The innovating country then becomes a net importer.

An advantage of the product cycle theory is that it satisfactorily explains the so-called Leontief paradox. According to the Heckscher–Ohlin theory of trade, US exports should, in general, be more capital intensive than US imports (because the US is relatively abundant in capital). In 1953, however, Leontief demonstrated that US exports were more labour-intensive than US imports. A partial explanation for this is that, relative to other countries, the US is well endowed with skilled labour and that US exports are 'skilled-labour intensive' while US production of import-competing goods is 'unskilled-labour-intensive'. According to product cycle theory, which is characterized by a shift from labour intensity to relative capital intensity, the US exports the products at a skilled-labour-intensive stage of production and imports them when the stage of production becomes relatively capital intensive, thus resolving Leontief's paradox.

Walker (1979), on the basis of a number of rigorous tests, has suggested a reasonable degree of confirmation of the technology gap theory. He did, however, suggest a number of important shortcomings, most notably a rather naive view of the mechanisms behind the transfer of production from one country to another, ie imitation was over-emphasized and monopoly powers and capital mobility were under-emphasized. Walker then proceeded to test the more detailed product cycle theory for textile machinery, chemicals and consumer electronics. While textile machinery was a 'non-conformist', chemicals and consumer electronics largely conformed with this theory.

On the basis of data for a single branch of industry, agricultural implements, Rothwell (1981) concluded that

... market leaders in Europe are nationally owned, home-based companies. Most of these companies have been in existence for thirty years and more, and there is little evidence of any shift in production facilities 'off-shore'. It seems that where maintaining competitiveness depends on the continual improvement of product performance, and where there is no marked convergence towards a 'standard' model, product-cycle theories of international trade do not apply. Little advantage – except perhaps a reduction in production and foreign distribution costs – is to be gained from shifting the main operation to a low labour cost country. Rather, the advantage lies in maintaining production at centres of technical expertise and in contact with local markets demanding innovative products.

Agricultural implements trade approximates more to the technology-gap model. Because the dominant manufacturing mode is one of batch production, dynamic production economies are rather more important than scale economies. As a result, close and continuous interaction between product development and design personnel and those involved in production planning and design, was seen to be a significant factor in ... [competitive] success ...

Further, in his detailed case study of the plastics industry, Freeman (1963) also emphasizes the importance of technological leadership to competitiveness: 'Technical progress results in leadership in production in this industry, because patents and commercial secrecy together can give the innovator a head start of as much as 10–15 years.'

In a more general test, Soete (1979) attempted to establish a relationship, in a statistically rigorous way, between technical change and export competitiveness in manufactured goods. He regressed exports per head of forty industries in 1974 against cumulative US-registered patents per head for the period 1963–76 for all OECD countries (excluding Iceland, New Zealand and, of necessity, the United States because the patenting data were available only for *foreign* countries registering patents in the US. (see Pavitt and Soete, 1980).). The results of this analysis are shown in Table 1.8. It can be seen that for most capital goods industries, where technical change is relatively strong,

Table 1.8   Inter-country regression results for 40 SIC industries (1974)

Industry	United States SIC	t-value b coefficient	R^2	(United States) Applied R&D/ value added
*(1) Significant results**				
Drugs	283	12.12	0.89	9.05
Special industrial machinery	355	12.13	0.89	1.33[a]
Metalworking machinery	354	11.99	0.88	1.00
Engines and turbines	351	8.40	0.79	11.07
Instruments	88	8.24	0.78	7.65
Electrical transmission and distribution equipment	361, 3825	7.88	0.77	8.23
Ordnance, guided missiles	348, 376, 3745	7.50	0.76	43.48
Electrical industrial apparatus	362	7.30	0.74	6.18
Industrial inorganic chemicals	286	5.86	0.65	3.08[b]
Office and computing machinery	357	5.42	0.61	18.79
Communications and electronics equipment	366, 367	4.49	0.52	22.45
Aircraft	372	4.34	0.51	19.13
Electrical lighting, electrical equipment	364	4.17	0.48	3.70[c]
Soaps, cleaning products, etc	284	4.07	0.48	3.12[d]
Construction machinery	353	4.13	0.47	3.12
Miscellaneous chemical products	289	3.68	0.42	3.12[d]
Fabricated metal products	34	3.48	0.41	2.73
General industrial machinery	356	3.52	0.40	1.33[a]
Industrial organic chemicals	281	2.92	0.31	3.08[b]
Petroleum products	13,29	2.79	0.30	1.33[a]
Miscellaneous machinery	359	2.67	0.30	1.33[a]
Motor vehicles	371	2.81	0.30	8.43
Railroad equipment	374	2.71	0.28	3.83[c]
Refrigeration and service machinery	358	2.51	0.25	1.33

(2) Non-significant results

Radio and TV receiving equipment	365	2.20	0.23	2.44
Plastic materials	282	2.21	0.22	7.92
Miscellaneous electrical equipment	369	2.24	0.22	3.70[c]
Electrical household appliances	363	2.16	0.21	3.70[c]
Rubber products	30	1.82	0.18	2.09
Textiles	22	1.59	0.15	0.7
Farm machinery	352	1.62	0.12	3.08
Miscellaneous transportation equipment	379	1.53	0.12	3.83[c]
Stone, clay, glass products	32	1.32	0.11	1.13
Non-ferrous metal products	3336, 3398, 3463	1.33	0.11	0.87
Ferrous metal products	331, 332, 3399, 3462	1.30	0.10	0.61
Food	20	0.99	0.08	0.58
Agricultural chemicals	287	1.08	0.07	3.51
Motor and bicycles	375	0.61	0.06	3.83[c]
Paints and allied products	285	0.52	0.03	3.12[d]
Ship and boat building	373	0.47	0.03	3.83[e]

* Significant at the 1 per cent level.
[a] R&D/value added figures were only available for the group of SIC 355, 356, 358 and 359.
[b] R&D/value added figures were only available for the group of SIC 281 and 286.
[c] R&D/value added figures were only available for the group of SIC 363, 364 and 369.
[d] R&D/value added figures were only available for the group of SIC 284, 285 and 289.
[e] Estimated.
[f] R&D/value added figures were only available for the group of Standard Industrial Classifications.
(*Source*: L. Soete, 1979)

significant results are obtained. For most consumer goods and intermediate goods industries, where technical change is weaker and often based on the diffusion of innovations that have occured in the capital goods sector, non-significant results are obtained. Thus, according to this analysis, in a large number of sectors and countries, international competitiveness is based to a large extent on technical change.

It is clear from the above empirical and statistical results, in the face of increasing international competition – which includes competition between the industrialized countries on the one hand, and a gradual improvement in the competitiveness of a number of developing countries on the other (especially the newly industrializing countries) – that greater importance must be attached in the advanced market- economy countries to the improvement of the trade position in more complex products. For many of these countries this means that their trade position must be improved in the long term principally through concentration on the production of technologically advanced goods. Increasingly they will be less able, in general, to compete on price with low-technology and mature standardized products from developing countries, and this has clear implications for reindustrialization and technology policies in the advanced nations.

Of course, while there undoubtedly is a link between 'embodied technological change' and trade performance, the question still remains as to the extent to which the competitiveness of a nation's industry is influenced by its innovative activities. From the research that has been carried out to date, it would appear that this link is more valid for some countries than for others. The comparative advantage of Dutch industry, for instance, appears to lie primarily 'in those sectors of Dutch industry that make intensive use of human capital and raw materials'. The technology factor, as approximated by relative R&D expenditures, was shown to have no effect on patterns of sectoral trade in the Dutch case. In supporting the previous positive result for human capital, an investigation carried out by *Fortune* (Koekkoek and Mennes, 1982) indicated that a positive link existed between the relative export position of Dutch industry and the number of technicians and people with an education in natural sciences in the different industrial sectors.

We point out the Dutch case not because it proves that there is no relationship between 'embodied technological change' and export performance, but to show that seeking correlations between the two – in this case using relative R&D expenditure as a proxy for embodied technology – is not always as straightforward as it might appear. Indeed, as the data in Table 1.5 showed, the Netherlands is a net importer of technological know-how, the proper utilization of which would rely heavily on the human capital contained within the importing companies. A similar, but very much stronger case could be made for Japan.

Another approach employed to evaluate the importance of technological change in trade is to determine the position of a country's industry in the production of high-technology products. We showed such data in Table 1.4, which gave the specialization coefficients for high-technology products for the EEC, the US and Japan; in Table 1.9 we give similar specialization coefficients for eight EEC nations spearately. This illustrates that although the position of a number of countries such as West Germany, France and the UK worsened somewhat, the decline was nowhere as severe as in the Netherlands.

Table 1.9   Specialization coefficients for high-technology products

	1963	1970	1980
Netherlands	1.05	0.83	0.69
Belgium	0.67	0.77	0.79
Denmark	0.58	0.60	0.66
FRG	1.21	1.06	0.99
France	1.00	1.06	0.93
Italy	0.84	0.83	0.63
Ireland	0.43	0.67	1.03
United Kingdom	1.05	0.92	0.94
EEC	1.02	0.94	0.88

(*Source*: EEC, 1982)

In both the neo-technology theories of trade we see that competitive advantage, at least initially, is associated closely with technological leadership. For some product types, continued competitiveness depends on maintaining technological leads; for others, notably those in which the possibilities for product change diminish and products become more or less standardized and suited to continuous or mass production, competitive advantage shifts towards factors of production (low cost), distribution and servicing, often to be found outside the original innovating country.

Taking a longer-term view we can see how the competitive advantage of Britain in the eighteenth and nineteenth centuries – based on technological leadership in textiles and textile technology and later in iron and steel – was eroded first by advances in steel production taken up more vigorously in the US and Germany, and then by the introduction of electricity and the automobile in the US and the growth of the modern chemical industry in Germany, with their associated production of machine tools and new machines (Ray, 1980).

Referring to this change in British fortunes, Soete (1983) makes an extremely important point:

This dramatic change in fortune from an absolute technological leadership producing, e.g. in the mid-19th century more steam engines than the rest of the world put together, has of course many causes, but it is no doubt related to the rapid international diffusion of British technologies, which were hampered in their internal domestic diffusion.

Thus, it is not the creation of technological leadership in itself that affords a nation its competitive advantage, but the rate and level of diffusion of the technology into economic use (Pavitt and Soete, 1982), that is, the degree to which the nation appropriates the benefits of its technological advances before international diffusion occurs and other nations catch up; or, in other words, how long it can hang on to its technological monopoly position and thus its monopoly profits.

The Kondratiev Cycles

During the past five year or so it has increasingly been mooted by a growing number of economists that over the last forty years the world economy has undergone a cycle of structural changes that in some ways parallels earlier cycles in economic activity (Mensch, 1979; Freeman, Clark and Soete, 1982; Freeman, 1981; van Duijn, 1983. For an interesting critique, see Rosenberg and Frischtach, 1983.) The idea of a more or less regular occurrence of the type of structural crisis we are experiencing today is generally associated with a Russian economist, N. D. Kondratiev, who expounded his theory in the 1920s (although the idea had originally been formulated in some detail by a Dutch economist, J. van Gelderen, in 1913). Kondratiev based his theory on a statistical analysis of a set of price and production time-series data for the period 1790–1920 for the US, France, Germany and England. The three major long-term cycles Kondratiev identified during this period were: 1790 to about 1850 (approximately sixty years) with a peak between 1810 and 1817; 1850 to 1895 (approximately forty-five years) with a peak around 1875; a third cycle starting in about 1895 with its peak between 1914 and 1920.

While Kondratiev did not explicitly include technology as a causal factor in long-wave formation, he did suggest that when a major wave of expansion was under way, inventions that had remained dormant would attract investment and begin to find commercial application. It was the economist Joseph Schumpeter in *Business Cycles* (1939) who first advanced the notion of radical technological innovations as a major factor in the recurrent crises of structural adjustment. To be sure, Schumpeter stressed the uniqueness of each cycle, pointing to such important exogenous factors as wars and harvest failures; nevertheless the most important feature was innovation, and Schumpeter spoke explicitly of technological revolutions being the driving force of economic growth.

According to Schumpeter it was entrepreneurs who, seeing new profit opportunities, vigorously exploited the emerging techno-economic combinations. This led to a 'swarming effect' of imitators – an entrepreneurial bandwaggon – with an associated wave of new investment, which in turn generated boom conditions. As competition increased, firms began gradually reducing their margins to remain competitive, the time for technological monopoly profits being well passed. Before the system could reach a stable equilibrium, a new wave of innovations would occur with major destabilizing effects. Schumpeter called this a process of creative capital destruction, and deemed it sufficient to engender Kondratiev-type cycles.

Freeman et al have addressed this issue in some detail:

Schumpeter justified his view that technical innovation was 'more like a series of explosions than a gentle though incessant transformation' on three grounds. First, he argued that innovations are 'not at any time distributed over the whole economic system at random, but tend to concentrate in certain sectors and their surroundings', and that consequently they are 'lop-sided, discontinuous, dis-harmonious by nature'. Secondly, he argued that the diffusion process was inherently a very uneven one because 'innovations do not remain isolated events, and are not evenly distributed in time . . . on the contrary, they tend to cluster, to come about in bunches, simply because first some and then most firms follow in the wake of successful innovation'. Thirdly, he maintained that these two characteristics of the innovative process implied that the disturbances it engendered could be enough to 'disrupt the existing system and enforce a distinct process of adaptation' (see Fels, 1964, pp.75–77).

Hardly anyone would deny the truth of Schumpeter's first proposition. It is confirmed by a great deal of empirical research on the uneven distribution of

R&D, patents, inventions and innovations between the various branches of the economy (Baker, 1976; van Duijn, 1981). The differences between rates of growth of various branches of production are well-known and obvious, as is the fact that some industries decline whilst others grow rapidly. Moreover, it is also universally agreed that many of these structural changes are the result of technical innovation. The decline of the canals and horse transport and the rise of the railways is an obvious case, followed by the rise of the internal combustion engine and the decline of the railways. Changes in the pattern of energy production and distribution are another related and obvious case. No one would deny that the social and economic changes arising from these major processes of technical innovation were sufficient to entail substantial problems of structural adaptation, especially for those countries which already had a large capital stock and pool of skilled labour devoted to the exploitation of the older systems of technology (Freeman et al, 1982 p33 and 34).

According to Kuznets (1940), for the innovations to be capable of causing Kondratiev-type economic cycles, they would need to be such that their effects would permeate throughout the whole economic system and be far reaching. Schumpter pointed to such major innovations: textiles and related innovations which he associated with the first Kondratiev; railways, iron, coal and construction which he

Figure 1.8   A simple schematic of the Kondratiev Waves

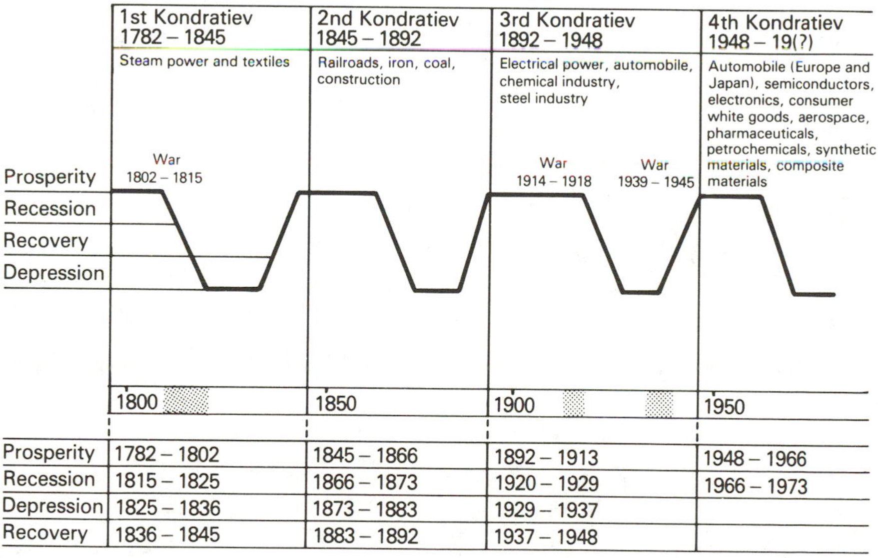

	1st Kondratiev 1782 – 1845	2nd Kondratiev 1845 – 1892	3rd Kondratiev 1892 – 1948	4th Kondratiev 1948 – 19(?)
Prosperity	1782 – 1802	1845 – 1866	1892 – 1913	1948 – 1966
Recession	1815 – 1825	1866 – 1873	1920 – 1929	1966 – 1973
Depression	1825 – 1836	1873 – 1883	1929 – 1937	
Recovery	1836 – 1845	1883 – 1892	1937 – 1948	

(*Source*: R. Rothwell, 1982)
a6NB: This diagram shows simply fluctuations over time and does not attempt to indicate the relative magnitudes of the economic upswings and downswings for the different Kondratievs. In practice, of course, the base line will rise from left to right as the average level of world economic activity has risen considerably during the period covered.

associated with· the second Kondratiev; and electrical power, the chemical industry and automobiles which he associated with the third Kondratiev (see Figure 1.8).

We turn now to a discussion of the fourth Kondratiev wave. Soete (1978) has illustrated clearly that the relationship between manufacturing output and employment in the EEC nine (taken together) has undergone a series of structural changes during the period 1950–78. Soete (1981) later presented data illustrated changes in the relationship between manufacturing output and employment for various EEC countries separately and for the US and Japan. The data presented in Figure 1.9 are an updated version of Soete's earlier data, and show the relationship between manufacturing output and employment for the EEC nine and for Britain and Germany separately: the structural changes that have taken place are rather obvious (Rothwell and Soete, 1983). Taking the data for the nine EEC countries we can distinguish three distinct periods:

Figure 1.9   Industrial output and employment, EEC – 9 (1962 = 100)

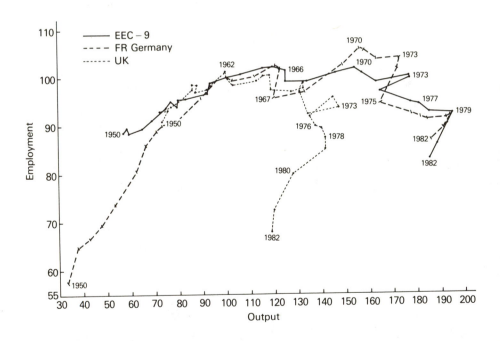

(*Source*: Rothwell and Soete, 1983)

– the period 1950 to 1964, which is characterized by high growth in industrial output (7 per cent annual rate) accompanied by an important creation of employment (1 per cent annual average growth rate);

- the period 1964 to about 1970, which is characterized by high growth in industrial output (6 per cent annual average rate) and employment stagnation (jobless growth);
- the period from about 1970 to 1980, characterized by low and stagnant growth in industrial output (1 per cent annual average rate) accompanied by employment loss (between 1973 and 1978 employment fell at an average annual rate of 1.8 per cent.) (deployment).

Figure 1.9 also illustrates how, because of lack of growth in industrial output, the onset of the decline in manufacturing (deployment) began in the UK in about 1968. In the case of West Germany, which enjoyed a relatively high rate of growth in industrial output throughout the 1960s, the phenomenon of deployment began about four years later.

If we turn now to the relationship between investment and employment, Figure 1.10, taken from Clark (1979), plots change in manufacturing employment per unit of manufacturing investment in the UK for the period 1930 to 1977. It can be seen that during the period 1930 to the mid-1950s the relationship was positive and growing; from the latter half of the 1950s to 1964 it grew increasingly less positive; from 1964 onwards it became negative and manufacturing investment in the UK then became associated not with employment creation, but with employment loss.

Figure 1.10   Employment change per unit of investment (smoothed), UK manufacturing.

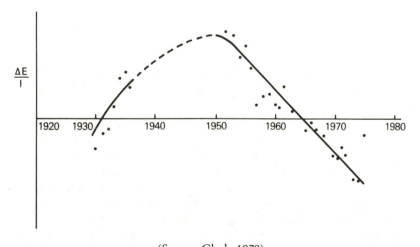

(*Source*: Clark, 1979)

The data in Figure 1.10 can be taken to suggest a change in the ratio of expansionary investment to rationalization investment. Mensch et al (1980) have pointed to a similar pattern in the West German manufacturing sector. During the 1950s and early 1960s, investment aimed at expansion was sufficiently high in relation to that aimed towards rationalization that job creation was greater than job displacement. In the mid-1960s the productivity effects of rationalization investment began to dominate and increased industrial output could be attained with more or less no increase in employment, thus establishing a period of jobless growth. From the beginning of the 1970s, rationalization investment effects swamped expansionary investment effects, and increased output was achieved with a reduced labour force.

It is important to point out that the 'deployment' of the 1970s was not associated with rapidly increasing manufacturing productivities. Indeed, during the 1970s, productivity growth actually declined in most of the advanced market economies (see Table 1.10). Increasing manufacturing unemployment was due to a growing mismatch between productivity growth and the (reduced) rate of growth in output (demand). What these data show is that fundamental structural changes have taken place in the relationship between manufacturing output and manufacturing employment, and between investment in manufacturing and manufacturing employment, during the thirty-year period 1950 to 1980.

Table 1.10   Average annual growth rates of labour productivity (GDP per man hour)

	1950–60	1960–70	1970–80
France	4.3	5.1	3.8
West Germany	6.6	5.2	3.6
Italy	4.3	6.3	2.5
Japan	5.7	9.6	4.3
UK	2.3	3.2	2.4
US	2.4	2.4	1.5

(*Source*: Data taken from Freeman, Clark and Soete (1982), Table 8.2, p148)

Since we earlier termed the last forty years or so the fourth Kondratiev the question now is 'What role has technological change played in the structural changes that have taken place during this period?' First, we can say that perhaps the most notable feature of the past thirty-five years has been the emergence and rapid growth of a bunch of new technology-based industries associated with advances in science and technology of the previous twenty years or more. These new technology-based industries – notably electronics, semiconductors, synthetic materials, petrochemicals, agrochemicals, composite materials, pharmaceuticals and aerospace – generated new areas of techno-economic activity and the growth of new markets. The wealth generated by the emergence of these new high-technology industries caused an associated boom in demand for both capital goods and for consumer durables, resulting in the rapid growth in the capital goods supply industries, as well as in the automobile and consumer electronics and white goods industries.

We can represent the pattern of evolution of these new industries by the simple schema presented in Table 1.11 (Rothwell and Zegveld, 1982). In the dynamic growth phase (1945 to about 1964) production was undertaken in small and initially relatively inefficient units, and many new entrepreneurial firms, both innovators and imitators, entered the race. The focus of research and development was largely on the introduction of, and major improvements to, radically new products. As the markets for these products grew rapidly, firms acquired new and improved forms of production machinery in order to meet demand. Manufacturing investment was thus directed mainly towards the creation of new products and the expansion of manufacturing capacity. While productivity grew rapidly, output (demand) grew even faster and many new jobs were created.

Table 1.11   Model of Postwar Industrial evolution

1945 to approximately 1964 – dynamic growth phase
Emergence of new industries based largely on new technological opportunities.
Production initially in small units.
Emphasis on product change and the introduction of many new products.
Rapidly growing new markets.
Some market regeneration in traditional areas, eg textiles.
New employment generation (output growth greater than productivity growth).
Competitive emphasis is mainly on product availability and non-price factors.

Mid to late 1960s – consolidation phase
Increasing industrial concentration and growing static scale economies.
High dynamic economies.
Introduction of organizational innovations.
Increasing emphasis on process improvement.
Some major product changes, but based mainly on existing technology.
Rapid productivity growth.
Markets still growing rapidly.
Output growth and productivity growth in rough balance (manufacturing employment more or less stable).
Competitive emphasis still mainly on non-price factors.

Late 1960s to date: maturity and market saturation phase
Industry highly concentrated.
Very large production units, often vertically integrated.
Some product change, but emphasis predominantly on production process rationalization.
Increasing organization rationalization, including foreign direct investment in areas of low labour cost.
Growing automaticity.
Stagnating and replacement markets.
Productivity growth greater than output (demand) growth.
Rapidly growing manufacturing unemployment.
Where products are little differentiated, the importance of price competition is high.

(*Source*: R. Rothwell and W. Zegveld, 1982)

The increasingly well-established industries rapidly began to gain in production expertise and continued to acquire more efficient manufacturing equipment from capital goods suppliers. Production units increased in size, thus achieving scale economies, and mergers and takeovers occurred increasingly frequently. Management learning took place and organizational innovations were introduced. From the early to late 1960s the industries thus underwent a period of consolidation during which productivity increased rapidly as firms moved down the learning curve. There was still a great deal of product innovation, but now mainly within established technological regimes. At the same time, market demand continued to expand at a high rate, and productivity growth and output growth were roughly in balance. This was the period of jobless growth in output.

As the industries matured and industrial concentration increased, productivities reached historically high levels. At the same time demand growth began to decline as markets saturated and became increasingly ones of replacement. Technological opportunities for radical product innovation also diminished, as did the possibilities for entrepreneurship and the creation of new technology based firms. Investment was directed less towards output expansion and more towards increasing production efficiency and reducing labour requirements as firms fought to maintain both margins and price competitiveness. Productivity increase, albeit at a reduced level, began to outstrip demand growth and manufacturing jobs were shed. Simultaneously firms increasingly began to locate the production of mature products in areas of low labour cost, further reducing employment in the advanced nations.

Several years into this 'maturity and market saturation' phase, along came the energy crisis with its accompanying effects of reducing real disposable incomes and increasing inflation. This effectively accelerated the crisis of stagnation into the crisis of stagflation with resultant high unemployment. During this period governments began to introduce counterinflationary measures which were at the same time counterexpansionary, effectively reducing demand even further.

If we look for examples of the pattern of industrial evolution outlined above, we can see industries that have passed through all three phases in the case of electronics (Freeman, Clark and Soete, 1982) and semiconductors (Rothwell, 1983) and an example of an industry in the second phase is the case of computer-aided design (Kaplinsky, 1983). Certainly when we look at the synthetic fibres, consumer electronics, petrochemicals, consumer white goods and automobile industries we can see them struggling to cope with overcapacity in stagnant markets – good examples of industries in the 'maturity and market saturation' phase.

Having discussed the pattern of evolution of the 'new' (start-of-cycle) industries of the past forty years, it is important that the contribution to economic growth of the 'old' (end-of-cycle) industries is not ignored. There is little doubt, for example, that the steel, textiles and construction industries – all long established – played their part in the postwar economic recovery. Significantly, in all three industries, major innovations played an important role, eg continuous casting of steel and oxygen steelmaking; synthetic fibres, carpet tufting machinery and shuttleless weaving in the textile industry; systems building in the construction industry. Currently the three industries, following an extended period of rapid growth, are now suffering from massive overcapacity.

As Schumpeter himself pointed out, of course, major exogenous nontechnological factors play a crucial 'triggering' role in the major upswings (or downswings) that characterize the Kondratiev cycles, a good example being World War II. This (and the build up to the war in the 1930s) focused massive resources onto major new technologies and spawned the new industries of the 1950s and beyond. At the same time, it helped to overcome potential institutional and social barriers to the implementation of technological change, and this is an extremely important point. Indeed, as Chesnais (1982) has pointed out, Schumpeter (in *Business Cycles*, 1964, p 279) stated that it had become necessary for him to drop the practice of

treating the institutional framework of society, the attitudes of individuals and groups, and the policies resulting from a given social pattern as data of our economic process, and changes in these data as external factors. We will glance at the social process as a whole and in doing so adopt the convenient, though possibly inadequate, hypothesis of Marxism, according to which social, cultural, political situations and the spirit in which and the measures by which they are met, derive from the workings of that capitalist machine. Our cyclic schema lends itself to this view, not only because of the length of its longest wave, which brings long-run social changes within the reach of business-cycle analysis, but also because it stressed that kind of economic change that is particularly likely to break up existing patterns and to create new ones, thereby breaking up old and creating new positions of power, civilisations, valuations, beliefs, and policies which from this viewpoint are no longer 'external'.

Perez has taken up this general theme and extended it further by postulating that Kondratiev's long waves are not a strictly economic phenomenon, but rather the manifestation, measurable in economic terms, of the harmonious or disharmonious behaviour of the total socioeconomic and institutional system (on both the national and international levels):

A structural crisis (i.e. the depression in the long wave), as distinct from an economic recession, would be a visible syndrome in a breakdown between the dynamics of the economic subsystem and the related dynamics of the socio-institutional framework. It is, in the same movement, the painful and conflict-ridden process through which a dynamic harmony is re-established among the different spheres of the total system (Perez, 1983).

Although we discuss policy implications in some detail below, it is worthwhile pointing out here that both Schumpeter's and Perez's statements do have profound implications for policy; perhaps the most significant is that they imply the necessity for going beyond policies that relate only to technological change. In other words, it simply is not enough to expand the frontiers of scientific knowledge and technological advance if the institutional framework is locked into the exploitation of mature technologies, and if attitudes in society are such as to retard the diffusion into use of major new products. Clearly policies towards reindustrialization must tackle all these areas.

At this point it is worthwhile attempting to link the Kondratiev cycles to the issue of changing patterns of international trade, in particular using the notion of the 'leading technological activity country' (Soete 1983). It is clear that in the case of the first (textiles) Kondratiev, Britain was technologically the lead country and as a consequence appropriated the benefits of its innovative activity through obtaining a very large share of world trade in textile goods. At the same time, Britain took steps to prevent textile machines being exported to competitor countries, eg Switzerland. Britain maintained its technological lead during the early years of the second (railways) Kondratiev, which again was reflected in a large share in world trade. By the time of the third Kondratiev, however, Britain had lost her technological lead to the US and Germany and progressively retreated to trading in 'captive' Empire markets.

Soete (1981) has discussed the dynamics of international competition in terms of technological 'catching up' whereby the leading technological activity nation progressively loses its lead through the international diffusion of technology:

The major factor underlying the importance of international competition within the technical change – employment debate is of course the international diffusion of technology. For sure, technology acquires only commercial value through 'appropriation'. Its international diffusion is thus neither free and costless, nor immediate. Technological 'assets' represent monopoly power, and it has been shown that a large proportion of the OECD's manufactured exports is dominated by these technological assets. Yet there is little doubt that technological appropriation is highly imperfect at the international level. Today, new technology gets diffused rather rapidly, and allows generally speaking the other developed, 'imitating' countries 'to catch up'.

The international diffusion of technology has been a crucial factor in the development and economic growth of most developed countries. Particularly when a clear technological leader can be identified (e.g. the US since the 2nd World War), there seems to be scope for a process of rapid 'catching-up' growth, where the mere existence of a technological gap may provide a sufficient incentive for rapid economic growth. According to Gomulka (1971), one can actually consider two sorts of diffusion mechanisms: the first, the free exchange of scientific and technical information follows directly from the technological gap ('technological gap will be thought of as a pump of diffusion', p.11), the second consists of the actual import of technology and its diffusion in the country. It is in the first instance the latter which will be most effective for successful industrialization. Japan's success in following such a strategy is well-known: in 1950 it imported technology for less than $3 million, in 1963 for nearly $150 million, and in 1979 for more than $2800 million. At the same time its research expenditures rose from $129 million in 1953 to $1060 million in 1964 and $14200 million in 1977/78. It is the gradual shift of its 'endogeneous' technological effort from an auxiliary role to the import of technology, to autonomous technological development, which seems to be the crucial characteristic of Japan's emergence as a technological leader (Soete, 1981 p105 and 106).

It is the ability to acquire technology that results in very rapid productivity and economic growth rates in the catching-up countries. However, according to Soete, as the technology gap narrows, and increasing numbers of countries draw near to the technological frontier, productivity (and economic) growth slows and is determined by the rate of advance of the technological frontier itself. International competition intensifies, and the once laggard countries spend increasing sums on 'indigenous' technological development. Internationally, there is a great deal of duplication of R&D effort. As a result of these factors, the rate of return to inventive and innovative activity diminishes:

As mentioned before however, to the extent that the resulting increase in international technological competition reduces the rate of return to technology, most countries find themselves in the paradoxical situation of spending more on 'autonomous' research while the price for the import of technology has actually slowed down. As each country's 'technological assets' represent less and less monopoly power, so that the monopoly rent it can earn on its technology exports starts declining, it will finally be the degree of technological success, the relative labour costs, the availability of skills, and the extent to which government support is provided, which will determine which country(ies) will eventually emerge as the new technological leader(s). A process of 'divergence-growth' (Pavitt, 1979, 1980) will be set in motion, which will last till the newly created technological gap is sufficiently large to provide a sufficient incentive for the 'lost-out' countries to catch up (Soete, 1981 p110 and 111).

Of course, where the new technology gap is generated by the emergence of one or more fundamental new technologies capable of generating substantial economic growth, this may trigger a new Kondratiev cycle and the emergence of new leader–laggard combinations, which subsequently pass through the competitive (catching-up) dynamic described by Soete. In view of this, it is appropriate to pose the question, 'What of the future?' Can we detect developments in technology or areas of techno-economic activity which might form the basis of the next upswing?

The answer to the latter question is 'yes'. Possibilities currently being mooted (and in some instances already the objective of a great deal of technical development activity and some industrial exploitation) are:

– biotechnology (biomass, single cell protein, bio-engineering).
– energy-related technologies (heat pumps, solar energy systems).
– electronic office equipment.

- advanced information technology (including fibre-optics and satellite communications).
- advanced medical electronics and new forms of implants (biocompatible materials).
- photochemistry.
- coal gasification and liquafection.
- exploitation of ocean resources (the ocean bed, aquaculture).
- robotics technology.
- new agrochemicals for the regeneration of marginal land.

POLICY IMPLICATIONS

The question now, of course, is what is the relationship between our discussion of 'cycles' and the requirements of technology policy? We can see that the concept of technology-related cycles is relevant at the level of individual products (product cycle) at the level of industrial branches (industry cycle) and at the level of the national (and world) economy (Kondratiev cycle). The concept of technological cycles is also relevant to the discussion of comparative advantage in international trade. So we can see immediately that the concept of technology-related cycles at all levels implies in the first instance the importance of technology policies at the national and subnational levels. If the current recessionary trend is indeed associated with diminishing technological (and therefore market) possibilities, then one of the first aims of technology policy must be the identification, stimulation and diffusion into use of new technologies on which future economic growth – the next growth cycle – can be based. A second important aim must be to utilize technology to help solve the problems of saturation and decline in existing industries. This means the search for major innovations to regenerate demand via radical product changes, and the continued search for product improvements as well as for increased production efficiency to reduce – or at least retard the increase in – real prices to maintain international price competitiveness, especially with mature products facing strong competition from the newly industrializing countries. In other words, technology policy must be geared to the stimulation of the 'sunrise' industries while at the same time addressing the problems of the 'sunset' industries.

This raises a number of important questions. The first relates to resource allocation and specifically how to decide on the proportion of available resources to be devoted to assisting the end-of-cycle industries and that to be dedicated to the generation of front-end industries, and this will, of course, depend to a large extent on the current industrial structure. The second problem relates to the social impact of applying technological change for the purposes of improving the efficiency of end-of-cycle industries; this will inevitably mean the greater adoption of automated (laboursaving) devices such as robots, thus increasing unemployment at a time when unemployment levels generally are deemed unacceptably high. Certainly it will be many years before the employment creating effects of the newly emerging techno-economic combinations will create sufficient employment seriously to dent current high unemployment levels. Thus we might very well see regenerative effects slowed down due to (understandable) social resistance to the adoption of rationalization-type technological changes. At the same time social resistance to change, or even simply indifference, might act to slow down the rate at which new technologies are introduced and new products are diffused into social use. In terms of those sectors in which governments should attempt to extend and regenerate the industry cycle, this would depend on the national appropriability of the benefits of regenerative activities. On the face of it, technology-gap industries might, in general, offer the greatest possibilities of appropriability, although radical innovations might effectively reverse the direction of comparative advantage in mature product cycle industries. Hoffman and Rush (1980) have suggested that this might well happen in the areas of garment production and electronics assembly as the result of the adoption of microelectronics-based production machinery in the former, and the increasing use of microelectronics components in the latter, by firms in the advanced economies.

A second potential barrier to change relates to the structure of industrial branches, and this is important both in industrial regeneration and new industry formation. An example relating to the former can be found in the European textile industry. The British textile industry is now highly concentrated and vertically integrated, a structure developed to capitalize on economies of scale in production and marketing to meet new waves of competition from less developed countries in the 1960s. This structure has not proved altogether successful since the production technology (textile machinery) is readily available to all producers (ie there is a lack of national 'appropriability') making labour costs a strong element of competition with mass-produced products – precisely the type of product the British textile industry structurally is best adapted to produce. The Italian textile industry, based on small decentralized production units, has proved better able to adapt to low-cost competition. The West German textile industry, which had initially evolved along the lines of the British, underwent considerable organizational changes in the 1970s leading to the emergence of smaller, more specialized (non-mass market) and market-oriented production units which resulted in a considerably more competitive industry. The greater inherent structural flexibility of the Italian and West German firms has enabled them to move to areas of specialist production, eg industrial textiles, and to the production of customer-oriented fashion products. Small size, with its associated manufacturing flexibility, has enabled these firms to respond rapidly to changes in fashion.

A further example of this process can be found in the emergence of the US semiconductor and computer-aided design (CAD) industries. In both cases, while the initial inventive and innovative activity occurred in the R&D laboratories of major companies (the innovations being destined mainly for own-use), rapid growth and market diffusion came about through the medium of many new, small spin-off firms (Rothwell, 1983; Kaplinsky, 1982). The small firms appeared culturally better adapted to applying the new technologies to a variety of new applications (see Chapter 6 for more detailed discussion). However, in most advanced market economies R&D activity and output is dominated by major corporations. If, as the model of Abernathy and Utterback implies, technological and managerial efforts in end-of-cycle industries are geared towards the efficient production of dominant designs, with their associated technological and attitudinal rigidities, the structural and cultural adaptation necessary to enable such firms to enter new fields might prove difficult to attain.

An additional major potential barrier to the regeneration of established industries relates to the level of accumulated fixed capital associated with current modes of production. In other words, end-of-cycle companies are unable or unwilling to write off existing capital stock while at the same time developing or adopting new techniques, and a good illustrative example of this, which also illustrates a number of problems relevant to our general theme, can be found in the nineteenth century chemical industry in Britain.

In the eighteenth and early nineteenth centuries the alkali industry was of prime importance because of its links with the washing and bleaching of textiles. Until the early part of the nineteenth century alkalis were obtained from natural sources (mainly the burning of seaweed) despite the fact that a method for synthetic production had been known since the 1780s, the so-called Leblanc process that had been submitted to a competition organized by the French Academy. It was not until the late 1820s that the Leblanc process was first commercially adopted in Britain, and by 1850 it formed a central part of the British chemical industry.

Despite the fact that the Leblanc process was highly wasteful of sulphur, calcium and chlorine, British output rose between 1860 and 1880 by some 300 per cent, during which period British companies introduced many improvements. In the middle of the nineteenth century, however, a new and more elegant method of alkali production was developed. While this new process was initially wasteful of expensive ammonia in the form of ammonium chloride, a Belgian chemist, Ernest Solvay, devised a method of obtaining free recyclable ammonia in 1863. Despite many initial scale-up problems, by the 1870s Solvay-produced alkalis were able to undersell those produced by the Leblanc process by 20 per cent:

The reasons for the greater efficiency of the Solvay process are significant. Whereas the Leblanc process was a batch process involving the mixing and heating of materials in [individual] vessels, Solvay's was a continuous flow process. This meant labour costs were lower and the whole process could be better controlled. More importantly, the Solvay process used cheaper raw materials and very efficiently recycled and re-used 'waste' products. It was the Solvay process that the newly industrialised nations adopted and with which they soon contested British supremacy. *Despite the obvious advantages of the Solvay process British managers, who had a large investment in Leblanc plant, were unwilling to abandon it*, [author's emphasis]. Instead, they responded to the challenge in a number of ways: by increasing efficiency through process improvement; by concentration through the merging of companies to form the United Alkali Company, thus facilitating economies of scale; and through entering into price fixing agreements with British Solvay producers (Yu, 1982).

Because of this response, from the mid-1980s onwards British competitiveness declined and Germany took the lead. Between 1890 and 1900 British exports of alkalis were more or less halved. The crucial factor in the divergent fortunes of the British and German industries was the difference in the rate of diffusion of Solvay technology between the two countries. For example, in 1882, 1887 and 1900, the Solvay process accounted for 44 per cent, 75 per cent and 90 per cent respectively of German soda production. The corresponding figures for Britain were 12 per cent, 22 per cent and 40 per cent. Thus, unlike the Germans, British manufacturers were constrained in the adoption of the Solvay process because of the high levels of capital and skills locked into the much more firmly established Leblanc process, and this despite the fact that a great deal of the pioneering development work on the Solvay process was done by Mond in Lancashire.

As well as illustrating our original point, the alkali industry case also demonstrates the so-called 'sailing ship effect', named following the work of Gilfillan (1935) who showed that most of the important improvements to the sailing ship occurred after the introduction of the first steam ship. A similar phenomenon occurred in the thermionic valve industry following the invention of the transistor, when new and improved forms of vacuum tube were developed by established manufacturers. It illustrates how established companies can become locked into existing technological trajectories. Rather than attempting to capitalize on the possibilities offered by the emergence of a superior new substitute technology, they vigorously defend their position through the accelerated improvement of the old technology (ie extending the product cycle).

The public policy implications of the above example are twofold. In the first case, governments might wish to offer financial assistance for the accelerated scrapping of existing capital stock associated with the 'old' technology and for the purchase of the 'new'. In the second case they might be involved in funding research and development associated with the new technology within the scientific and technological infrastructure (creating not just new knowledge, but also a cadre of new skills) as well as offering selective development grants to individual companies.

A further barrier to radical change is likely to lie in structural mismatches and rigidities obtaining in major national R&D institutions. In some countries, for example, collective industrial research institutions, often founded many years ago, are industry-specific and designed to meet the needs of the industries of earlier Kondratievs (textiles, steel, footwear). The practices adopted by such institutions (standards, validation, manufacturing support) and their skill profiles – locked into the requirements of the old industries – generally are not suited to involvement in the creation of radical innovations. In most countries – a notable exception being the US – universities culturally are poorly adapted to the generation (spin-off) of new small firms based on high technology.

A fourth problem relates to the structure of capital markets. These, while being reasonably well adapted to the support of ongoing activities in existing companies (via, for example, stock markets), are generally poorly adapted to the provision of risk (Schumpeterian) capital necessary for the creation of new technology based firms producing major new products. Not only do existing institutions (banks, building societies, insurance companies) lack the cultural propensity to invest in high-risk start-ups, they generally lack the skills necessary to make realistic judgements concerning the viability of such firms. At the same time, because of declining profits, end-of-cycle firms are less able to fund the high levels of R&D necessary for the creation of major regenerating innovations, and capital for such high-risk technological ventures might not be forthcoming from conventional sources of finance (see Chapter 5).

Clearly, a prime aim of technology policy must be to help overcome the technological, institutional and cultural rigidities discussed above. In the case of technology, governments can play an important role in the generation of new generic technologies on the basis of which new industries will be formed. In other words they have an important part to play in the early stages of the longer-term industry cycle and in the creation of generic technologies which will act as an 'envelope' for the many shorter-term product cycles that are the primary concern of individual companies. In the case of major national R&D institutions, governments have the prime responsibility for restructuring skill profiles and for shifting the basis of funding to direct R&D efforts into the newly emerging generic fields. In the case of capital provision, governments clearly can redirect their already considerable support for industry more closely towards meeting the requirements of new technology based companies and for major diversification projects in existing companies. In the case of institutional culture, governments face a more difficult task. While they can, even in the relatively short term, redirect technological and financial flows, they are liable to find that institutional change takes rather longer to achieve. It is, nevertheless, as Nelson and Winter have emphasized, an essential task that must be addressed:

... the hunt for appropriate policy instruments will not be an easy one. Macro measures will not do; thus, proposals like a general R & D tax credit (which has been quite fashionable in recent discussions in the US) are beside the point. Policies need to be designed to influence particular economic sectors and activities. Regarding these, the key policy will be to augment or redesign institutions rather than to achieve particular resource allocations per se. Improving the railroads does not look like an objective that can be met through funding a few specified R & D projects. Rather, the policy search must be for a set of institutions that will allocate resources appropriately over a wide range of circumstances and time (Nelson and Winter, 1977 p 40).

A further potential constraint to the diffusion of new technology which might be of prime concern to governments, is the infrastructural one. In certain instances government's role might not be the actual provision of the infrastructure itself, but rather providing the legislative framework within which the infrastructure is established. Good examples of this are the need for regulations to govern the provision and distribution of satellite television and the laying down of cables as a basis for the information society of the future.

It is important also that governments establish a coherent regulatory framework to control the externalities of industrial production. In other words governments have the prime responsibility for establishing rules that protect the health and safety of workers and consumers, as well as the physical and ecological environments and the wellbeing of society in general. This might, of course, require a good deal of scientific and technical research by government agencies to enable them properly to understand the risks associated with new technological developments in industry (eg biotechnology), in order that they can establish meaningful rules. It is important that government regulatory agencies acquire, or at least gain access to this necessary expertise, otherwise they might well establish regulations that are inadequate, meaningless or overstringent thus, in the latter case, potentially stifling further industrial development activity. There is a great deal of evidence to suggest that regulatory activity in the United States during the 1960s and 1970s had a marked negative impact on the prosperity of firms to invest in high-risk innovatory activities. This was more often due to the uncertainties associated with the regulatory formulation and implementation system than with the actual regulations themselves (Rothwell, 1980; Rothwell, 1981(b); National Academy of Sciences, 1980).

One of the prime justifications for governmental involvement in funding scientific and technological developments for industrial exploitation is to underwrite the high risks and considerable costs associated with the development of radical technologies, both of which individual companies might be unable or unwilling to bear alone. Individual companies might also be unwilling to participate in fundamental research in particular because they believe the appropriability of the benefits of such work is low, especially where they have to contract out basic research to public laboratories in, for example, universities. There are also areas in which market imperfections justify government intervention, such as health care, environmental protection and care of the elderly. In each of these areas, private rates of return on investment in technological developments might sometimes be insufficient to induce companies to participate (Stout 1981). In such cases governments again will be expected to underwrite at least some of the costs of development and production.

Finally, technological change, and policies towards stimulating technological developments are, by themselves, insufficient to ensure either the structural transformation of industry or international competitiveness, or both. Policies must be adopted that tackle the full range of activities from technological development through to market exploitation. In other words, we require technological innovation policies. In Chapter 2 we discuss the process of technological innovation and the factors that influence it, and in Chapter 3 we describe the elements of technological innovation policy as well as their evaluation.

REFERENCES

Abernathy W J and Utterback J M 1978 Patterns of Industrial Innovation. *Technology Review* **80** (7) June/July

Aho C M and Rosen H F 1980 Trends in Technology-Intensive Trade with Special Reference to US Competitiveness. Science and Technology Indicators Conference, OECD, Paris, 15–19 September

Baker R 1976 *New and Improved – Inventors and Inventions that have Changed the Modern World*. British Museum Publications

Chesnais F 1982 Schumpetarian Recovery and Schumpetarian Perspective: Some Unsettled Issues and Alternative Interpretations. In Giersch H (ed) *Emerging Technologies*. J C B Mohr (Paul Siebeck), Tubingen

Clark J 1979 A Model of Embodied Technical Change and Employment. (Mimeo), Science Policy Research Unit, University of Sussex

Colombo U 1977 Innovation in Europe. Paper presented at a Symposium organized by the Science Policy Foundation and the Commission of the European Communities, Brussels, 14–16 April

EEC 1982 *The Competitiveness of European Community Industry*. Brussels

Fels R (ed) 1964 Abridged edition of Schumpeter J A *Business Cycles*. McGraw Hill, New York

Freeman C 1963 The Plastics Industry: A Comparative Study of Research and Innovation. *National Institute Economic Review* **26**: 22–60

Freeman C (ed) 1981 Technical Innovation and Long Waves in World Economic Development. *Futures* **13**, (4) Special Issue

Freeman C Clark J and Soete L 1982 *Unemployment and Technical Innovation*. Frances Pinter

Gershuny J I 1982 Social Innovation: Change in the Mode of Provision of Services. *Futures* December: 496–516

Gershuny J I 1983 *Social Innovation and the Division of Labour*. Oxford University Press

Gilfillan S 1935 *Inventing the Ship*. Follet, Chicago

Haustein H-D 1980 Lighting Industry: A Classical Case of Innovation. IIASA, Working Paper No. WP-80-12 January. Laxenburg, Austria

Hirsch S 1965 The United States Electronics Industry in International Trade *National Institute Economic Review*. **34**

Hoffman K and Rush H 1980 Microelectronics, Industry and the Third World. *Futures* August

Horn E-J 1983 Technological Balance of Payments and International Competitiveness. *Research Policy* **12**: 91–103. North-Holland Publishing Company, Amsterdam

Kaplinsky R 1982 Firm Size and Technological Change in a Dynamic Context. (Mimeo) Institute of Development Studies, University of Sussex

Kaplinsky R 1983 *The Impact of Technical Change on the International Division of Labour: The Illustrative Example of CAD*. Frances Pinter

KoekkoeK and Mennes 1982 Revealed Comparative Advantage in Manufacturing Industry: The Case of the Netherlands. (Mimeo) Erasmus University, Rotterdam

Mensch G 1979 *Stalemate in Technology*. Ballinger, Cambridge, Mass., USA

Mensch G, Kaash K, Kleinknecht A and Schnapp R 1980 Innovation Trends and Switching Between Full and Under-Employment Equilibrium, 1950–1978. International Institute of Management, Discussion Paper Series, Berlin. January

National Academy of Sciences 1980 *Antitrust, Uncertainty and Technological Innovation*. Washington, DC

Nelson R and Winter S 1977 In Search of a Useful Theory of Innovation. *Research Policy* **6**: 36–76

OECD 1983 *Science Resources Newsletter* **7**: Science and Technology Indicators Unit, OECD, Paris

Pavitt K Technological Innovation and Industrial Development, Part I (1980); Part II (1981). *Futures* December and January

Pavitt K and Soete L 1980 Innovative Activities and Export Shares; Some Comparisons Between Industries and Countries. In Pavitt K (ed) *Technological Innovation and British Economic Performance*. MacMillan

Pavitt K and Soete L 1982 International Differences in Economic Growth and the International Location of Innovation. In Giersch H (ed) *Emerging Technologies*. J C B Mohr (Paul Siebeck), Tubingen

Peck M J and Goto A 1981 Technology and Economic Growth: The Case of Japan. *Research Policy* **10**: 222–243

Peters T J and Watterman R H 1982 *In Search of Excellence*, New York, Harper and Row

Perez C 1983 Structural Change and the Assimilation of New Technologies in the Economic and Social Systems. International Seminar on Innovation, Design and Long Cycles in Economic Development. Royal College of Art,

Department of Design Research, London, 13–15 April

Posner M 1961 International Trade and Technical Change. *Oxford Econ. Papers* **13** No.(3) October: 323–41

Ray G 1980 Innovation in the Long Cycle. *Lloyds Bank Review*, (135): 14–28

Rosenberg N and Frischtack C R 1983 Technological Innovation and Long Waves. *American Economic Review, Papers and Proceedings* May

Rothwell R 1980 The Impact of Regulation on Innovation: Some US Data. *Technological Forecasting and Social Changes* **17**: 7–34

Rothwell R 1981 Non-Price Factors in the Export Competitiveness of Agricultural Engineering Goods. *Research Policy* (10): 260–88

Rothwell R 1981 Some Indirect Impacts of Regulation on Innovation in the US. *Technological Forecasting and Social Change* **18**: 57–80

Rothwell R 1982 Innovating Towards Prosperity. *Chelwood Review* Christmas issue

Rothwell R 1983 Innovation and Firm Size: A Case for Dynamic Complementarity. *Journal of General Management* **8**: (3) Spring

Rothwell R and Gardiner P 1982 The Role of Design in Competitiveness. Paper presented to International Conference on Design Policy, Royal College of Art, London, 20–23 July. Published in *Long-Range Planning* (1984) *17*, No. 3, P. 78–91, as Design and Competition in Engineering

Rothwell R and Soete L 1983 Technology and Economic Change. *Physics in Technology* **14** (6) November: 270–7

Rothwell R and Zegveld W 1981 *Industrial Innovation and Public Policy*: Frances Pinter (Publishers) Ltd

Rothwell R and Zegveld W 1982 *Innovation and the Small and Medium Sized Firm*. Frances Pinter (Publishers) Ltd

Schumpeter J 1939 *Business Cycles*. McGraw Hill, New York and London

Soete L 1978 International Competition, Innovation and Employment. Six Countries Programme Workshop, Paris, 13–14 November. (Mimeo) Science Policy Research Unit, University of Sussex

Soete L 1981 Technical Change, Catching Up and the Productivity Slowdown. In Granstrand O and Sigurdson J (ed) *Technological and Industrial Policy in China and Europe*. Research Policy Institute, Occasional Paper Series No 3, University of Lund, Sweden

Soete L 1983 Long Cycles and the International Diffusion of Technology. International Seminar on Innovation, Design and Long Cycles in Economic Development, Department of Design Research, Royal College of Art, London, 13–15 April

Stout D 1981 The Case of Government Support for R&D and Innovation. In Carter C (ed) *Industrial Policy and Innovation*. Heinemann

van Duijn J J 1983 *The Long Wave in Economic Life*. Van Gorcum, Assen, Netherlands

van Gelderen J 1913 Springvloed: Beschouwingen over industiele ontwickkeling en prijsbeweging. *De Nieuwe Tijd* **18** (4, 5, 6) April-June

Vernon R 1966 International Investment and International Trade in the Product Cycle. *Quarterly Journal of Economics* **80**: 190–207

Walker W 1978 *Industrial Innovation and International Trading Performance*. JAI Press, Greenwich, Conn, USA

Yu H Y 1982 *The Dynamics of Technological Leadership and Economic Development*, M Phil Thesis, Science Policy Research Unit, University of Sussex

CHAPTER TWO

The Process of Technological Innovation: Patterns and Influences

THE INNOVATION PROCESS

In this chapter we shall deal with the process of technological innovation itself. It is clearly desirable that policy makers have some knowledge of the innovation process if they are to formulate and promulgate realistically measures designed to enhance national innovative capabilities. But before we begin it is worthwhile making a clear distinction between 'invention' and 'innovation', which are often the subject of a great deal of confusion. A useful definition of invention is: 'The creation of an idea and its reduction to practice'.

Here 'reduction to practice' implies a rough laboratory test using typically a handbuilt model in order to prove the principle involved; it does not imply the construction of a well-developed, preproduction prototype in a manufacturing company. Thus invention is an act of technical creativeness involving the description of a novel new concept that would normally be suitable for patenting. It is not, in itself, an act suggesting movement towards commercial exploitation of the new combination; the latter, in fact, is the process of innovation:

Industrial innovation includes the technical, design, manufacturing, management and commercial activities involved in the marketing of a new (or improved) product or the first commercial use of a new (or improved) process or equipment (Freeman, 1974).

In other words, industrial innovation involves the commercialization of technological change, and invention is simply one element, albeit an important one, in the overall innovation process. As our definition suggests, however, innovation does not necessarily imply the commercialization of only a major advance in the technological state of the art (a radical innovation) but it includes also the utilization of even small scale changes in technological know-how (an improvement or 'incremental' innovation).

In practice, of course, radical and incremental innovations often will be closely linked, and a radical innovation will pave the way for an extended series of improvements, the sum total of which can have as marked an influence on the innovation's commercial performance as did the original breakthrough. It might also pave the way for a wave of innovations in other fields as, for example, did the transistor. In competitive terms, while the introduction of a major new combination can afford the originator significant technical and market leads, continued success depends on the ability of the firm to improve continuously the performance of the new device. The evolution of the innovation is part of a cumulative learning process within the firm and by customers. It would be rare for a firm to be able to appropriate completely the benefits of a radical innovation to such a degree as to exclude competition across its total life cycle. In some countries, perhaps most notably the United States, anti-trust legislation would make such complete appropriation even more difficult.

Technological innovation is generally a dynamic, iterative process rather than a one-off event. This is illustrated in Figure 2.1, which suggests that a successful new design involves only a temporary balance of price and non-price characteristics and continued success requires frequent adjustments to this balance. Moreover, it suggests that innovation is a process involving not only the innovating company but its customers also, especially during its latter phases.

A good example of this process can be found in the development of the enormously successful Sulzer weaving machine. This was a radical design innovation – the world's first shuttleless loom – that passed

Figure 2.1   Innovation as an Iterative Design Process

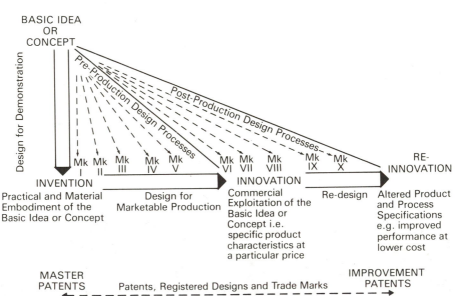

(*Source*: Rothwell and Gardiner, 1983.)

through ten prototype stages over many years before the commercial launch of the Mark 11 version. Throughout its development the Sulzer loom was tested regularly in the weaving mills of potential customers and it was feedback from these that provided much of the impetus for further redesign. Finally, in line with our model (Figure 2.1), the Sulzer loom underwent many design improvements during subsequent years that enabled it to maintain its competitive lead. Indeed, while the Mark 11 was a machine for producing plain cotton-staple goods only, it was explicitly designed with its later transformation into a more universally applicable machine in mind (Rothwell, 1976). In this respect, like the Boing 747 with its many derivatives, and the Cortina car which evolved into a broad range of models, the Sulzer loom can be said to be a 'robust' design (Rothwell and Gardiner, 1984).

Some over-simplified early 'models' of innovation, in fact, emphasized the causal role of scientific and technological advance and were generally linear; these can be summarized by Figure 2.2(a), which is the so-called 'technology-push' model of innovation. According to this model, discoveries in basic science lead eventually to industrial technological developments which result in a flow of new products and processes to the market place.

Figure 2.2   Two extreme models of the innovation process – the 'traditional' views

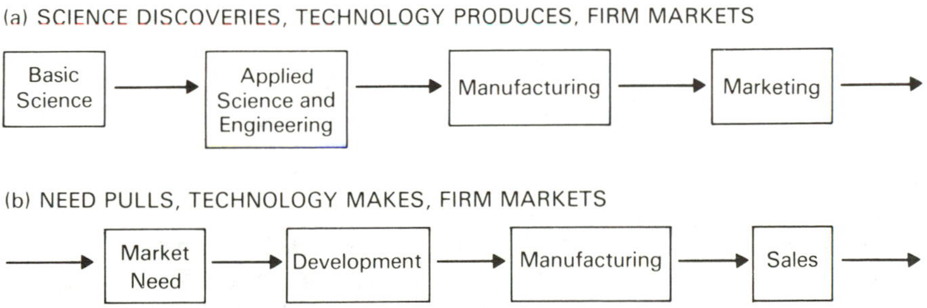

(a) SCIENCE DISCOVERIES, TECHNOLOGY PRODUCES, FIRM MARKETS

Basic Science → Applied Science and Engineering → Manufacturing → Marketing →

(b) NEED PULLS, TECHNOLOGY MAKES, FIRM MARKETS

→ Market Need → Development → Manufacturing → Sales →

(*Source*: Rothwell, 1983)

From the early to mid-1960s onwards, largely as the result of a growing number of empirical studies and descriptions of actual innovations, the role of felt need in innovation began to be emphasized, which led increasingly to the adoption of the linear 'need-pull' model of innovation shown in Figure 2.2(b). Here, innovations arise as the result of a perceived, and often clearly articulated market need.

During the past decade, both the pure technology-push and need-pull models of innovation have increasingly been regarded as extreme and untypical examples of a more general process of coupling between science, technology and the marketplace (Mowery and Rosenberg,

1978). In the first case, it is obvious that more R&D has not necessarily resulted in more innovation. In the second case, overemphasis on market needs can result in a regime of technological incrementalism and lack of radical innovation (Hayes and Abernathy, 1980). Moreover, the relative importance of technology-push and need-pull might vary considerably during different phases of the industry cycle.

Figure 2.3   Interactive model of the innovation process

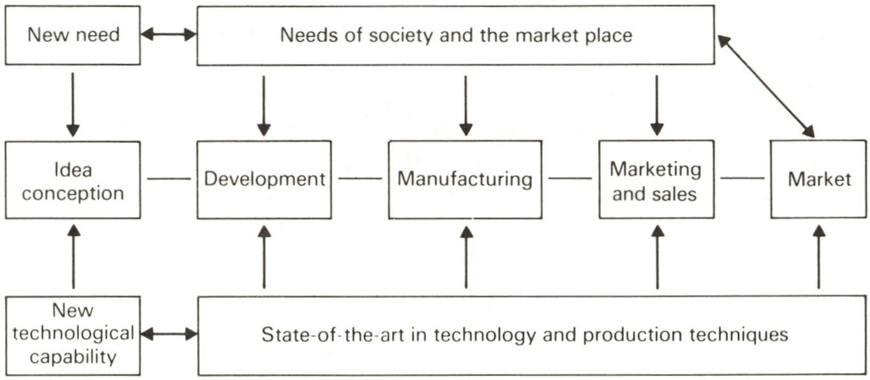

(*Source*: Rothwell, 1983)

A more representative model of industrial innovation is given in Figure 2.3; this is the so-called 'interactive model'. According to this model innovation is regarded as a logically sequential, though not necessarily continuous process, that can be subdivided into a series of functionally separate but interacting and interdependent stages. The overall pattern of the innovation process can be thought of as a complex net of communication paths, both intra-organizational and extra-organizational, linking together the various inhouse functions and linking the firm to the broader scientific and technological community and to the marketplace. In other words the process of innovation represents the confluence of technological capabilities and market needs within the framework of the innovating firm.

Despite the increasing acceptance of the interactive model of innovation, it nevertheless remains clear that many governments – and indeed many industrial companies – continue to adhere, at least implicitly, to the technology-push model. This is reflected in the emphasis in most countries on funding R&D – often to the neglect of other areas, such as demand – in the belief that more R&D does indeed result in more innovation. While we might, without too much difficulty, accept a close connection between development and innovation, we might question the extent to which the results of basic research, in the form of scientific advance, contribute to technological innovations in industry. Is basic scientific understanding a prerequisite to technological progress? If so, is the gap between scientific advance and industrial technological application decreasing? These questions, which are clearly important from the point of view of public policy, are addressed in the following sections.

THE DISCOVERY–INNOVATION TIME LAG

An interesting and long-standing debate in the innovation field centres on the question of whether or not the lapsed time between scientific discovery or invention and industrial innovation (commercialization) is decreasing. Mensch (1979), for example, has suggested, on the basis of his observed bunching of innovations during the depression periods of the Kondratiev cycles, that a 'depression accelerator' effect can occur which shortens the time between invention (including basic discovery) and commercialization. A second, and more general, factor is the rapid growth during the twentieth century of industrial R&D laboratories (Freeman, 1974). This internalization of scientific and technological activity by mainly large companies (who can also forge good contacts with researchers in universities and government research establishments) greatly increases their ability to capitalize on scientific advance and invention, which might be considered to have great potential for reducing the gap between discovery and innovation.

The question is, of course, has the expected shortening in discovery–innovation gaps occurred? Unfortunately, as we shall see below, the evidence on this point is far from conclusive. Enos, for example, on the basis of his study of thirty-five innovations, found the following time gaps (data taken from Giarini and Loubergé, 1978):

  – Pre-1900 (12 innovations) ; 12.5 years
  – 1911–40 (11 innovations) ; 15.8 years
  – post-1941 (12 innovations) ; 12.5 years

Cook and Morrison (1961) also provide inconclusive data which are listed in Table 2.1. They conclude:

Although the *frequency* of innovation has certainly increased in the last 150 years [a conclusion supported by Mensch], it is unlikely that one could demonstrate any significant *general* shortening in the time-span of the initial concept to innovation chains.

In contrast to the results in Table 2.1, Hafstad (1966) has presented data which suggest that a definite shortening has occurred in the discovery–innovation time gap: photography – 112 years; telephone – 56 years; radio – 35 years; radar – 15 years; television – 12 years; atomic bomb – 6 years; transistor – 5 years.

Table 2.1   Time gaps: original idea to innovation

Innovation	Time gap	Approx. date
Cotton gin	Months	1800
Vulcanization of rubber	2–3 years	1840
Railroad air brake	1–2 years	1868
Telephone	5 years	1880
Electrolytic aluminium	2 years	1886
X-rays	Weeks	1896
Ductile tungsten	3 years	1910
Nylon	6 years	1930
Hybrid corn	About 20 years	1930s
Radar	Few years	1935–1937
Penicillin	12 years	1940s
Transistor	4–5 years	1945–1952
Uranium mobile power	16 years	1954

(*Source*: Cook and Morrison, 1961)

These latter results, which contrast sharply with Cook and Morrison's for the telephone and for radar, highlight perhaps the major problem inherent in such exercises (after that of obtaining a statistically significant sample), ie do we measure the period from a basic scientific advance – and if so which – or from the clear invention of a practical principle. As Giarini and Loubergé (1978) point out, the former is frought with many difficulties. Commenting on Hafstad's results, they point out that:

The year 1725 was chosen for photography because that was when it was first discovered that silver salts turn black under the influence of light and not as previously thought under the influence of heat. But the beginnings of photography could equally well have been set back to the discovery of silver salts in 1565 or to the invention of the camera obscura in the year 1000, or alternatively, set at the date of the first photograph in 1822.

Giarini and Loubergé go on to make a further highly significant point:

Moreover, discoveries are rarely the result of sudden inspiration. They are mostly the outcome of a long search taking many decades and progressing step by step with occasional leaps ahead. Any prediction as to when a discovery will be made is . . . almost entirely arbitrary. And the example of the argument as to whether the main credit for the discovery of nuclear energy should go to Madame Curie, Neils Bohr or Oppenheimer or Fermi, shows how complex the background to the discovery may be.

From the point of view of public policy, perhaps the most notable contribution to this debate was that by Cook and Morrison who pointed to the role of need factors in shortening the discovery–innovation gap:

Even a casual inspection of the examples can leave little doubt that a major factor in shortening the time-gap is the *intensity* with which the *need* for the innovation is *actually felt* by the *potential user*.

Cook and Morrison point to four degrees of felt need and provide examples of each:

- Need felt in advance: examples where an urgent and explicit need was felt by the potential user before the innovation and acted to shorten the time gap, are the cotton gin, radar, paper and high-yield penicillin.
- Need felt only after the discovery or invention: examples of where the customer did not realize he had a need until after the concept, device, process or system was made, but realized his need *quickly* and shortened the time gap, are X-rays, wireless, photography, telegraph and hybrid corn.
- Need not felt until long after the discovery or invention: examples in which a lack of explicit felt need on the part of potential users caused the innovation to progress slowly – usually combined with difficulty in determining or recognizing the technical adequacy and economic attraction of the innovation, or because satisfactory alternatives were already in successful use, thus making the situation strictly a competitive one – are the rocket motor, magnetic recording, catalytic cracking and the fluorescent lamp.
- Negative need, or actual objection: an example in which one group of potential customers felt a negative need and delayed the innovation resulting in a long time gap is the sewing machine.

It might be concluded from the above that public bodies can accelerate the application of scientific and technological advance in certain desired directions both by the clear articulation of unmet public needs, current and future, and through disseminating information concerning identified needs elsewhere in society. In other words, governments might become involved in establishing not only technical information services, but market information services also. This conclusion is consistent with the results of a recent analysis by Nelson (1982) who, on the basis of descriptions of the role of the US government in the development of seven major industrial sectors, emphasized the important role played by public procurement agencies. Finally, as we shall discuss later, governments might have a role to play in helping to overcome various societal and institutional barriers to the acceptance of new technology, thereby accelerating rates of commercial application.

THE ROLE OF SCIENTIFIC ADVANCE IN TECHNOLOGICAL INNOVATION

While it is clear from the previous section that it is not possible to provide a definite answer to the question of shortening discovery –innovation time gaps, it is clear that scientific advance often does play an important role in technological innovation. However, to what degree science plays a direct role in innovation, or to what degree it plays a more diffuse enabling role, is far from clear. Nor is it by any means certain that scientific advance necessarily precedes technological development and commercial application. Indeed, as we shall see later, Rosenberg suggests that the flow is often in the opposite direction and, if this is true, it renders much of the scientific discovery–application time-lag debate meaningless.

The historian of science Derek de Solla Price (1965) was one of those who seriously questioned the proposition that scientific advance is a necessary prerequisite to technological innovation. He argued that science and technology are essentially two separate worlds, that the contact between them is spasmodic and occasional and that technology 'feeds on itself' for long periods without any major influence from science. Indeed, Price pointed out that the 'actors' associated with these two activities (science and technology) are different, as are their aims. Scientists are concerned primarily with generating scientific publications, in other words with generating knowledge, and thereby gaining kudos amongst their peers. Engineers are concerned with patents and blueprints, in other words with generating artefacts offering commercial benefits. Price used the simile of two dancing partners to illustrate the nature of the science–technology interaction, who both have their own steps even while dancing to the same tune; occasionally they will come together and be in step, usually they will be out of step.

Freeman (1974) later took up Price's model and argued that while it might well have been a true description of the science–technology interaction during the nineteenth century, it fails to describe adequately the relationship today. Today's relationship he sees as being much more 'intimate', arguing that the professional R&D department is both a cause and a consequence of this intimacy. Certainly, given the growing employment of scientists in industrial R&D during this century, with their ability to 'plug-in' to an 'invisible college of peers' working in universities and government research laboratories, while at the same time pursuing their own, albeit more directed, research interests, Freeman's claim would appear to have some validity. The question remains, of course, as to whether we can muster sufficient empirical evidence to support or refute this claim.

During the 1960s two well-known and detailed attempts were made in the United States to determine the role that fundamental, 'non-mission oriented' research plays in technological innovation. These are TRACES (Illinois Institute of Technology, 1968) and Project Hindsight (Sherwin and Isensen, 1966). The former investigation was based on tracing key scientific events which contributed towards five major technological innovations. The latter was a study of 'recent' science and technology that had been utilized by the US Department of Defence in the development of twenty post-World War II weapons systems.

Table 2.2   Distribution of research and development events by type of event

	Non-mission orientated	Mission orientated	Development and application events
	(%)	(%)	(%)
Research institutes and government	10	15	10
Industry	14	54	83
Universities	76	31	7
Total	100	100	100
% of all events	70%	20%	10%

(*Source*: Illinois Institute of Technology, 1968)

Table 2.3   Distribution of R&D events according to organizational source, and to type of event

Distribution of all R&D events	
Department of Defence Laboratories	39%
Federal Institutions (except Department of Defence)	2%
Industry	49%
Universities	9%
Foreign	1%
TOTAL	100%
Distribution by type of event	
Undirected research	0.3%
Applied research	7.7%
Technology	92%
TOTAL	100%

(*Source*: Sherwin and Isensen, 1966)

The results of TRACES and Hindsight are shown in Tables 2.2 and 2.3 and they are, at first sight, apparently contradictory. According to TRACES, 70 per cent of the key events which contributed to the five major innovations studied were 'non-mission research events'; according to Hindsight undirected (non-mission or fundamental) research played an extremely minor role in the development of the twenty weapons systems. However, the apparently minor role played by undirected research reported in the Hindsight study is almost certainly due largely to the fact that the investigation began with 1940 and deliberately chose to exclude the pool of basic knowledge assembled before 1940. The significance of this omission is demonstrated by the results of TRACES which showed that 90 per cent of all non-mission research events were completed at least ten years before the innovation. Clearly, the starting point is crucial.

Cynical observers might point out, in addition, that since TRACES was funded by the National Science Foundation, an organization responsible for funding non-mission research in the US, it might not be altogether surprising that such research was found to be crucial to technological innovation. Hindsight, on the other hand, was funded by the Department of Defence, an organization involved in funding mission-oriented research and technological development; again, perhaps not surprisingly, the results confirmed the importance of such directed R&D. Moreover, TRACES was almost certainly undertaken in response to the results of the Hindsight project.

Another US study – this time undertaken by the US National Academy of Science (NAS) (1965) – yielded results supporting those of TRACES. The NAS study investigated scientific publications which announced practical discoveries in chemistry, and the basic research results which led to these discoveries were, on the basis of cited references, traced back to their origins. Publications relating to sixteen different industrial discoveries included two-hundred-and-forty citations; 65 per cent of these referred to university research, 31 per cent to industrial research and 4 per cent to other sources. Further, 67 per cent referred to fundamental science journals and books, 22 per cent to applied journals, 10 per cent to patent publications and 1 per cent to other sources.

Few, of course, will be surprised to learn that basic scientific research makes a significant contribution to technological developments in chemicals, a science-based industry which itself performs basic research. A study in the UK, however, yielded results which suggested that university chemistry research has played only a relatively minor role in industrial chemical innovation. The study set out to determine the relationship, over a period of time, between university research in organic chemistry and the use by British industry of the results of this research (Langrish, 1974). The technique used was to study the institutional origins of abstracts produced by the *Journal of the Society of Chemical Industry*, which for eighty years or more has produced abstracts of the world's literature that might be of relevance to industrial chemists. The study showed that there had been a marked change during the period in the main institutional sources of abstracts, from European universities (mainly German) in 1884 to American industry in 1952. Since the end of the nineteenth century foreign industry has been the major source of inputs with, in 1952, UK industry being the second most important source. UK universities have consistently been the least, or the second least, important source of inputs.

Langrish offered two alternative hypotheses as to why the importance of university research has apparently declined: (1) industry has increasingly taken over its own research; (2) a new branch of science is only useful to industry in its early days (for example, the early days of astronomy as a science were linked with economically important attempts at improving navigation but it has hardly been useful since then).

Langrish then states:

The relationship between university research and industry may well be a function of the degree of development of the area concerned. Once a new area has been established, the aim of science is to understand; the aim of technology is to make it work, and industry has been very successful at making things work without too much reliance on understanding.

On the basis of Langrish's data for the chemical industry, it might be postulated that in certain areas of science the role of universities is to make the initial fundamental breakthrough, followed by many years of basic research to understand the *nature* of the process; the role of industry is commercially to utilize the breakthrough, concentrating on understanding and harnessing its *effects* while being largely unaware of their causes. Given the very rapid growth in industry R&D during this century, moreover, it might also be suggested that without a very considerable inhouse R&D capability, industry would be largely unable either to utilize the potential of the breakthrough or to enhance this potential progressively. Industry has thus needed increasingly to take over the relevant fields of research itself. At the same time the universities have gone on to open up new fields of research, perhaps paving the way for the next generation of industrial applications.

The results of a study by Gibbons and Johnston (1974), in contrast to those of Langrish, suggested that university scientific research in the UK does make a significant *direct* contribution to industrial R&D; it is, perhaps, this direct input that is not captured by Langrish's citation technique. Gibbons and Johnston identified (in the early 1970s) 887 units of information input that contributed to the solution of technical problems encountered during thirty recently completed or ongoing industrial innovation projects. Three hundred of these information inputs were from external sources, of which 107, or 36 per cent, could be classified as 'scientific' information. Of these 107 scientific inputs, 36 came from the scientific literature (which might be expected to contain a strong university representation, ie an indirect university input), 8 from scientific textbooks, 11 from scientific handbooks, 4 from scientists met at conferences, 18 from scientists in government research establishments and 30 from scientists in universities. Thus, about 10 per cent of the total information inputs from external sources for technical problem-solving at the thirty industrial R&D projects derived directly from university scientists.

Clearly, the important issue of the role of university research in industrial technological change requires further careful research, preferably treating each research field separately, or on a sector by sector basis. This would allow for variations in linkage according to the 'age' of the scientific field or of the industrial technology (Rothwell, 1982).

Turning back to the United States, in a follow-up study to TRACES, 'The Interactions of Science and Technology' (NSF, 1973), a study similar to TRACES was undertaken but which went very much further than TRACES and analysed the factors which are conducive to successful technological innovation. Ten major innovations were studied in detail, and the relative numbers of non-mission orientated research events, mission orientated research events, development research events and non-technical events which contributed to the innovation were determined. The results indicated that of more than five hundred 'significant' events (ie 'an occurrence judged to be important to the development of the technical innovation or its further improvements, as reported in a published paper, presentation or reference to research'), about 40 per cent were non-mission orientated, about two-fifths were mission orientated, about one-fifth were development research and about 5 per cent were non-technical. Of the ninety 'decisive' events ('occurrences that provide a major impetus to the innovation or its further improvement...') about one-sixth were non-mission orientated, about half were mission orientated, about two-fifths were development events and 1 per cent were non-technical events.

We can see from the results of TRACES II that the study attempted to take into account the relative significance of the different events, ie 'significant' and 'decisive'. While non-mission research made an important contribution to 'significant' events, mission-oriented (applied R&D) made the major contribution to the 'decisive' events.

Having described briefly the results of a number of studies that set out to determine the relationship between science and technology, it might appear strange to question their validity. Nevertheless, the question has to be asked whether it is meaningful, with the complex interactive process of technological innovation, to talk of identifying discrete 'events' and attempting to measure with any degree of precision their relative significance. Perhaps the most telling comment on this point was made by Mowery and Rosenberg (1978):

Indeed, the pervasiveness of uncertainty in the innovation process is ignored by most of the empirical studies. This is particularly true of the studies that have as their unit of analysis some group of selected innovations, and that attempt to reconstruct the history of such innovations: Hindsight, TRACES and the Battelle study are prominent examples. The attempt to decompose neatly the complex, stochastic, and uncertain process which is that leading to innovation into a set of events that can simply be cumulated to yield an innovation, is as gross an oversimplification as is the 'black box' approach of the surveys of business firms. To attempt such a reconstruction, and further to attempt to ascribe relative importance to the various categories of research events, seems fallacious.

Without doubt, the seminal contribution to the debate on the relationship between science and technology, is the paper 'How exogenous is science?' by Nathan Rosenberg which is included in his book *Inside the Black Box* (Rosenberg, 1982). The core theme of this paper is 'that technological concerns shape the scientific enterprise in various ways'.

Of course, the underlying assumption in the various studies described in this and the previous section, is that the nature of progress is such that science tends to influence technology, rather than vice versa, because scientific understanding precedes technological advance. Rosenberg questions this widely held assumption:

One of the more misleading consequences of thinking about technology as the mere *application* of prior scientific knowledge is that this perspective obscured a very elemental point: technology is itself a body of knowledge about certain classes of events and activities: it is not merely the application of knowledge brought from another sphere. It is a knowledge of techniques, methods, and designs that work, and that work in certain ways and with certain consequences, even when one cannot explain exactly why. It is therefore, if one prefers to put it that way, not a fundamental kind of knowledge, but rather a form of knowledge that has generated a certain rate of economic progress for thousands of years. Indeed, if the human race had been confined to technologies that were understood in a scientific sense, it would have passed from the scene long ago (Rosenberg, 1982, p.143).

According to Rosenberg, there are many areas even today where technological progress occurs in the absence of a full understanding of the underlying scientific principles. In these cases, technological change is largely an ad hoc process in which knowledge is accumulated through trial and error. A good example of this is the aeroplane, which has developed extensively despite the lack of any adequate theories of turbulence and compressibility.

Rosenberg argues persuasively that the normal overall pattern of development has been one in which technology precedes scientific understanding and in which scientific activity largely is directed towards understanding and explaining the principles underlying established technological phenomena. In other words technological advance largely determines the scientific agenda. Given the economic incentives underlying technological advance, this pattern is, according to Rosenberg, hardly surprising. Of course, Rosenberg does not argue that technology always precedes science, but that empirical evidence suggests that in general this has been the case.

It might be, of course, that gaining a basic scientific understanding of an established technological phenomenon will greatly enhance the scope and accelerate the pace of technological change. For example, copper oxide and silicon rectifiers were being used before Shockley's research threw some light on the phenomenon of electronic conduction in doped semiconductor materials, out of which grew the modern semiconductor industry; animal breeders had succeeded in producing many different forms of livestock and domestic animals before the discovery of DNA paved the way to understanding the possibilities of genetic engineering. In both cases, the use of instrumentation – the result of technological developments – was crucial in furthering basic scientific understanding.

So we can see that just as the innovation process itself is complex and stochastic, so too is the interaction between science and technology. Each feeds on the other, the 'impact vector' swinging first this way and then that, its direction changing over time and the relative importance of science and technology at any one time being different in different areas of techno-economic activity. Considering the impact vector as unidirectional, running always in one direction or the other, clearly is naive and fails to embrace the uncertainties and the complexities of the real world of technological innovation. Unfortunately, this conclusion is of little assistance to public policy makers who might wish to allocate national resources between scientific and technological institutions. Perhaps the best advice to be offered here is the suggestion that, first, resource allocation be preceded by a thorough analysis of the nature of, and relationship between, science and technology in each field, as well of the evolving pattern of societal and market needs, and to make organizational and institutional arrangements which promote strong interaction.

PUSH OR PULL

It should be clear from the foregoing sections that we subscribe neither to the simple linear technology-push nor the simple linear need-pull models of innovation. Technological innovation is, as Mowery and Rosenberg (1979) have shown, generally too complex a process to be described by a simple chain of causality in one direction or the other. It is, nevertheless, worth briefly outlining the major arguments in this area, less from the point of view of specific products or processes, but rather more from the viewpoint of the evolutionary dynamics of new generic technologies or industrial branches.

It was probably the work of Schmookler (1966) which pointed most strongly to the importance of demand factors in innovation. Based on a highly detailed study of the evolution over time (1840–1950) of patents and investment mainly in four capital goods industries in the United States (railroads, petroleum refining, agriculture machinery and paper making) – but also, although to a lesser extent, in a number of consumer goods industries – Schmookler's work led him to the conclusion that market growth and market potential were the main determinants of the rate and direction of inventive activity. Schmookler summarized his principal conclusions as follows:

... the most striking and most significant result of the entire study . . . concerns the relation of capital goods output to the number of capital goods inventions. The relation is evident in time series involving a single industry, and in cross sections relating to several industries. When time series of investment (or capital goods output) and the number of capital goods inventions are compared for a single industry, both the long-term trend and the long swings exhibit great similarities, with the notable difference that lower turning points in major cycles or long swings generally occur in capital goods sales before they do so in capital goods patents.

. . . The possibility that the results reflect the effect of capital goods inventions on capital goods sales is grossly implausible. In the time series comparisons, trend turning points tend to occur in sales before they do in patents and long swing troughs in sales generally precede those in patents. Moreover, trends and long swings in investment in the industries examined are adequately explained on other grounds.

. . . The fact that inventions are usually made because men want to solve economic problems or capitalise on economic opportunities is of overwhelming importance for economic theory. Hitherto, many economists have regarded invention – and technological change generally – as an *exogenous*, and some even thought, an *autonomous*, variable. It was exogenous in the sense that it was not controlled by economic variables. According to some, it was exogenous in a particular sense, it was autonomous, its own past entirely determining its future.

These views insofar as they were of a substantive nature rather than merely a methodological convenience, are no longer tenable . . . the belief that invention, or the production of technology generally, is in most instances, essentially a non-economic activity is false . . . the production of inventions, and much other technological knowledge, whether, routinised or not, . . . is in most instances as much an economic activity as is the production of bread (Schmookler, 1966, pp.204–208).

As we saw in Chapter 1, the work that stressed most strongly the role of technology in innovation and economic change, was probably that of Schumpeter (1910; 1943). In the first case Schumpeter stressed the importance of exogenous science and invention which, via the medium of entrepreneurial activity, led to the growth of new industrial branches and new areas of demand (the Schumpeter I model); in the second case he emphasized the role of endogenous science and technology in the R&D laboratories of major companies – strongly coupled to exogenous science and technology – which again led to new patterns of production and new market structures (the Schumpeter II model).

Thus we are faced with a dilemma. Two eminent economists, both operating with detailed time series data, reach apparently diametrically opposed conclusions. Fortunately a detailed piece of research undertaken in the late 1970s at the Science Policy Research Unit provided some of the answers to this dilemma. The research, carried out by Walsh, Townsend, Achilladelis and Freeman (1979), provided a detailed critique of Schmookler's methodology, pointing in particular to the problems of employing only aggregate patent statistics and failing to gain an understanding of major discoveries and inventions that can influence profoundly whole sectors or subsectors of industry. Furthermore, they looked at an industry that was more science and R&D intensive than those considered by Schmookler, namely the chemical industry: more specifically they looked in detail at four subsectors; plastics, dyestuffs, pharmaceuticals and petrochemical intermediates. The indicators employed were scientific papers, patents, investment and production.

Walsh et al set out to test four models of innovation: the demand-led model (after Schmookler); the model of technology and demand-led science (after Hessen, 1931); Schumpeter's model of entrepreneurial innovation (Schumpeter I); and Schumpeter's model of innovation managed by large firms (Schumpeter II). These models are set out in Figures 2.4, 2.5, 2.6 and 2.7 respectively, which are taken from Walsh et al. (The Schumpeter I and II figures were based on the earlier diagrams of Phillips, 1971).

Figure 2.4   Schematic representation of Schmookler's model of demand-led invention.

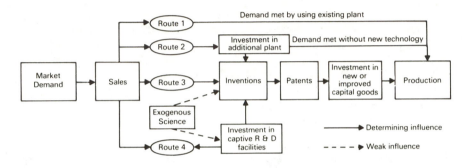

Figure 2.5   Schematic representation of Hessen's model of technology and demand-led science.

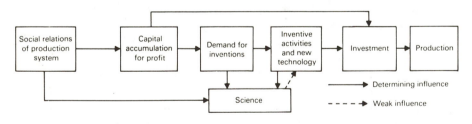

Figure 2.6   Schematic representation of Schumpeter's Model of entrepreneurial innovation (I)

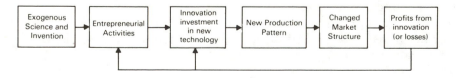

Figure 2.7   Schematic representation of Schumpeter's Model of large firm managed innovation (II)

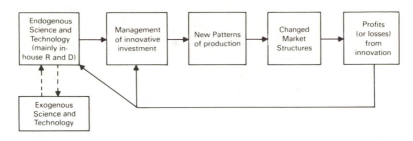

(*Source*: Walsh et al, 1979)

Among the most important conclusions of the study are the following:

Take first of all Schmookler's model of market demand leading and determining the scale and direction of inventive activity. There is some support for a weak version of this theory but little to justify a strong version. At the major turning points in economic activity we found only limited evidence to support the view that either the expansion of the market (or its contraction) clearly *preceded* (pre-dated with a significant time-lag) a change in the scale of inventive activity. Some of our evidence directly contradicted Schmookler's theory in that an upsurge of inventive (and occasionally even scientific) activity clearly preceded the growth of the market. This was the case with both plastics and dyestuffs in the period 1925–1935, and it was also the case with drugs in the 1930s. However, a weaker version of the theory could be justified on the grounds of intelligent long-term *anticipation* of future market demand stimulating inventive activity in these cases.

A weaker version of the Schmookler theory could also find support from the post-war evidence of similar long-term patterns between the various time series. There was a powerful upward movement of production and investment in all the main product groups we are considering and this was accompanied in every case by an upward surge of similar scale and duration in the number of patents and scientific publications. To this limited extent the statistical evidence provides some support not only for Schmookler but for all the four models which we are considering. There is clearly some fairly close association between scientific activities, inventive work, production and investment in each of the various sectors (Walsh et al, p 22).

In the case of dyestuffs, and using nineteenth-century data, Walsh et al found some support for Schmookler's theory:

Here we did find one clear-cut case of demand leading innovation. Paradoxically this is an instance usually cited by supporters of science-push, and even supporters of demand theories have made an exception in this case. Our re-examination of this period shows that the original growth of dyestuffs patenting clearly followed the growth of demand from the textile industry and especially the UK textile industry (then by far the largest in the world) (Walsh et al, p 23).

Later, however, with the mergence of the increasingly dominant German synthetic dyestuffs industry, a counter-Schmookler pattern emerged, and supply factors became much more significant. This was brought about by endogenous R&D in the expanding laboratories of the major German synthetics producers and by the drive for German self-sufficiency prior to the First and Second World Wars, which led to accelerated efforts in Germany to develop new synthetic materials to overcome its dependence on imported natural raw materials, which in turn led to a great deal of basic and applied scientific research.

Commenting on Hessen's highly deterministic theory of technology and demand leading basic science, Walsh et al state :

Whilst our evidence would not support a purely deterministic view of demand leading invention or technology leading science, it would certainly be consistant with a theory which postulated an interdependent or shifting relationship. There do appear to be some periods when technology leads and some when science leads, and others when the indicators move very close together. In these circumstances we would expect not only similar patterns (although with varying leads and lags), but also that publications themselves would reflect a degree of convergence of science and technology. This is indeed the case. Derek Price (1965) himself, while maintaining in general that technologists did not seek to publish like scientists, but to patent or to design, made an exception for chemistry and electronics, where there is substantial publishing activity by technologists, much of it linked directly or indirectly to fundamental science. In an interesting citation study of 'Science-Technology Coupling in Electronics' Liebermann (1978) found that for industry authors publishing in the *Transactions of the IEEE* references to the basic science literature from *Physical Review* were slightly more recent than those of university authors. He concludes from his study that in electronics the 'science-technology coupling has remained strong over the past two decades, as a consequence of the continued birth of new science-related technologies within the solid-state field'. Thus it appears that the coupling between the scientific and technological sectors proceeds over time like a series of overlapping waves, as various ties form and then gradually die out.

These findings are remarkably similar to our own and the institutional mechanism which Lieberman suggests is one in which the links between the most fundamental research and applied technology are made by intermediaries who are able to communicate with both. Our own study and his suggest that such people are to be found mainly within industry and especially within industrial R&D Departments (Walsh et al, p 27).

Perhaps the above quotation highlights the most significant result of Walsh et al's study, and that is the evidence of 'two-way linkages with strong reciprocal influences'. In some cases demand might lead to technological activity (and production), followed by basic research to understand the fundamental mechanisms involved (a sort of 'Rosenberg model'); in other cases the results of prior scientific research might be a necessary prerequisite for inventive and then innovative activity, which might then be followed by further basic research better to understand the mechanisms involved. Walsh et al term this derivative scientific activity 'gap-filling' science.

In general, Walsh et al see their overall findings as being more consistent with the theories of Schumpeter than with those of either Schmookler or Hessen.

Schumpeter Mark I suggested that exceptional creative entrepreneurs deriving ideas from an exogenous science background undertook risky innovative developments to launch new products and change existing market structures. They often anticipated rather than followed demand.

Schumpeter Mark II postulated that 'endogenous' science and technology, mainly within the R and D laboratories of the large firms had increasingly substituted for the mechanism of the 'exogenous' inventor setting up in business. He did not however rule out the possibility of the Mark I mechanisms continuing to operate within a climate increasingly dominated by large-scale corporate R and D. According to our findings, this is almost exactly what has happened in the chemical industry since the 19th Century. Men like Perkin and Baekeland coming from an academic background were able to make a fortune from their own discoveries by establishing their own firms. Sometimes these chemist-inventors worked with partners who had greater commercial experience, sometimes they acquired this knowledge themselves, but they laid the foundations for the modern chemical industry, whilst at the same time, as Schumpeter argued, they completely disequilibrated the previous market structures and destroyed some traditional trades in older materials.

As however the new chemical firms grew up and consolidated their new markets they made an extraordinarily important social innovation – the captive industrial R and D laboratory. This meant that they were no longer so vulnerable to the 'creative destruction' brought about by exogenous science and technology through new entrepreneurs. They themselves learnt the trick of institutionalising this process. By earning exceptional profits on their major innovations they were able to finance scientific and technical activities on such a scale as to retain the ability to generate successive new waves of invention and innovation, or at least to keep fairly close behind the leaders (Walsh et al, pp 27–28).

Thus we might conclude from the work of Walsh et al that the relationship between science, technology and the marketplace is rarely unequivocally unidirectional, nor is it a simple one, and within particular branches of industry causality can switch from being mainly in one direction to being mainly in the other. The linkages between science, technology and the marketplace are complex, interactive and multidirectional, the dominant driving force varying over time and between one branch of industry and the next. Innovation is, as we suggested earlier, a process of coupling, and it should be a primary aim of policy to forge the necessary links, adjusting the balance of resources to match the pattern of requirements for each technology or industry at its particular stage of development.

TECHNOLOGICAL TRAJECTORIES

It is probably true to say that most of the emphasis in the literature on technological innovation during the 1960s and 1970s was on innovations at the level of the firm. This reflected a growing interest on the part of researchers and policy makers alike in understanding the managerial and other factors associated with successful and unsuccessful innovations. By and large most of these empirical studies were descriptive and lacked theoretical underpinning.

Economists, in contrast, continued to take a broader and more theoretical view of technological change, dealing mainly with process changes and attempting to measure the contribution of 'technical change' to manufacturing productivity growth. In this case technological change, and indeed the firm, were treated as a 'black box' and behavioural and organizational factors largely ignored.

During the 1970s Richard Nelson and his colleagues at Yale University began the search for a theory of innovation that might link together better the 'micro' and 'macro' worlds that previously had been treated largely as separate entities. This work culminated in the seminal paper 'Towards a Useful Theory of Innovation' published by Nelson and Winter in 1977 (greatly extended in Nelson and Winter, 1982):

This essay presents an overview of selected aspects of prevailing theoretical understanding of innovation and attempts to sketch some directions that would seem fruitful to follow if we are to achieve a theoretical structure that can be helpful in guiding thinking about policy. We are using the term innovation as a portmanteau to cover the wide range of varigated processes by which man's technologies evolve over time. By theory we mean a reasonably coherent intellectual framework which integrates existing knowledge, and enables predictions to go beyond the particulars of what actually has been observed. It seems apparent that if scholarly knowledge is to be helpful to deliberation about possible policy directions, theory must be wide enough to encompass and link the relevant variables and their effects, and strong enough to give guidance as to what would happen if some of these variables changed (Nelson and Winter, 1977).

In their paper, Nelson and Winter developed the concepts of 'natural trajectories' and 'selection environments'. (More recent work by Gardiner (1984) has identified a number of distinctive 'design trajectories' in aeroplanes and automobiles during the past 50 years.) Taking first natural trajectories:

. . . it may be that there are certain powerful intra project heuristics that apply when a technology is advancing in a certain direction, and payoffs from advancing in that direction that exist under a wide range of demand conditions. We call these directions 'natural trajectories'. If natural trajectories exist, following these may be a good strategy (Nelson and Winter, 1977).

Thus the rate and direction of technological advance might be determined not only (as economists would contend) by demand conditions but also, as Rosenberg (1972) puts it, through the operation of certain 'technological imperatives'. In the semiconductor industry, for example, we can see that both technological and market forces drove semiconductor developments along the paths of more reliable, smaller, less energy-intensive and cheaper devices. Clearly these developments satisfied the evolving needs of the aerospace, military and computer markets well, but it would have been surprising if accumulated technological and production learning had not moved developments along similar paths.

Nelson and Winter make the more general point that:

While natural trajectories almost invariably have special elements associated with the particular technology in question, in any era there appear to be certain natural trajectories that are common to a wide range of technologies. Two of these have been relatively well identified in the literature: progressive exploitation of latent scale economies, and the increasing mechanisation of operations that have been done by hand (Nelson and Winter, 1977).

A good illustrative example of natural trajectories can also be found in the pattern of developments in textile machinery during the postwar era. The principal development trends during this period have been geared towards three main ends: increasing the productivity of individual units of production; reducing the number of operations required in a given production sequence; increasing the amount of automatic transfer between operations (Rothwell and Zegveld, 1979). The many radical and incremental innovations in textile machinery during the past thirty or so years have been directed largely towards satisfying these ends (Rothwell, 1976) which, between them, have established the agenda of both public and private R&D programmes.

Turning now to selection environments,

We propose the concept of a 'selection environment' as a useful theoretical organiser. Given the flow of new innovations, the selection environment (as we are employing the terms) determines how relative use of different technologies changes over time. The selection environment influences the path of productivity growth generated by any given innovation, and also it feeds back the influence strongly of the kinds of R & D that firms and industry will find profitable to undertake (Nelson and Winter, 1977).

Nelson and Winter point to two basic classes of selection environment: market and non-market. In the first case, not surprisingly, the nature of demand acts as a filter for selecting projects for development from a larger portfolio of possibilities. Firms will innovate in areas which yield them the maximum appropriability of benefit from their R&D efforts.

In the second case, the motivations of firms in a non-market sector, according to Nelson and Winter, cannot simply be presumed to be monetary profit, and they offer as examples the relationship between a doctor and his patient:

The doctor is not supposed to make his decisions regarding the use of a new drug on the basis of whether this will profit him, but rather on his expectation of how this will benefit his patients. Further, he is supposed to know more about this than his patients, [and the] relationship between a public sector agency, like a school system, and its clientele (students and parents), and sources of finance (mayor, council and voters) [which] simply does not have an arms' length distance quality that marks the relationship between seller and potential buyer of a new car. . . . The public sector agency is expected to play a key role in the articulation of values, and to internalise those and work in the public interest of its own violation.

A second non-market selection element that can influence the choice of technology (as well as its rate of development) is government regulations. These can effectively filter out harmful developments and accelerate the search for more socially desirable alternative (eg the discontinuance of development and marketing of cyclamates in the US and the shift in development effort towards 'natural', high-intensity nonsucrose sweetners). There exists compelling evidence that in some branches of technology (eg pharmaceuticals) government regulations can have a powerful influence on both the rate and direction of technological change (Rothwell, 1979).

The work of Nelson and Winter does, we believe, indeed lay the foundations of a useful theory of innovation. The concept of natural trajectories of technological change (technological trajectories) aids us in taking not so much a 'macro', but rather a 'meta' view of technological change, enabling us to look beyond what is happening at the level of individual projects and firms. The concept of selection environments assists us in understanding why, given a set of possible trajectories within a rather broad technological regime, certain pathways are preferred. It is important also to note that public institutions and public policy are themselves potentially important elements of the selection environment.

TECHNOLOGICAL INTERRELATEDNESS AND INTERSECTORAL FLOWS

In his paper 'Technological Interdependence in the American Economy', Rosenberg states:

Innovations hardly ever function in isolation. Time and again in the history of American technology, it has happened that the productivity of a given innovation has turned on the question of the availability of complementary technologies. Often these technologies did not initially exist, so that the benefits potentially flowing from invention A had to await the achievement of inventions B, C or D . . . The growing productivity of industrial economies is the complex outcome of large numbers of interlocking, mutually reinforcing technologies, the individual components of which are of very limited economic consequence by themselves. The smallest relevant unit of observation, therefore, is seldom a single innovation but, more typically, an interrelated clustering of innovations (Rosenberg, 1979).

Rosenberg offers a number of examples of technological interdependence, highlighting instances where the practical use of a particular invention was delayed until a complementary development(s) enabled its implementation:
- It was not until the development of cheap, high-quality steel that the potential of the compound steam engine was realized.
- It was not until the development of suitable machine tooling methods that alloy steels realized their full potential.
- Many advances in metallurgy were required before the jet engine could be put into general use.

To the above we might add the crucial 'enabling' contribution that computer aided design (CAD) made to the rapid development of large scale integrated circuits (the development of CAD systems themselves owing much to previous developments in computing and in semiconductors) and the need for the development of new and modified forms of textile processing machinery before the commercial potential of synthetic fibres could be realized by textile manufacturers.

Rosenberg's concept of technological interdependence is of great significance to technology policy, especially in the area of technology choice. Unless policy makers understand the interrelatedness (where it exists) between apparently separate fields of technology, technological bottlenecks are likely to occur and progress in the chosen field delayed.

Other important issues are those of technological linkages between sectors and the pervasiveness of certain types of innovation. These issues have been addressed by Townsend et al (1981) on the basis of data relating to the sectors of production and use of some 2300 innovations introduced by UK companies between 1945 and 1979. From a cross-tabulation of sectors of production and use of innovations (involving only cases where ten or more innovations were involved and accounting for a total of 1383 innovations), Townsend et al found that twenty-four out of the forty-two flows identified were intersectoral rather than intrasectoral. The most significant of these flows are illustrated in Figure 2.8.

Townsend et al then went on to investigate the pervasiveness of producer innovations, and their results are shown in Table 2.4 for thirty-four sectors of industry. In the Table the third column shows the percentage of innovations produced in a sector that were first used in other sectors, the fourth column shows the number of sectors at which

Figure 2.8 Intersectoral linkages

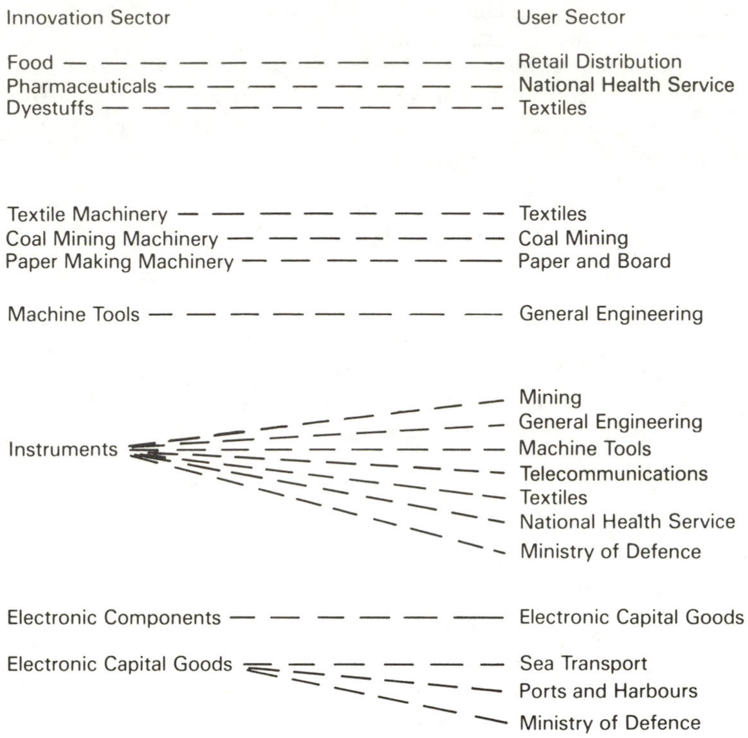

Innovation Sector   User Sector

Food — — — — — — — — — — — — Retail Distribution
Pharmaceuticals — — — — — — — — — National Health Service
Dyestuffs — — — — — — — — — — — Textiles

Textile Machinery — — — — — — — — — Textiles
Coal Mining Machinery — — — — — — — — Coal Mining
Paper Making Machinery — — — — — — — Paper and Board

Machine Tools — — — — — — — — General Engineering

                                                        — Mining
                                                        — General Engineering
Instruments   — Machine Tools
                                                        — Telecommunications
                                                        — Textiles
                                                        — National Health Service
                                                        — Ministry of Defence

Electronic Components — — — — — — Electronic Capital Goods

Electronic Capital Goods   Sea Transport
                                                        Ports and Harbours
                                                        — Ministry of Defence

(*Source*: Townsend et al, 1981)

50 per cent or more of the innovations of the sectors outside the producing sectors were first used, and the fifth column the total number of outside sectors in which the innovations were used.

Innovations produced in thirteen of the sectors found applications in ten or more outside sectors, the average number of sectors of application being just under ten. The sectors with the highest degree of pervasiveness in terms of the number of sectors of first use were instruments (44 sectors); electronic capital goods (23 sectors); electronic components (18 sectors); plastics and plastic processing (17 sectors), and electronic computers (16 sectors).

Only two sectors find applications for their outside innovations in just one sector: textile machinery and cement. A much larger number find at least 50 per cent of their innovations concentrated in one sector: food products, pharmaceuticals, detergents, dyestuffs, machine tools, coal-mining machinery, industrial plant, broadcasting equipment, other electrical equipment, tractors, leather and footwear. In a number of cases, no first uses at all were within the sector of production: pharmaceuticals, mining machinery, industrial furnaces and plastics (Townsend et al, 1981).

Table 2.4   The Spread of first use of innovations from each sector

Sector	No. of Innovations	Percentage first used outside sector	No. of sectors in which 50% of outside use is reached	No. of outside sectors in which Innovation is Used
Food	65	44.6	1	3
Pharmaceuticals	82	100.0	3	7
Detergents	20	20.0	1	2
Plastics	70	87.3	4	17
Dyestuffs	51	86.3	1	7
Iron and steel	99	34.3	2	12
Aluminium	39	53.8	3	11
Machine tools	165	96.4	1	13
Textile machinery	222	99.5	1	1
Mining machinery	116	100.0	1	2
'Other' machinery	65	96.9	3	17
Industrial plant	22	100.0	1	5
Instruments	328	93.0	6	44
Electronic components	109	94.5	2	18
Broadcasting equipment	48	31.2	1	4
Electronic computers	54	66.7	3	16
Electronics capital goods	90	91.1	4	23
'Other' electrical	39	94.9	1	6
Shipbuilding	51	43.1	2	8
Tractors	38	50.0	1	2
Motor vehicles	77	20.8	2	7
Textiles	88	33.0	3	10
Leather (and footwear)	35	20.0	1	3
Glass	40	82.5	3	9
Cement	22	40.9	2	1
Paper and board	29	72.4	4	13
Plastics products	30	100.0	4	17

Note: 1) For all relevant minimum list heading (MLH) codes see table 4.4.
    2) Sectors with 20 or more innovations included Total = 2094
(*Source*: Townsend et al, 1981)

The intensity and pervasiveness of intersectoral linkages in technology were predominantly due to producer/user relations rather than to diversification by firms. Diversification accounted for only eighteen of the forty-six cases identified, and for only 18 per cent of the sample of innovations.

Largely on the basis of the above data, and adopting a more systematic approach, Pavitt (1983) has developed a three-point classification of companies on the basis of their role in technological change: supplier-dominated firms, production-intensive firms and science-based firms.

Supplier-dominated innovations are found mainly in traditional sectors of industry such as textiles, construction and agriculture. The firms in these industries make little contribution to technological change themselves, but buy in technology from suppliers.

Production-intensive firms evolve from the supplier-dominated category. They are large firms that produce standard bulk materials using continuous-flow techniques, or consumer durables (including vehicles) using mass-production techniques. Because of the high costs of production breakdown in these firms, they build up strong engineering skills oriented towards production processes, skills which themselves become an important source of changes in process technology. They also make a significant contribution to upstream innovation in machinery and instrumentation.

The science-based firms are technologically highly specialized and founded on key scientific discoveries in electricity, electromagnetism, semiconductors (the electronics industry), chemical synthesis and biological synthesis (the chemical industry). Their products are, however, highly pervasive and find application in a wide range of user sectors.

Four important conclusions of Pavitt's analysis were as follows (Pavitt, 1983):

– Technical change in firms is cumulative and specific. Outside sources of general knowledge and specific technology must be matched by inhouse competence if they are to be effectively assimilated.

– Trajectories of technological development in firms are strongly influenced by their principal activities, and can be classified and explained in terms of three categories: supplier-dominated, production-intensive and science-based.

– Firms in these three categories have different potentials and directions for technical change, and these largely determine their possibilities for technology-based diversification.

– Firms in the same three categories respond to, and require, different patterns of supporting government policies.

In his second category Pavitt included machinery suppliers. Firms in this area perform their own R&D and increasingly many are adding electronics skills to their traditional skills in mechanical engineering. They vary in size from small to very large companies, and the number of sectors they supply varies enormously. Textile machinery manufacturers, for example, supply just one user sector (textile industry), while machine tool manufacturers supply many branches of industry. Machinery suppliers are a key factor in the productivity growth of their user industries. Where the capital goods industries are technologically laggard, however, new developments can, as Pavitt has suggested, originate in the production- intensive category of user companies, a good example being the development of robotics in automobile manufacturing in Italy.

Just as Rosenberg's work suggested the need for technological interdependencies to be taken into account by governments committed to technological selectivity, so Pavitt's work suggests the need for policy makers to take into account technological interdependencies between different branches of industry. Thus, in certain cases, sector-specific policies might be inappropriate, intersectoral relationships imposing the need for balanced and coordinated development programmes to be undertaken in technologically linked (supplier/producer/user) sectors.

Finally in this section it is worthwhile briefly examining a further technological linkage mechanism between users and producers, and that is the role of the user in the innovation process. Even firms in Pavitt's first category (supplier-dominated), users, while not actually manufacturing process equipment themselves, can nevertheless make a significant contribution to technological change in the supplier. A study of innovations in the European textile machinery industry, for example, showed that while the technologically more radical innovations arose largely in the R&D laboratories of major machinery companies, many of the incremental innovations originated as the result of user learning in textile mills (Rothwell, 1976).

It was, without doubt, the work of Eric von Hippel that first focused attention on the role of the user in the innovation process (von Hippel, 1976, 1977, 1978). Von Hippel's researches in the scientific instruments industry showed that, from a total of 111 innovations, 76 per cent originated as the result of inventive activity on the part of the user. Shaw (1983) found a similar pattern for innovations in the UK medical instruments industry: in a sample of thirty-three innovations, twenty-five were transferred from the user to the manufacturer via a process of continuous and multiple interaction.

In attempting to explain his results, von Hippel utilized the concept of the appropriability of innovation benefit as a predictor of the functional locus of innovation (von Hippel, 1979). Commenting, for example, on the work of Berger (1975) and Boyden (1976), who found, in the plastics and plastics additive industries respectively, that all the innovations studied derived exclusively from the manufacturer, he states:

As noted earlier Berger and Boyden have, for example, sampled plastics and plastics additive innovations respectively and have found all of these to have been developed by product manufacturers rather than by product users. I suspect that further research would show this locus explicable in terms of the ability of users and manufacturers to appropriate output-embodied benefits from these categories of innovations. A particular plastic or additive is typically not essential to users since other materials exist which can do the job at a (usually minor) cost premium. To the manufacturer, however, a plastics and additive innovation which provides such a slight cost advantage might mean that major users of other materials (steel, aluminium, other plastics, etc.) replace these with the innovative material and quickly become major customers, thus allowing the innovator to capture significant output-embodied benefit (Von Hippel, 1979).

While we would agree that the appropriability of benefit is a crucial factor in determining the locus of innovative activity, we would add a second factor, that of the locus of state-of-the-art expertise. It is not, for example, surprising that medical researchers are the source of a significant percentage of medical instrument innovations since they are involved in state-of-the-art medical research which often necessitates building new monitoring and measuring equipment in collaboration, in the UK, with medical physicists and technicians. The same is true of chemists in university and government laboratories who often invent and build new analytical equipment to further their researches. Medical researchers are not normally in the business of instrument manufacturing, and they can best appropriate the benefits of their inventive activity through buying back professionally manufactured, easy to use and reliable instruments from manufacturers to whom they have transferred their invention. The manufacturer, on the other hand, appropriates the benefits of his design, engineering and manufacturing efforts via instrument sales. It would, of course, be unusual for the instrument manufacturer to contain the necessary level of medical research skills to enable him to make the initial invention, although he can remain 'plugged in' to the inventive medical researcher and utilize him as a part of the subsequent instrument development process once the original invention has been transferred.

Since much of the state-of-the-art research in many fields and in many countries is performed in universities, government laboratories and other public sector institutions, clearly the above results have implications for public policy. Specifically, they again highlight the need for effective linkage mechanisms to facilitate in this case the transfer of user-inventions to manufacturing companies. In many countries, of course, such mechanisms already exist, although whether or not they operate effectively is another matter.

FACTORS IN SUCCESS AND FAILURE

The literature on factors affecting the success and failure of innovations is simply too extensive to be comprehensively covered here, and we can do no more than offer a brief summary of some of the more important points that have emerged from the many empirical studies in this field. Table 2.5 lists a number of the key factors associated with success and failure or delay in innovation, taken from a comparative analysis of nine major studies undertaken during the 1960s and 1970s. (Rothwell, 1977. See also Cooper, 1980).

Table 2.5 illustrates clearly that there are no magical formulae for innovatory success, and it is more or less possible to sum up the results of the various studies by saying that success is a matter of 'good

Table 2.5 Factors associated with success and failure delay in industrial innovation

Success	Failure/delay
External or market related communications factors	
1. Good marketing-related communication and effective collaboration with the firm's environment to determine users' requirements. Active collaboration with customers during development.	1. Lack of market research: failure to interact with potential customers and ignorance of competitors' likely strategies. Lack of publicity and sales effort.
Internal communication factors	
2. Good internal cooperation and coordination between R&D, production and marketing functions to meet precise user requirements.	2. Lack of contact between functions. Internal transfer problems.
Internal management systems factors	
3. Careful project planning and control.	3. Inadequate project evaluation and control.
Technical factors	
4. Efficient development work. De-bugging before commercial launch.	4. Poor or incomplete development work. Many technical problems in use.
Top management style factors	
5. The will on the part of top management to innovate. Participative, flexible management style.	5. Project not taken seriously by top management or integrated into company strategy. Bureaucratic, inflexible procedures.
Economic resources factors	
6. Provision of good after-sales service and user-education facilities.	6. Insufficient resources committed to educating users. Poor after-sales service.
Key individual factors	
7. Existence of committed key individuals such as product champion, business innovator, technical innovators (inhouse entrepreneurs).	7. Business innovator too junior; product champion too junior – unable to overcome internal resistance to change.

(*Source*: Based on Rothwell (1977) who analysed 9 studies addressing factors determining success in innovation)
(*Adapted from*: A. E. Johne, 1982).

common sense' and 'overall management competence'. We shall deal with a number of the success factors separately below.

Understanding and meeting user needs The need to gain an imaginative understanding of user needs, and of interpreting them in the design of a new product or process, is obvious. Nevertheless it is evident from the many empirical studies in this area that firms are very often deficient in this respect. For whatever reason, they are simply unable to establish the optimum performance and price combination from the point of view of the eventual user, and this is the most frequently quoted cause of failure.

Effective coupling with the marketplace This is essential in establishing the optimum performance and price combination. In some industries it means actually involving the customer in the development process. Indeed in certain industries, as we have seen, the user will often play a very significant and sometimes the major role in invention and early prototype construction. It is also important, of course, to keep in touch with supplier innovations in materials and components.

Effective internal coupling This is especially important with respect to linking effectively the R&D and marketing functions; in other words ensuring that development activity is clearly directed towards meeting user needs. It is also important with respect to linking the design and development function to the manufacturing function in order to ensure that products are designed to be efficiently and reliably manufactured (Rothwell, 1980). This is one area in which the Japanese, for example, are particularly strong (Shoenberger, 1983).

Effective coupling with external sources of scientific and technological expertise Whilst there is no substitute for inhouse technical skills, it is nevertheless important to complement these skills when necessary with external expertise. The ability to identify external expertise in specific areas and to do this rapidly can often make a crucial contribution to innovatory success.

Gifted and committed intrapreneurs These are the so-called product champions, business innovators and technological gatekeepers (Rothwell et al, 1974; Rothwell, 1975). The product champion enthusiastically supports the innovation, especially during critical phases. He remains committed to it when things appear to be going wrong and others are thinking of abandoning ship. The business innovator plays the key managerial role of integration, coordinating the efforts of those involved in the project especially from functionally separated departments. The technological gatekeeper plays an invaluable role in bringing technological information into the firm and in disseminating it throughout the firm. Whether or not these key individuals can operate effectively is a function of both corporate culture and structure.

Efficient manufacturing procedures The importance of eliminating technical bugs before commercial launch is obvious. Nevertheless, it is a message that did not appear to reach many would-be innovators to their cost, and again it is an area in which the Japanese have great comparative strengths.

Efficient aftersales service and user education Selling a new product is not simply a matter of transferring a piece of technology, but rather of offering an economic package. Servicing and spares supply are important components of this package; so too is user education. It is crucial to train users in the right uses and limitations of a new device, otherwise if they do misuse it and it malfunctions they will, with some justification, blame the supplier and not themselves.

It can be seen that all the factors listed in Table 2.5 are concerned with what the firm actually did or did not do during the innovation project; in other words they are all project execution variables. To these we can add a second set of factors that outline essentially the preconditions for corporate innovation, ie that define a corporate framework in which innovation can take place.

The first of these factors is top management commitment to, and visible support for, innovation. Top management visibility is absolutely crucial, especially in the case of major innovations, to overcoming the barriers and resistances to innovations that often exist in companies. For example, people committed to one area of production might resist moves to new areas and it is a top management function to facilitate such shifts. This is especially important within the framework of reindustrialization.

The second factor is the importance of having a long-term corporate strategy in which innovation plays a key role. Innovation should not be an ad hoc process, but one that has direction and purpose. It might be that firms are sometimes compelled to innovate in response to unexpected competitive actions, in response to sudden market shifts, or in response to the emergence of a significant new technological capability, but such cases should be the exception rather than the rule. Firms need a strategy in order to obtain synergies between R&D projects, manufacturing projects and marketing projects. Properly planned, one project can contribute to the next project and so on. In order words a coherent strategy enables firms to build on past successes and to capitalize effectively on emerging strengths.

The third factor is the need for an associated long-term commitment to major projects, based not on criteria of short-term return on investment, but on considerations of future market penetration and growth. There is a good deal of evidence to suggest that many firms, particularly in the United States and the UK, increasingly have adopted a 'cash flow' view of development activity, and as a consequence have focused increasingly on short-term projects that yield quick returns, while innovation, and especially major innovation, requires a longer-term view, and at least some of the firm's projects should be funded with 'patient' money (Hayes and Abernathy, 1980).

The fourth factor is corporate flexibility and responsiveness to change. In some industries production sequences have tended to become increasingly specific with respect to the production of dominant product designs. This means that they become more and more rigid and less able to accommodate product changes. In other words, because of increasing inflexibility in production, it is often seen as being too expensive to introduce product improvements. It seems likely that the introduction of flexible manufacturing systems will largely overcome this problem, enabling innovative firms to offer not just a single dominant design, but a 'family' of designs having a broad range of operation characteristics to appeal to a wide range of customers. We should also recognize that technological innovations might require organizational and market innovations to facilitate their implementation, and again this is especially the case with radical innovations. Management must accept this and the company should be sufficiently flexible to accommodate it.

The fifth factor is top management acceptance of risk. Innovation is inherently a high-risk undertaking and one of the few things we can be sure about is that there will be failures. Management must accept this, and not use one failure as an excuse for withdrawing from the innovation race altogether. In addition, attempts should be made to learn the lessons of failure through analysing unsuccessful projects, which many firms fail to do. Associated with this is the need for termination criteria. Potential failures can continue for a considerable period under their own momentum with extremely high costs in lost opportunities for more promising projects, and it is essential that top management accept the responsibility for the termination of failing projects.

The final factor is the creation of an environment within the firm in which entrepreneurship can flourish and innovations occur. The literature on this point is copious (for a review see Johne, 1982), but it appears to point to two distinct modes of organization, one conducive to, and one inimical to, inhouse entrepreneurship: these have been termed 'organic' and 'mechanistic' respectively. The following comments from the literature more or less describe what organic and mechanistic mean:

Taking first 'organic':
    Freedom from rigid rules.
    Participative and informal. Many views aired and considered.
    Face to face communication. Little red tape.
    Interdisciplinary teams. Breaking down departmental barriers.
    Emphasis on creative interaction and aims.
    Outward looking. Willing to take on external ideas.
    Risk accepting.
    Flexibility with respect to changing needs, threats and opportunities.
    Non-hierarchical.
    Information flows downwards as well as upwards.

Turning to 'mechanistic':
    Rigid departmental separation and functional specialization.
    Hierarchical.
    Bureaucratic.
    Many rules and set procedures.

Formal reporting.

Long decision chains and slow decision making.

Communication via the written word.

Much information flows upwards, little information flows downwards.

The organic type of organization seems best suited to the early creative aspects of innovation. The mechanistic form is probably best suited to effective production and distribution, and a major problem lies in making the shift from the organic to the mechanistic form as the project develops. A number of large organizations, especially in the United States, have recognized the need to create organic forms internally as vehicles for innovation, and many have adopted a variety of so-called new venture techniques to this end (Roberts and Wainer, 1971; Roberts, 1977; Rothwell, 1975b).

It would, of course, be surprising if innovatory success or failure could be explained in terms of one or two factors only, and an important result of many of the innovation studies is their emphasis on multi-factor explanations. In other words, success is rarely associated with doing one or two things brilliantly, but with performing all operations competently and in a well-balanced and coordinated manner.

A significant fact to emerge from these innovation studies is that, outside the United States (where public procurement and regulations have been important), governments have rarely been seen to play a major determining role in either success or failure. In some instances this has undoubtedly been a function of the research methodologies employed, which have often concentrated solely on firm-specific factors. It might also point to a more fundamental factor, which is that innovatory success or failure, in practice, is determined largely by the actions of management. The implication of this, of course, is that in the case of specific innovation projects in firms, there are inherent limitations to what innovation policies can achieve. While governments can, to be sure, create a national environment conducive to innovatory endeavours, while they can supply certain inputs to the innovation process and act as an innovation-receptive market, and while they can remove certain barriers to innovation, in the final analysis success depends on the propensities and abilities of industrial managers. In other words, while governments can act to complement the innovatory endeavours of technically progressive managers (establish the necessary 'enabling conditions'), they can do little in the face of incompetence or simple indifference. Policy makers would do well to bear this in mind.

Finally, all the major studies of success and failure in innovation greatly emphasize the importance of intrafirm and extrafirm linkages. They support the interactive model of innovation shown in Figure 2.3, ie innovation as a process of communication. Establishing efficient internal linkages is, of course, a prime function of management, as is establishing appropriate mechanisms for linking the firm to the marketplace and to external sources of scientific and technological expertise and advice. With regard to the latter, moreover, there exists an important role for public policy in facilitating linkages between the publically funded scientific and technological infrastructure and industry (as well, of course, as forging more effective links between universities and collective industrial research institutions). If, as we suggested in Chapter 1, we are now experiencing the emergence of a new wave of generic technologies, the establishment of effective linkages between the infrastructure and industry must be a core element of public innovation policy.

REFERENCES

Berger A 1975 *Factors Influencing the Laws of Innovation Activity Leading to Scientific Instrument and Plastics Innovation.* Unpublished, S M Thesis, Sloan School of Management, MIT, Cambridge, Mass. June

Boyden J 1976 *A Study of the Innovation Process in the Plastics Additives Industry.* Unpublished S M Thesis, Sloan School of Management, MIT, Cambridge, Mass., January

Cook L G and Morrison W A 1961 *The Origins of Innovation.* Report No 61-GP-214 June. General Electric Company, Research Information Section, New York, June

Cooper R G 1980 *Project Newprod: What makes a new product a winner?* Quebec Industrial Innovation Centre, Montreal, Canada

Freeman C 1974 *The Economics of Industrial Innovation.* Penguin Modern Economics Texts

Gardiner P 1984 Design Trajectories for Aeroplanes and Automobiles during the past 50 years, in Freeman C (ed) *Innovation, Design and Long Cycles in the Economy* London, Royal College of Art.

Giarini O and Loubergé H 1978 *The Diminishing Returns of Technology.* Systems Science and World Order Library, Pergamon Press

Gibbons M and Johnston R 1974 The Roles of Science in Technological Innovation. *Research Policy* **13** November

Hafstad L 1966 The Role of Industrial Research. *Science Journal* September

Hayes R H and Abernathy W J 1980 Managing our way to Economic Decline. *Harvard Business Review* July-August

Hessen B 1931 The Social and Economic Roots of Newton's Principle. In Bukharin N (ed) *Science at the Crossroads: Papers from the Second International Congress of the History of Science and Technology, 1931.* (revised edition) F. Cass

Illinois Institute of Technology 1968 *Technology in Retrospect and Critical Events in Science (Project TRACES).* NSF-C535, Washington DC

Johne A 1982 Innovation, Organization and the Marketing of High Technology Products, Ph.d. Dissertation, University of Strathclyde, Department of Marketing

Langrish J 1974 The Changing Relationship Between Science and Technology. *Nature* **23** August

Liebermann M G 1978 A Literature Citation Study of Science-Technology Coupling in Electronics. *Proceedings of the IEE* **66** (1) January

Mensch G 1979 *Stalemate in Technology*. Ballinger, New York

Mowery D C and Rosenberg N 1978 The Influence of Market Demand Upon Innovation: A Critical Review of Some Recent Empirical Studies. *Research Policy* **8** April

National Academy of Science 1965 Chemistry: Opportunities and Needs. NAS, Washington

Nelson R (ed) 1982 *Government and Technical Change*. Pergamon Press, New York

Nelson R and Winter S 1977 Towards a Useful Theory of Innovation. *Research Policy* **6**: 36–76

Nelson R and Winter S 1982 *An Evolutionary Theory of Economic Change*. Cambridge, Mass./London

Pavitt K 1983 Patterns of Technological Change – Evidence, Theory and Policy Implications. Papers in Science, Technology and Public Policy, Science Policy Research Unit, University of Sussex

Phillips A 1971 *Technology and Market Structure*. Lexington Books, Lexington

Price D 1965 Is Technology Historically Independent of Science? *Technology and Culture* **6** (4)

Roberts E B 1977 Generating Effective Corporate Innovation. *Technology Review* **80** (1)

Roberts E B and Wainer H A 1971 Some Characteristics of Technical Entrepreneurs. *IEEE Trans on Engin. Management* EM-13, 3

Rosenberg N 1972 *Technology and American Economic Growth*. Harper Torch Books, New York

Rosenberg N 1979 Technological Interdependence in the American Economy. *Technology and Culture* January: 25–50

Rosenberg N 1982 *Inside the Black Box*. Cambridge University Press

Rothwell R 1975 Intracorporate Entrepreneurs. *Management Decision* **13** (3)

Rothwell R 1975b From Invention to New Business Via the New Ventures Approach. *Management Decision* **13** (1)

Rothwell R 1976 The Sulzer Weaving Machine: A Case Study of Successful Innovation. *Textile Institute and Industry* May

Rothwell R 1976b *Innovation in Textile Machinery: Some Significant Factors in Success and Failure*. Science Policy Research Unit, Occasional Paper Series No. 2, University of Sussex

Rothwell R 1977 The Characteristics of Successful Innovators and Technically Progressive Firms. *R&D Management* **7** (3) June

Rothwell R 1979 *Government Regulations and Industrial Innovation*. Report to the Six Countries Programme on Innovation, TNO, PO Box 215, 2600 AE Delft, The Netherlands

Rothwell R 1980, 'It's not (just) what you make, it's how you make it', *Design*, (Design Council, London) March

Rothwell R 1982 The Commercialisation of University Research. *Physics in Technology*, **13** (6) November

Rothwell R 1983 *Information and Successful Innovation*. British Library Report No. 5782

Rothwell R Freeman C Jervis P Horsely A Robertson A B and Townsend J 1974 SAPPHO-Updated: Project SAPPHO Phase II. *Research Policy* **13** (3)

Rothwell R and Gardiner P 1983 The Role of Design in Product and Process Change. *Design Studies* Special Engineering Issue, July

Rothwell R and Gardiner P 1984 Tough Customers: Successful Designs, *Design Studies* Special Issue on Innovation, December (edited by R Roy)

Rothwell R and Zegveld W 1974 *Technical Change and Employment*. Frances Pinter

Schmookler J 1966 *Invention and Economic Growth*. Harvard University Press, Cambridge, Mass.

Schoenberger R J 1982 *Japanese Manufacturing Techniques: Nine Hidden Lessons in Simplicity*. The Free Press

Schumpeter J J 1910 *Theorie der Wirtshafthichen Entwicklung*. Dunsher and Humboldt, Leipzig

Schumpeter J J 1943 *Capitalism, Socialism and Democracy*. Harper and Row, New York

Shaw B 1983 The Role of the User in the Generation of Innovations in the UK Medical Equipment Industry. (Mimeo) School of Management, Polytechnic of Central London, Marylebone Road, March

Sherwin W S and Isensen R S 1966 *First Interim Report on Project Hindsight*. CFSTI, Washington

Townsend J Henwood F Thomas G Pavitt K and Wyatt S 1981 *Innovations in Britain since 1945*. Occasional Paper Series No. 16, Science Policy Research Unit, University of Sussex

von Hippel E 1976 The Dominant Role of Users in the Scientific Instrument Innovation Process. *Research Policy* 5 (3)

von Hippel E 1978 Users as Innovators. *Technology Review* 80 (3) January

von Hippel E 1979 Appropriability of Innovation Benefit as a Predictor of the Functional Locus of Innovation. Sloan School of Management, MIT, Working Paper 1084–79, June

Walsh V Townsend J Achilladelis and Freeman C 1979 Trends in Invention and Innovation in the Chemical Industry. Report to SERC (Mimeo) Science Policy Research Unit

CHAPTER THREE

Evaluating Policies for Technological Innovation*

TECHNOLOGICAL INNOVATION POLICY

For many years governments have been formulating and implementing both industrial policies (investment grants, taxation policy, industrial restructuring, public ownership) and science and technology policies (technical education, patents, infrastructurally based pure and applied research). In general these policies have been formulated and implemented by separate departments within the central government bureaucracy and, not surprisingly, they have often developed more or less independently and in a largely uncoordinated manner.

More recently, and certainly from the recessionary mid-1970s onwards, governments in the advanced market economies have become increasingly involved in the creation of policies towards technological innovation (Rothwell and Zegveld, 1981). This reflects a growing belief on the part of governments that one means of at least partially overcoming the effects of high energy costs and stagnating markets for many major product groups (eg the automobile, colour television, agricultural tractors, merchant ships, etc), and therefore of breaking out of the current recessionary cycle, is the stimulation of technological innovations in industry.

Just as our definition of the process of technological innovation (Chapter 2) included all the steps from invention to the marketplace, so technological innovation policy is concerned with the whole gamut of activities from research through to marketing and sales. Technological innovation policy is thus an integrative concept, and we can define technological innovation policy as being essentially a fusion of science and technology policy and industrial policy. Government policies to stimulate technological innovation are many and varied, as are the tools designed to satisfy policy aims, and a list of policy tools is given in Table 3.1, which generally can be grouped under three main headings (Rothwell, 1982).

* This chapter is based largely on Rothwell R. 1982. *Evaluating the Effectivness of Government Innovation Policies.* Report to the six Countries Programme on Innovation, Six Countries Secretariat, TNO, PO Box 215, 2600, AE Delft, The Netherlands.

1. Supply – provision of financial, manpower and technical assistance, including the establishment of a scientific and technological infrastructure.
2. Demand – central and local government purchases and contracts, notably for innovative products, processes and services.
3. Environmental – taxation policy, patent policy and regulations (economic, worker health and safety and environmental), ie those measures that establish the legal and fiscal framework in which industry operates.

Table 3.1   Classification of government policy tools

Policy tool	Examples
Public enterprise	Innovation by publicly owned industries, setting up of new industries, pioneering use of new techniques by public corporations, participation in private enterprise.
Scientific and technical	Research laboratories, support for research associations, learned societies, professional associations, research grants.
Education	General education, universities, technical education, apprenticeship schemes, continuing and further education, retraining.
Information	Information networks and centres, libraries, advisory and consultancy services, data bases, liaison services.
Financial	Grants, loans, subsidies, financial sharing arrangements, provision of equipment, buildings or services, loan guarantees, export credits.
Taxation	Company, personal, indirect and payroll taxation, tax allowances.
Legal and regulatory	Patents, environments and health regulations, inspectorates, monopoly regulations.
Political	Planning, regional policies, honours or awards for innovation, encouragement of mergers or joint consortia, public consultation.
Procurement	Central or local government purchases and contracts, public corporations, R&D contracts, prototype purchases.
Public services	Purchases, maintenance, supervision and innovation in health service, public building, construction, transport, telecommunications.
Commercial	Trade agreements, tarrifs, currency regulations.
Overseas agent	Defence sales organisations.

(*Source*: Rothwell and Zegveld, 1981)

Which of these measures are used, and in what combination, varies a great deal from country to country depending on national perceptions of techno-economic threats and opportunities and, to some extent, on the prevailing national political philosophy. Table 3.2, which provides an analysis of policy recommendations by type of tool based on innovation policy statements in six countries in the late 1970s, shows the types of policy tool most preferred in the different countries, as well as those that are largely ignored. For Canada, Japan and the Netherlands the most favoured tool is the scientific and technical one, for Sweden education, for Britain financial and taxation and for the United States legal and regulatory. In the case of the United States this reflects a deep concern about the economy being overregulated, while the British emphasis on financial and taxation measures appears to stem from the preoccupation with obtaining a healthy environment for industry to operate in. These two contrast with the other four countries, which seem to prefer to deal more directly with the inputs to the process of innovation.

Table 3.2   Analysis of policy recommendations by type of tool

Type of tool	Canada	Japan	The Netherlands	Sweden	United Kingdom	United States
1. Public enterprise	0	0	0	1	1	0
2. Scientific and technical	7	7	9	3	4	4
3. Education	3	1	5	11	4	3
4. Information	2	2	8	2	3	8
5. Financial	5	2	6	5	6	4
6. Taxation	1	0	0	1	6	13
7. Legal and regulatory	0	0	6	1	0	46
8. Political	2	4	2	3	4	2
9. Procurement	4	0	2	2	3	11
10. Public services	0	0	1	0	3	0
11. Commercial	2	1	1	0	0	3
12. Overseas agent	0	0	0	1	2	0
Total	26	17	40	30	36	94

(*Source*: Rothwell and Zegveld, 1981)

So far we have dealt with innovation policy tools rather than the national philosophies underlying their use, and consideration of national strategies towards innovation highlights a number of important differences in this respect. Perhaps the most significant difference lies between those nations that have a clear-cut, long-term strategy towards the development and exploitation of specific high-technology product groups and new technologies, and those that do not. In Japan and France (see Tables 3.3 and 3.4) and to a lesser extent in Sweden, Canada and West Germany, there is a clear emphasis on attempting to identify potentially important new industrial sectors. These nations appear to have accepted that structural change to their economies (via major technological innovations) is to be actively pursued, arguing that greater advantage is to be gained from exploiting changes in the new world economic order rather than steadfastly resisting these changes through measures seeking to protect ailing industries. In other words, they lay emphasis on the structural transformation of the industrial base towards newer, more technology-intensive sectors and product groups; that is, their policies contain a strong 'reindustrialization' component.

Table 3.3   Areas of interest to Japanese industry

New Products	Energy industries	Advanced, high-technology industries
Optical fibres	Coal liquefaction	Ultra-high-speed computers
Ceramics	Coal gasification	Space developments
Amorphous materials	Nuclear power	Ocean developments
High-efficiency resin	Solar energy	Aircraft
	Deep geothermal generation	

(*Source*: Japanese Ministry of International Trade and Industry)

Table 3.4   Strategic high-technology priorities in France

Strategic Industry	Objectives	Overall actions planned
Electronic office equipment	To achieve 20–25% world market share, and avert an anticipated $2bn trade deficit in 1985	In strategic sectors, the government will negotiate development contracts with individual companies, setting specific goals for sales, exports and jobs. Firms that make such commitments will receive tax incentives, subsidised loans, and other official aids.
Consumer electronics	To create a world-scale group including TV-set and tube makers that will each rank among the top three globally. To eliminate the $750 million trade deficit in such products.	
Energy-saving equipment	To ensure that government grants to companies and households to install such equipment are spent primarily on French products.	
Undersea activities	To recapture second place in the world after the USA.	
Bioindustry	Objectives not yet defined.	
Industrial robots	Objectives not yet defined.	

These six industries together are expected to add $10bn in sales and to double their workforce to 135 000 by 1985.

(*Source*: *Business Week*, 30 June, 1980, p140.)

Other countries appear not to possess an explicit long-term strategy towards technological development and market exploitation. In these countries (notably the United States) strategy appears to be left largely in the hands of private companies. Policy tools are available to assist would-be innovative firms, but technology choice is mainly by managers, the direction of technology being determined by market forces.

According to a recent policy statement by Mr Patrick Jenkin, Minister of State for Industry, the UK appears to be in an intermediate state between the latter and the former type of country (Elliot, 1982): while the British government remains apparently committed to a 'market forces' policy, the Department of Industry has established a set of strategic aims that include, centrally, the adoption by British industry of certain key technologies (Table 3.5).

Table 3.5   UK Department of Industry strategic aims

DOI strategic aims

Central aim: A profitable, competitive and adaptable UK productive sector

Climate	Efficiency	Innovation
Social climate which values productive industry.	Human skills in industry equal to competitor.	Gear research and inward technology to UK needs.
Fiscal regime which encourages new enterprise.	Expose state-owned industries to competition by privatization.	Standards to raise UK design and quality performance.
Regulatory framework to promote competition and new firms.	Reduce UK regional disparities in resource utilization.	Awareness and rapid adoption of key technologies.
Elimination of trade obstacles.	Inward investment and collaboration with foreign companies.	Public purchasing to promote innovation and competitiveness.
	Technical support for UK companies in world markets.	
	Selective aid to raise UK output and performance.	

(*Source*: J. Elliot, *Financial Times*, 16 November 1982)

There are several points of direct relevance to the theme of policy evaluation to be drawn from the above discussion. As Gibbons (1982) puts it,

Firstly, the range of policies is extremely large and, as formulated, are seldom directed at a single objective or even at a single government department. In other words, innovation policies involve multiple objectives and multiple actors. To some extent this is a feature of a good deal of government policy but the effects are more difficult to handle in the case of innovation policy because these policies involve as an intrinsic element non-governmental organisations mainly firms, trade unions, and banks.

Many firms will, of course, possess their own innovation policies that might not always align with those of government. It might be, in fact, that governments can learn much about innovation policy from the more successful – and technically progressive – of the firms in the private sector.

This complexity is increased as Nicholson (1982) has pointed out, by the growing international nature of innovation policy, with organizations such as the EEC, the OECD and the UN involved in policy analysis and, in the case of the EEC, in aspects of policy formulation and implementation in certain areas (eg the European steel industry).

POLICY EVALUATION

At the same time that governments have been involved in implementing a rapidly growing number of measures to increase national rates of technological innovation and to enhance long-term national innovation potential, concern over the effectiveness of these policy initiatives has grown apace. Given the high direct costs of innovation policies such concern is understandable, especially during a period of increasingly severe budgetary constraints. The costs of losing potential opportunities by misconceived or misapplied policies involving the inefficient use of highly skilled technical and managerial manpower, can also be high. There is then a pressing need for a greater understanding of the factors influencing policy effectiveness in order to enable governments to increase their efficiency. During the past five years or so a number of public policy evaluations have been undertaken by J. Irvine and B. Martin (1980, 1981, 1983; Martin and Irvine 1981, 1983; with Pavitt K 1982) of the Science Policy Research Unit which are relevant to the theme of evaluating technological innovation policies. They cover a wide range of issues from evaluating 'big science' to international programmes of R&D support. Apart from these, however, few policy initiatives in technological innovation have been subjected to systematic and objective assessment regarding their efficacy, and innovation policy today might generally be said to be more an object of faith rather than understanding. The current widespread interest in evaluating the effectiveness of public policies towards technological innovation is, therefore, both timely and crucial.

While, as stated above, it is true that there have been few *systematic* evaluations of national policies towards technological innovation, that is not to say that we are entirely ignorant regarding the types of problems that, in a rather general sense, such policies have suffered from in the past. Below are summarized a number of the principal difficulties of national technological innovation policies identified by the authors in their detailed overview of the subject (Rothwell and Zegveld, 1981).

Firstly, there has often been a lack of market know-how amongst public policy makers, and according to Golding (1978) and Little (1974) there exists evidence to suggest that government funds often have gone to support projects of high technical sophistication but of low market potential and profitability. As well as often having lower market potential, projects funded by governments have also tended to involve higher technical and financial risks than those funded wholly by industrial companies. That government backed projects involve high technical risk might, of course, be taken as justification for government involvement in the first place: The problem governments face is to identify high-risk projects that also have high market potential, yet it is doubtful whether government policy makers generally possess the competence to assess market prospects satisfactorily.

Secondly, subsidies have in the past tended to assist mainly large firms, an imbalance that can and should be redressed. This tells us nothing, of course, about the effectiveness of those subsidies that have been made to small firms. In the case of large firms, evidence from Canada and West Germany suggests that funds often have gone in support of projects that are relatively small and sometimes of dubious merit which the companies would not finance by themselves. The Enterprise Development Program in Canada (Rothwell and Zegveld, 1981 p 199), which will support only projects that represent a significant risk to the firm, represents an explicit attempt to avoid financing marginal projects in large firms.

Thirdly, governments often have tended to adopt a passive, rather than an active, stance towards information dissemination. As a result, policy measures have been taken up largely by a limited number of 'aware' (usually large) companies.

Fourthly, there has been a general lack of practical knowledge or imaginative conceptualization of the process of industrial innovation by policy makers. As a result, they have tended to adopt an R&D-oriented view of innovation, often to the detriment of other important aspects of the process, eg innovation-oriented public purchasing.

Fifthly, there has sometimes been a lack of interdepartmental coordination – and sometimes cooperation – between the relevant organizations and agencies involved in the policy process. This can result in lack of complementarity between different initiatives, and might also lead to the propagation of contradictory measures. That this is true in other areas of public policy is amply demonstrated in Table 2, Chapter 4 for the US.

Finally, there has been a tendency for innovation policies to be subjected to changes in political philosophy rather than to changing national or international economic needs or conditions. Thus, in many countries policies have been subjected to a political cycle rather than to the dictates of economic, industrial or technological cycles.

In a survey seeking to determine the instrumentality of public technological innovation policies Goldberg (1981) showed there to be a marked paucity of empirical studies of policy effectiveness. This conclusion was supported by Gibbons (1982) who could point to only two major international studies, those of Allen et al (1978) and Rubenstein et al (1977). In the former study, while there were some variations between sectors of industry and between countries on the types of tools influencing firms, Allen et al were forced to conclude that in general

the most significant aspect of the study lies in its failure to detect any effects on project performance, of government attempts to stimulate innovation . . . If project success or failure can be taken as any measure of effectiveness of their actions, then little can be said to have resulted from all this /governmental/ expenditure of effort and money.

The results of the second study led the authors to draw essentially similar conclusions, again despite some differences between countries in managers' perceptions of the influence of government support for industrial activity. Thus,

. . . there are a number of basic and important perceptions among managers which are very similar across countries and which support our two secondary propositions that (1) government action to stimulate innovation is perceived as comparatively irrelevant and that (2) government actions generally delay the R D/I process. There is the belief that the effect of market forces and competition on the R D/I process outweighs by far the effects of government actions and that general government policies far outweigh the effects of specific incentive programmes. It is only in rare instances that the incentive programmes are perceived to have any direct effect on specific R D/I decision making. These commonly shared perceptions are joined by the feeling that the incentive programmes are in general too inflexible and too demanding in terms of required administrative details and liaison effects. In the administration of incentive programmes, governments are seen to be too slow and complex in their response to the needs of industry.

Despite this rather dismal picture concerning the lack of influence of government policy on technological change processes in industry, there is one important caveat to bear in mind. That is, both researches employed only one measure of effectiveness, namely the perceptions of industrial managers, and this might be an insufficient guide to reality. Certainly managers' perceptions of the influence of government policy can often be greatly biased, which was evidenced in the results of a Workshop on Government Regulation and Industrial Innovation jointly organized by the Six Countries Programme on Innovation and the US National Science Foundation in 1979. This showed the perceptions by managers in the US that direct regulatory impacts were almost always very large and negative were, with the exception of a few sectors of industry, considerably exaggerated (Rothwell, 1979). These perceptions were, moreover, largely responsible for the current US trend towards deregulation. There does, in fact, appear to be a general tendency for managers to overestimate the negative influences of governmental intervention and to understate its positive influences.

It is also essential that the outcome of a policy initiative be measured against its original intention. For example, while in some instances government regulations can have significant positive or negative influences on particular innovations or technologies, only seldom are regulations formulated that are designed with an explicit primary purpose to stimulate commercially oriented industrial technological developments. Thus, only in certain cases can regulatory policy be viewed as a direct and explicit element of technological innovation policy and in general it should not be assessed as such. Explicitly used as an arm of innovation policy, regulatory policy can, however, be a powerful enabling and even stimulating tool (see chapter 4), and in such instances should be assessed as such.

A more fundamental point, and one made by Gibbons (1982), is the suggestion that the Allen and Rubenstein studies did not evaluate policies, but rather they monitored them. In other words they were concerned with the question 'What happened?' rather than with the question 'What difference has it made?'. This distinction has clear methodological implications, the most significant perhaps being the need for comparative evaluations.

THREE STRANDS OF ANALYSIS

After Nelson (1974), Gibbons (1982) has identified three analytical traditions in rational policy analysis and provides, in all three cases, examples of use, each of which has implications for our current discussion of policy evaluation. This section is taken largely from Gibbons' paper.

The allocation of resources to science and technology

This tradition views the problem as stemming from past allocation of scientific and technical resources and proposes solutions in terms of the reallocation of R&D activities. Examples of this are:
  – Farina and Gibbons' (1976) analysis of the British Science and Engineering Research Council's policy of Selectivity and Concentration;
  – Irvine and Martin's (1978) international study of the effectiveness of basic research in radio and optical astronomy and high nuclear physics;
  – Irvine and Martin's (1981) later study of the effectiveness of the Norwegian system for the support of R&D activities in collective research laboratories.

Significant methodological aspects of these studies are as follows: In the first case (Farina and Gibbons), the research was clearly geared towards answering the question 'What difference did SERC's policy of selectivity and concentration make on the pattern of resource allocation?' In other words, it was a true evaluation of the effectiveness of a deliberate policy initiative rather than an exercise in monitoring change.

In the second case (Irvine and Martin) the researchers recognized the crucial importance of employing multiple partial indicators, unlike previous studies of the output of fundamental research, which were based normally on the use of national peer evaluation only. Irvine and Martin employed this in conjunction with citation analysis and a system of international peer evaluation. They then looked for convergence between these two partial indicators of performance.

In the third case, as well as using quantitative data on the inputs and outputs of the Norwegian R&D system, Irvine and Martin also elicited, in a structured manner, the perceptions of both the performers of R&D (collective research institute researchers) and the users of the output from R&D (industrialists). Again, they looked for convergence between these various partial indicators of effectiveness. In addition, seeking prescriptiveness from their results, they analysed the organizational structures and management practices of the Norwegian R&D system and determined how they had influenced the systems effectiveness.
Significantly, both Irvine and Martin's studies were comparative in nature.

The organization and control of economic activity

This tradition concerns itself primarily with institutional structures whose characteristics determine the way in which resources are allocated. The two main sets of emphasis within this tradition concern demand conditions ('examining what is worth what cost and what is better than what, and monitoring resource flows into the sector') and supply conditions ('evaluating the machinery that is supplying what is demanded').

The principal method utilized in demand side evaluation ('trying to evaluate what costs what') is cost–benefit analysis. An example of this is Gardiner's study of launching aid in the UK aircraft industry (Gardiner, 1975), which showed that the rate of return to public investment was small or nil, and which might be taken to indicate an ineffective allocation of resources or even, taking into account opportunity costs, a misallocation of resources. As Gibbons has pointed out, however, before making this judgement it is important to question whether the objective of the policy was to stimulate aero-engine development or to obtain a given return on public capital invested (Gibbons, 1982).

This raises the issue of the social rate of return to public investment in innovation and, indeed, one justification for public involvement in the first place is that private rates of return might be sufficiently low to deter private investment in areas of crucial long-term national interest.

In this respect Mansfield et al (1977) have illustrated that the public rates of return to industrial innovation often outweigh the private. In nearly a third of their cases the private rate of return was so low that 'no firm with the advantage of hindsight would have invested in the innovation, but the social rate of return was so high that from society's point of view the investment was well worthwhile'.

Turning now to supply side evaluation, Gibbons has offered Kogen et al's (1980) study of the commissioning of research in the DHSS as an illustrative example. This study shows how the organizational context in which DHSS funded researchers and policy makers interact, clearly influences the nature of that interaction. In this case, the policy making and scientific functions were effectively separated, the underlying assumption being

that policy makers and scientists belong to quite different knowledge systems and institutions and carry out their respective roles best when clear divisions of expertise and task are maintained; that policy makers are well able to formulate their research needs and that there is a strong, independent scientific community with research capacity and expertise to meet those needs under contracts with the department (M. Henkel et al, 1981).

One result of this institutional separateness, contrary to the above expectations, is that research commissioning is reactive rather than active; in other words, lack of scientific competence makes it extremely difficult for DHSS policy makers to play a positive role in commissioning specific policy-related research projects. What is the solution?

A number of alternative models might be conceived to the one described. We consider just one that will take into account some of the main arguments of this paper, that there are multiple authorities and multiple knowledge systems in health and personal social services research, and that a key issue in the promotion of policy related research is better understanding of the policy process and of the relationship between different forms of knowledge and action. Such an alternative model might be policy rather than science oriented and based upon *interaction* or *exchange*: interaction or exchange between the Chief Scientist, his scientific advisors, the research units and the policy makers (Henkel, et al, 1981).

Significant methodological implications of these studies are as follows:

- Before any meaningful evaluation can be undertaken, the precise policy aims of the intervention must be established, eg, in the case of aircraft launching aid, was it designed primarily to produce a high return to public investment or to stimulate aircraft developments?
- Public, as well as private rates of return to innovation policy-oriented public investment should, where possible, be included in any assessment of policy effectiveness. The former, however, might be highly diffuse and of longer-term perspective, and thus difficult to measure accurately or meaningfully.

- Policy assessment should, where the outcome is unfavourable, seek to discover the role played by institutions and their procedures in determining this outcome.

Public policy analysis

This third tradition promises a 'rational analysis to policy problems', which refers to (Nelson, 1974),

the laying out of alternative courses of action, of tracing their consequences in terms of benefits and costs, and identifying a best or at least a 'good' policy. The utility of such analysis was seen in terms of providing guidance for the policy maker so that he could choose more intelligently, from the range of alternatives presented, what needed to be done.

According to Nelson (1974),

. . . the scriptures of the policy analysis tradition have been marked by a shift of emphasis from before the fact analysis, to evaluation of programmes *ex poste*, to deliberate experimental development of policy.

Gibbons has explored a major example of a 'second phase' policy analysis, namely the comparative analysis by de Leon of the nuclear reactor programmes of six nations. The most significant methodological implication of de Leon's analysis is that it was conducted within an explicit framework of 'multiple actors, multiple objectives and different times'. For such major national programmes of technological development it is possible to suggest that (de Leon, 1976):

- different organizations and their objectives are particularly crucial or even predominant at certain stages of the design and dissemination process;
- different attributes are essential for the achievement of different objectives (a list of objectives and attributes of technology development are given in Table 3.6, de Leon);
- technology development programmes can be viewed as having multiple actors and objectives which mean that a single evaluative standard for a technology development programme is inadequate and potentially misleading;
- costs grow as development progresses and early uncertainties are resolved;
- successful development and dissemination of an efficient technology is largely determined by the cooperative and continual involvement of the developer, the vendor and the consumer.

In major national technology development programmes we can thus see the need for multiple success indicators, for comparative studies and for evaluation criteria suited to the different outcomes expected from, and the different institutions dominantly involved with, the various stages of the development process.

Table 3.6   Objectives and Attributes of Technology Developments

Objectives of Technology Developments
Science for Science's Sake
National Prestige
Development of Efficient Technology
Political Distribution
Attributes of Technology Developments
Active Scientific Community
Integrated Technology Delivery System
Concomitant Military Program
Early Starter
National R&D Heritage
Multiple Technology Options
Resources Invested

(*Source*: de Leon, 1976)

THE POLICY SYSTEM

It should be clear from the discussion so far – and especially from the last section concerning the three evaluation traditions identified by Nelson and illustrated by Gibbons – that an assessment of the effectiveness of government technological innovation policies should be carried out in the context of the overall policy system. This is especially true of evaluations seeking prescriptive utility.

At the simplest level we might represent the public policy process as in Figure 3.1 and this, straight away, suggests a useful definition of policy evaluation: 'Policy evaluation is concerned with measuring the degree to which explicitly stated government aims are met through the implementation of public policy initiatives.'

Figure 3.1 also illustrates the following points.
- Innovation is only one of a wide set of policies available to government in attaining various goals.
- There is a high degree of interdependence between goals.
- There are common elements between policies as well as many elements within each policy area.

We are thus dealing with a highly interdependent and interactive system and separating the various influences acting within this system might be difficult. We can, therefore, see at the outset that there may be severe problems of measurement as a consequence of the nature of the policy system itself. Further, in terms of policy effectiveness, tackling just one part of the system might not be sufficient, and constraints elsewhere might neutralize the positive influences of a particular initiative. Those involved in policy evaluation should be made explicitly aware of such possibilities from the start.

Figure 3.1   Public policy: goals, means, satisfaction

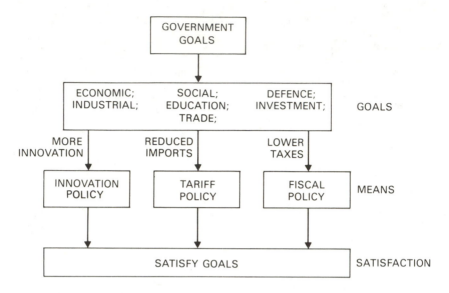

ASSESSMENT: MEASURING THE DEGREE TO WHICH GOALS ARE SATISFIED

Figure 3.2 offers a simple schema of the policy formulation and implementation process. The point of presenting this schema is to emphasize that the assessment of policy effectiveness has something to do with all five phases. In the first case, if the original analysis of national problems is wrong, then we might not expect a favourable outcome from subsequent initiatives based on this analysis. Second, given the establishment of appropriate aims, there is then the problem of formulating appropriate policies and of selecting appropriate tools. This will generally involve many actors who might represent different – and sometimes conflicting – interests, and attaining a reasonable balance between them might be impossible. For example, if political dogma outweighs economic considerations, we might well see the wrong policies established and the wrong tools used. The point is, we should be aware of these possibilities when assessing particular policy tools: there might be little inherently wrong with the tool or its mode of use; it might simply be the wrong tool.

Next we need to investigate the delivery system. Such factors as bureaucracy, lack of dissemination, lack of regional representation, and unclear or inappropriate decision criteria, can all invalidate the use of an entirely appropriate tool based on solid policy analysis. Finally, managers' expectations of the costs and benefits associated with the use of a policy tool will be instrumental in determining its rate of take-up, and evaluation should be concerned with eliciting these perceptions and discovering the reasons underlying them.

Figure 3.2   The policy formulation and implementation process

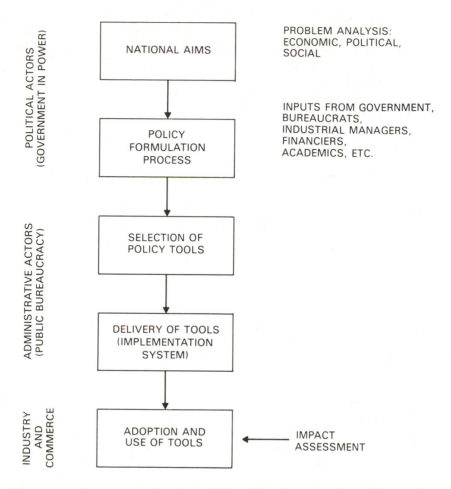

To summarize, any evaluation of the effectiveness of a policy tool or group of tools should include consideration of the complete policy system and its institutions.

SOME GUIDELINES FOR POLICY EVALUATION

This section is based on the discussions of the Six Countries Programme Workshop on the Evaluation of Innovation Policies and Instruments held in Windsor, UK, on the 22nd and 23rd November 1982. (For a Summary Report on the Workshop Proceedings, see Rothwell, 1983. Copies of the papers presented can be obtained from The Secretary to the Steering Committee, Six Countries Programme, PO Box 215

(TNO), 2600 AE Delft, The Netherlands.) It is not meant to be a technical discussion of policy evaluation techniques or practice, but rather a s_ of pragmatic guidelines for the use of those involved in policy evaluation. Before outlining the more specific issues that emerged from the Workshop discussions, we shall first summarize a number of general points that those involved in the evaluation of policies for technological innovation should bear in mind.

Because of the nature of the technological innovation process (its variation between industries, between firms of different sizes and between technologies; its technological, financial and marketing uncertainties) and of the actors involved, there are inherent limitations to what public policies can achieve. While they can enhance the performance of gifted managers, and while they can remove certain barriers to innovation, they are no panacea for success.

Industrial innovation is a high-risk undertaking and many projects inevitably will fail. Governments should be aware of this at the outset and be willing to accept the possibility – indeed the probability – of failure in companies taking up specific policy initiatives.

Because innovation is a dynamic process, the policy system should be sufficiently flexible and responsive to accommodate the possibility of rapid change. It should also be sufficiently flexible to accommodate different types of innovation produced in greatly differing contexts or, alternatively, be tailored to suit specific situations.

The highly interactive and interdependent nature of the policy system might itself impose certain limitations on the precision with which policy effectiveness can be measured. Because of this interactive nature, evaluations should encompass as much of the policy system as is practicable, rather than focus solely on individual elements within that system.

Policies do not implement themselves; nor does general awareness occur spontaneously. Governments must therefore adopt a positive approach to the dissemination of information regarding new initiatives and be willing to allocate sufficient resources to this end.

Evaluation is not a costless process and, if it is to be carried out successfully, might require the commitment of considerable resources. Governments must be willing to bear this cost; an inadequately performed evaluation can be as bad as no evaluation and even worse if the results are misleading. Because evaluation is expensive, it is unlikely that governments will be able, or willing, to assess all policy tools at the same time. The evaluation of policy tools should, therefore, be linked to major current policy concerns.

With certain policy initiatives, eg major national R&D projects, both the institutions involved with, and the output from, the initiative might vary over time. As a consequence governments must formulate evaluation criteria relevant to the different stages of the programme.

While the object of innovation policies is to change things for the better, it must be accepted that they can have the opposite effect. Large, prestigious lobby projects, that often lack market awareness might, for example, result in a misallocation of resources with the accompanying opportunity costs to other, more promising, areas. This re-emphasizes the need, from the outset, to take a rather broad view during policy evaluation.

Policy evaluation should look not only at the outcome of the use of specific policy initiatives, but also at the institutions involved in policy formulation and implementation and their *procedures*, as well as the relationships between them (interagency coordination; interdepartmental rivalry, etc). In other words, policy evaluation should be concerned not simply with the question, 'What change occurred as the result of policy?' but also 'why' and 'how' that change occurred. It is necessary to understand the network of interactions within the policy system before potential synergies can be capitalized and bottlenecks removed.

Governments should be honest at the outset (at least with themselves!) regarding the true objectives of an evaluation. Is it part of a legitimation process? Is it part of a process of budgetary cuts? Or is it an attempt genuinely to understand policy effectiveness and why? The reason underlying the evaluation decision will largely determine the use made of the results and, in some countries, their dissemination. In the longer term, the cynical political use of policy evaluation will tend to discredit the policy system as a whole.

Emphasis should be placed on forging links between the different institutions and actors involved in the policy formulation and implementation process (increased interdepartmental coordination) and between these and the user. While the user (industry) should clearly have a say in the policy formulation process, it should be recognized that managers often take a short-term view whereas policymakers often wish to look much further into the future. In the case of measures designed to induce changes in the shorter term, industry might have a major say and be regarded as the primary customer. For long-term measures designed to induce fundamental structural changes in industry, government must play the dominant role and be regarded as the primary customer.

In order to accommodate radical innovations, companies often need to adopt novel organizational forms, eg the new ventures initiatives. For its proper implementation, innovation policy might similarly require the adoption of novel institutional forms. In other words current institutions within the public administration, and those involved directly in implementation (eg government R&D laboratories), might need to adapt themselves to suit better the requirements of innovation policy, rather than vice versa. Traditional institutional structures and attitudes might impose limitations on the kinds of innovation policy the system can accommodate.

Turning now to the evaluation process itself, some of the major issues identified at the Workshop are addressed below.

Policy aims

Before any attempt can be made to evaluate the effectiveness of an innovation policy initiative, a clear statement must be made describing, unequivocally, the policy aims the initiative is designed to satisfy. If policy statements are 'fuzzy' regarding aims, any assessment inevitably will be a great deal 'fuzzier'. Where no primary aims are stated explicitly at the outset, the initiative might be justified on the basis of secondary or even tertiary effects which, clearly, would be misleading. (It was stated at the Workshop that failing programmes were often justified on the basis of secondary aims.)

The evaluators

A crucial issue is that of who performs the evaluation, and a number of suggestions were made on this point: government agencies, industry, academics, the institution under assessment, professional evaluation groups. A strong theme during the Workshop was that evaluation should not be left solely in the hands of those involved in policy formulation and implementation, because of potential problems of subjectivity in measurement and in interpretation.

If public bureaucracies are to be involved they might, to gain objectivity in measurement and credibility with the user, either create a central, autonomous staff function devoted to evaluation, as is done in the private sector, or create a central staff function to allocate evaluation to outside agencies and to monitor their progress.

In the case of industry, while managers should clearly have a say in evaluation, it must be recognized that they also can be highly subjective in their judgements. In the case, for example, of R&D credits, it is not inconceivable that managers would overestimate the benefit in order to ensure future cash support. Managers might also – especially in companies or industries with no strong traditions of innovativeness – emphasize the value of short-term measures to the detriment of those designed to induce longer-term changes. Finally, while managers might recognize the benefits accruing from the use of direct tools, they might fail to capture in their assessment the benefits from indirect, or environmental measures, eg inputs from the scientific and technological infrastructure.

The most favoured solution was the use of an entirely independent body of assessors, be they academics or professional consultancy groups. Or, perhaps, as Coleman (1972) has suggested, more than one group should be used, especially for major and/or politically sensitive evaluations.

It is also essential to address the question of the range of skills contained within the evaluator group. They should have expertise in the particular field under investigation (industrial, techno-economic, organizational) as well as expertise in the process of evaluation. The appropriate mix of skills will, of course, vary from project to project.

Manifestations of change

If the purpose of evaluation is to measure the changes induced by a particular policy initiative, then it is clearly necessary to determine those measurable factors that indicate the degree of change. If, for example, a measure is designed to increase the overall innovativeness of firms in a sector, or firms in a certain size category, is it possible to measure increased rates of innovation? Can this be measured directly? Does a figure for the current (prepolicy) innovation rate exist? Or is it necessary to measure innovation rates indirectly via, for example, R&D expenditures or patenting activity?

With specific or directed tools, measurement generally will be rather more straightforward than with environmental measures. It might, for example, be relatively straightforward to measure changes in R&D expenditure as a result of a scheme offering R&D credits. It would be more difficult to chart the effects of a reduction in corporation tax as an incentive to increased R&D and productivity-related expenditures, since they will be generally more diffuse. The problem of establishing causality is correspondingly greater. Even in the former case, firms might use the measure at least partially to reduce their future R&D costs. This means, of course, that ideally measurement should contain a strong element of comparison: the existence of a control group will greatly enhance the usefulness of the measurements.

There is then the question of measuring qualitative changes. As we have discussed, there are many problems in seeking solely the perceptions of managers as an index of effectiveness. Nevertheless, management perceptions are not unimportant, especially where quantification of policy impacts is difficult. This leads us back to the crucial point made earlier that multiple indicators of effectiveness should be sought, and that evaluation should be concerned with seeking convergence between these different indicators, between the opinions of different groups and between different quantitative measures or proxies where these exist.

One rather crucial qualitative change is company culture. In any evaluation it is important to ask the question, even in the absence of any measurable short-term quantitative indication of change within the firm, 'has government policy changed the culture of the firm?' In the longer term, changes in management attitude towards technological development will be of much greater significance than, say, take-up by the firm today of R&D credits. Without such cultural changes the firm, when R&D credits are discontinued, is likely to move back to its original (lower) level of R&D expenditure.

This leads to the question of the use of the various indicators as a measure of policy success, which implies the need, in the first place, for success criteria. In general, given that the tool is appropriate for meeting policy aims, success should take into account at least the following:

- utility from the point of view of actual users (effectiveness of the tool in use);
- diffusion of use amongst the population of potential users (take-up rate);
- representativeness of use among different classes of potential users (eg large or small firms);
- positive attitudinal changes induced in firms through take-up.

We turn now to the question of precision of measurement and completeness of data. It was felt overwhelmingly at the Workshop that, for the purpose of policy evaluation, great precision of measurement was not necessary and might in many instances be meaningless. Approximate results, complete enough to demonstrate causality, are sufficient. In terms of technique, the message was unequivocally 'keep it simple': evaluators should adopt a policy of 'sufficiency'; providing 'good enough' data at the right time. In short, evaluation is the art of the possible.

Timing of evaluation

As implied above, the timing of an evaluation scheme is a crucial factor in determining its success. There are two aspects to this: in the first case there is the question of how long does or should it take a particular initiative to have a significant and measurable impact; in the second case, and related to the first, if we wish to use the evaluation as a means of improving the initiative – ie establish a positive feedback loop – then how soon can this be achieved. From the point of view of improving the policy tool the answer is probably the sooner the better. It was also pointed out that evaluations take time and governments should not be in too much of a hurry to generate results; hurried results are likely to be poor results.

Explaining the outcome

One use of the results of a policy evaluation is simply to determine whether or not the policy initiative should continue. It was, however, felt strongly at the Workshop that policy evaluation should go further; that it should become a tool for positively improving the policy system. To achieve this, of course, the evaluation would have to answer not just the question, 'What happened as a result of the policy initiative?' but also the question, 'Why did this happen?' This would involve looking at

policy formulation, implementation and utilization and applying the following questions.
- Was the original analysis of the problem correct?
- Were the policy tools adopted appropriate to the solution of this problem?
- Was the implementation system adequate?
- Were the tools appropriately used in adoptor companies?
- If not, was this due to poor selection procedures or an inadequate system of monitoring?
- Did changing circumstances invalidate the original analysis?
- Why did some companies reject the use of the tool? . . . and so on.

Establishing feedback

An oft repeated theme of the Workshop was that the evaluation process – yielding 'what happened' and 'why' – should become an integral part of the policy system, and this was one of the most crucial issues raised. Built-in feedback from evaluation would result in a flexible and responsive policy system undergoing continuous adjustment and improvement. The achievement of this, however, would require commitment on the part of those involved in both policy formulation and delivery to the implementation of the results of evaluation. Because of strong lobbies and other entrenched interests, this might not be easily forthcoming. Whatever evaluation scheme is adopted, it must therefore be credible to all those involved in the policy system.

With built-in feedback timing would, of course, be crucial, as would the ability to identify points of maximum leverage within the policy system in order to achieve maximum change at minimum effort and at the appropriate time.

As an aid to both analysis and feedback, systematic data collection might be built into the policy initiative. This, if it is not too onerous – and clearly it must not be – might itself become a valuable tool for industrial managers as well as for public policy makers.

It was suggested earlier that evaluation and feedback should become more than the 'learning by doing' process outlined above: that an explicitly experimental policy system should be established along the lines of the US Department of Commerce's Experimental Technology Incentives Programme (Tassey, 1983). Here the policy system becomes itself part of a process of innovation. Whether or not public policy makers and administrators generally would wish to become, or are capable of becoming, part of such a system is, of course, another question entirely. However, in a highly imaginative series of experiments, the US National Bureau of Standards initiated such a system under the auspices of its Experimental Technology Incentives Programme (ETIP).

The aims of ETIP are succinctly stated in the Executive Summary of the final report as follows:

From 1972 to 1982 the Experimental Technology Incentives Program (ETIP) of the National Bureau of Standards carried out more than 200 experiments and studies better to understand how government policies impact private sector inventiveness and to improve these impacts.

ETIP adopted a strategy of experimentation with incremental changes in administrative policies and procedures in Federal agencies. Major components of this strategy included:

- Selection of agencies already inclined towards change where it was hypothesized the change, if properly planned and implemented, would result in an improved environment for private sector innovation;
- Collaborative problem-solving by involving all stakeholders in the planning, implementing, and evaluating of the experiment;
- ETIP's role of neutral third-party facilitator;
- Continuing feedback of data on the experiment's private-sector impacts for use in evaluating results and planning successive modifications and incremental changes; and
- Emphasis on transferring ETIP's skills, perceptions and methods to line agencies and institutionalising those changes found beneficial.

This strategy meant that ETIP served as both a catalytic agent for change and as a student of change and its effects (Herbert and Hoar, 1982)

This report offers a detailed evaluation of the effectiveness of the ETIP experiments in the areas of regulation, procurement, economic assistance and research and development and provides an assessment of the reasons underlying the effectiveness or lack of effectiveness of the various policy experiments.

Finally, we should emphasize that there is little sense in initiating evaluations solely of 'micro' policies which are undertaken in isolation from what is happening elsewhere. Evaluation, as we have implied before, should be concerned also with the complex network of relationships within the policy system, and specifically with their influence on overall policy effectiveness. Evaluations of 'micro' policies should be undertaken in the light of what is happening at the 'macro' level. An example of such an approach is the very thorough evaluation, after a three-year period of operation, of the West German R&D subsidy scheme directed towards small and medium-sized firms (Meyer-Krahmer et al, 1982) and there are examples of evaluations of major national R&D programmes in Keck (1977). For an overview of the experiences of various OECD members in policy evaluation see Hetman (1983). If we wish to move towards the formulation and implementation of a set of interrelated and complementary policy initiatives and thus towards a coherent technological policy, then the evaluation of such a policy must take into account the various horizontal (inter-micro) and vertical (micro–macro) links that the possession of such a policy implies exist. In short, coherent policies demand coherent evaluations.

REFERENCES

Allen T et al 1978 Government Influence on the Process of Innovation in Europe and Japan. *Research Policy* 7: 124–49

Braun E and McDonald S 1978 *Revolution in Miniature*. Cambridge University Press.

Coleman J S 1972 *Policy Research in the Social Sciences*. General Learning Press, Morristown, NJ

de Leon P 1976 *A Cross-National Comparison of Nuclear Development Strategies*. Rand Corp, Santa Monica, California

Elliot J 1982 Jenkin's Three Commandments. *Financial Times* 16 November

Farina C and Gibbons M 1979 A Quantitative Analysis of the SRC's Policy of Selectivity and Concentration. *Research Policy* 7: 301–338

Freeman C Clark J and Soete L 1982 *Unemployment and Technical Innovation*. Frances Pinter

Gardiner N 1975 *Economics of Industrial Subsidies*. Department of Industry

Gaudin T 1982 Chairman's Presentation at the Six Countries Meeting on Evaluating the Effectiveness of Innovation Policies, 22–23 November 1982, Windsor

Gibbons M 1982 The Evaluation of Government Policies for Innovation. Paper presented to Six Countries Programme Workshop, Windsor, 22–23 November

Goldberg W 1981 Explorations into the Instrumentality of Innovation Policy Research Report, International Institute of Management, Science Centre, West Berlin

Golding A M 1978 The Influence of Government Procurement on the Development of the Semi-Conductor Industry in the US and Britain. Six Countries Programme Workshop on Government Procurement Policies and Innovation, Dublin, Eire (PO Box 215, Delft, Netherlands)

Hayes R H and Abernathy W J 1980 Managing our way to Economic Decline. *Harvard Business Review* July-August: 67–76

Henkel M et al 1981 *The DHSS-Funded Research Units: The Process of Review*, Brunel University

Herbert R and Hoar R W 1982 *Government and Innovation: Experimenting with Change*. ETIP National Bureau of Standards, Washington DC (NBS-GCR-ETIP 82–100)

Hetman F 1983 *The Evaluation of the Effectiveness of Government Measures for the Stimulation of Innovation: State of the Art*. Workshop 6–7 June, OECD, Paris

Irvine J and Martin B 1980 A Methodology for Assessing the Scientific Performance of Research Groups. *Scientia Yogoslavica* 6(1–4): 83–95

Irvine J et al 1981 *Government Support for Industrial Research in Norway*. A Science Policy Research Unit Report, July

Irvine J and Martin B 1980 The Economic Effects of Big Science: The Case of Radio Astronomy. *Proceedings of the International Colloquium on Economic Effects of Space and Other Advanced Technologies, Strasbourg 28–30 April 1980*. European Space Agency, Paris

Irvine J and Martin B 1983 *The Economic and Social Impact of the ECSC Steel Research Programme. A SPRU Evaluation*. Commission of the European Communities, Brussels (to be published)

Keck O 1977 *Fast Breeder Reactor Development in West Germany, an Analysis of Government Policy*. (Doctoral dissertation) Science Policy Research Unit, Sussex University

Kogan M et al 1980 *Government's Commissioning of Research: A Case Study*, Brunel University

Little B 1974 *The Role of Government in Assisting New Product Development*. School of Business Administration, University of Western Ontario, London, Canada. (Working Paper Series No. 114, March).

Mansfield E et al 1977 Social and Private Rates of Return from Industrial Innovations. *Quarterly Journal of Economics* **91**: 221–240

Martin B and Irvine J 1981 Internal Criteria for Scientific Choice: an Evaluation of the Research Performance of Electron High Energy Physics Accelerators. *Minerva* XIX(3):408–32

Martin B and Irvine J 1983 *Perspectives on the Norwegian Institute for Energy Technology*. Ministry of Oil and Energy, Oslo (to be published)

Meyer-Krahmer F, Gielow G and Kuntze U 1982 *Innovations-forderung bei kleinen und mittleren Unternehmen*. Campus Verlag, Frankfurt and New York

Nelson R R 1974 Intellectualizing the Moon-Ghetto Metaphor: A Study of the Current Malaise of Rational Analysis in Social Problems. *Policy Sciences* **5**

Nelson R and Winter S 1977 In Search of a Useful Theory of Innovation. *Research Policy* **6**

Nicholson R 1982 Introductory Address to the Six Countries Programme Meeting, Windsor, 22–23 November

Oakey R P 1980 Regional Distribution of Innovative Manufacturing Establishments. *Regional Studies* **14**

Pavitt K 1982 Patterns of Technical Change: Towards a Taxonomy and a Theory. (Mimeo) Science Policy Research Unit, Sussex University

Pavitt K, Martin B and Irvine J 1982 *Final Report of the Project on 'CERN : Past Performance and Future Prospects'*. Social Science Research Council

Rosenberg N and Mowery D 1978 The Influence of Market Demand upon Innovation: A Critical Review of Recent Empirical Studies. *Research Policy* **8**

Rothwell R 1977 Characteristics of Successful Innovators and Technically Progressive Firms. *R&D Management* 7(3) June

Rothwell R 1979 *Government Regulation and Industrial Innovation*. Report to the Six Countries Programme (PO Box 215, TNO, 2600 AE Delft, The Netherlands)

Rothwell R 1981 Technology, Structural Change and Manufacturing Employment. *OMEGA* **9**(3):229–45

Rothwell R 1983 Firm Size and Innovation: A Case of Dynamic Complementarity. *Journal of General Management* Spring issue

Rothwell R and Zegveld W 1981 *Industrial Innovation and Public Policy*. Frances Pinter

Rothwell R and Zegveld W 1982 *Innovation and the Small and Medium Sized Firm*. Frances Pinter

Rubenstein A et al 1977 Management Perceptions of Government Incentives to

Technological Innovation in England, France, West Germany and Japan. *Research Policy* 6(4)

Tenbal M and Steinmuller E 1983 *Government Policy, Innovation and Economic Growth*. (Research paper 15.3). The Maurice Falk Institute for Economic Research in Israel, Mount Scopus, Jerusalem

Townsend J et al 1981 *Science and Technology Indicators for the UK: Innovations in Britain Since 1945*. (Occasional Paper Series No. 16, December) Science Policy Research Unit, Sussex University

Whiston T G 1982 *Environmental Regulations and the European Automobile Industry: Compliance Costs, Corporate Consequences and Productivity Issues* (Synthesis Report for OECD) Science Policy Research Unit, Sussex University

Zegveld W 1982 Towards a System of Support for Innovation. Presentation to the Six Countries Programme Workshop, Windsor, 22–23 November

CHAPTER FOUR

Elements of Technology Policy

A coherent policy towards industrial transformation and technological development ought to be structured along three main tracks. Firstly, there is the necessary social and economic environment to create favourable conditions for the development of industry and trade in general. Secondly, selected policies should be directed specifically at reindustrialization. Thirdly, policies should be designed to minimize the social cost of reindustrialization.

Policies to create favourable conditions for industry are aimed to create the environment in which industrial enterprises are able to function effectively. Some countries are giving relatively little attention to such policies and focus most of their attention on technology policies. Other countries, in contrast, adopt the opposite approach. In crude terms, reindustrialization and technology policies can be no substitutes for poor economic policies, and vice versa. The two should be complementary, and coherent policies towards reindustrialization contain elements of both.

GENERAL ECONOMIC POLICY IN AN INDUSTRIAL PERSPECTIVE

There are a number of essential conditions to be fulfilled for a new industrial potential to develop, and four factors are of decisive importance. In the first place there is the cost level. In particular, in some countries labour costs have risen more than productivity increases have warranted, which has corroded the competitive position of industry. Secondly, in spite of rising unemployment, the functioning of the labour market often makes it difficult and sometimes impossible to fill job vacancies. As a result of this, firms and countries are unable to take advantage of potential production and sales opportunities. In the third place, there are substantial mis-matches between what countries are able to offer on the world market on the one hand, and the structure of world market demand on the other.

One reason why industrial innovation is not progressing in an adequate way, is partly because – and this in the fourth factor – the capital position of firms has deteriorated through declining demand, by disproportional growth of costs and by low market prices for goods, especially those positioned at the end of the product life cycle.

Cost

Reenforcement of a country's international competitive position for existing, and also to a significant extent for new products, depends upon cost trends being brought under control. In this context wage cost, energy cost and cost relating to environmental regulations, either individually or combined, largely determine the competitive position of a significant number of major sectors of industry. Moreover, these cost categories are significantly affected by government policy.

Labour market

The poor match between supply and demand on the labour market can be considered as one of the problem areas currently confronting the development of industry. Any action to counteract the rigidity of the labour market calls for simultaneous action on both the supply and demand sides. The importance of a more flexible labour market is great, especially in the light of the necessity for industry to react quickly to a changing environment.

Investment, innovation and capital position

Cost being too high, and products positioned substantially at the end of the product life cycle, mean that the profit-generating capability, and thereby the possibility to invest in innovation, of end-of-cycle firms in particular is reduced. The problem of creating equity is all the more grave in view of the fact that it is often difficult for industry, especially start-up firms, to gain access to the capital market for the purpose of attracting equity capital. The tax system and the financial system need to be adjusted to cope with this fundamental problem (see Chapter 5).

REINDUSTRIALIZATION POLICY

Reindustrialization policy – after general economic policy the 'second track' of national policy – deals with industrial sectors, with main national priority areas and with generic technologies. We will concentrate here on policies for industrial sectors and on main national priority areas. Examples will be taken from the policies proposed in the Netherlands by the Advisory Committee on Industry Policy in 1981. The general approach adopted by the Advisory Committee can be applied also in other advanced market economies.

Sector development and technology

The report of the Scientific Council of Government Policy, *Place and Future of Netherlands Industry*, of 1980 pointed at the importance of a well-balanced industrial policy on sectoral structure. The report emphasized the need for an upgrading of the intermediate sectors (oil, chemicals, steel), a revitalization of the 'sensitive' sectors (clothing, footwear, furniture, etc) and a strengthening of the equipment sector (mechanical engineering and equipment manufacturing, electrical engineering, transport and instrument engineering). In order to stimulate sector development, it was important to understand the way in which technological change had played a role in the development of the current situation, and the extent to which new technological developments in the form of opportunities for products and processes could contribute to the improvement of the performance of the various sectors. The Wagner Commission's listing of the opportunities and threats facing Dutch industrial sectors can be employed as a guideline for other investigations of this kind (NICIP, 1981).

In the following Table (4.1), opportunities and threats for each group of industrial sectors are listed. The opportunities and/or threats are underlined where it is reasonable to assume that technological developments can play an ameliorating role. As the data show, the threats and opportunities vary widely from sector to sector. It seems also reasonable to assume that they will vary between different countries for the same sector. This means that the appropriate policies are likely to vary both between sectors and between nations.

Main national priority areas and technology

A reindustrialization policy is by definition selective. It selects what is to be stimulated and assigns proprities within that selection. This, however, must not lead to other promising initiatives being disregarded. Any selection, therefore, must not be exclusive, and policies must be flexible since new insights and developments may lead to change, to a reordering of priorities or to the emergence of new priorities. Two main problems are met in making these choices. First, industrial activity in most sectors and countries is extremely varied. Secondly, the number of objectives which economic policy has taken into account over the years has increased substantially. In addition to the traditional classic macroeconomic objectives, today we also apply criteria directed at energy, physical planning, environmental protection, and so on.

110

Table 4.1   *A. Intermediate or basic industries* (Industrial sectors: wood, paper, oil, chemical, building materials and base metal industry).

Opportunities	Threats
Manufacture of products having higher added value	Move away to primary producing countries
Availability of natural gas	Internal overcapacity
Cooperation between large-scale chemical companies. Allows inter alia inter-company supply	Increasing level of environmental charges
Bulk production based on large-scale operation	Competition-distorting support measures by other governments
Large and efficient production units	Energy-intensive production
	Small margin for R&D

B. Capital goods industry (Industrial sectors: Metal products, electrical engineering, and Transport equipment industry).

Opportunities	Threats
Supply of quality products and first-class service	*Heavy international competition in various submarkets where new product development requires very large R&D efforts*
Energy-saving equipment and environmentally acceptable technologies represent new opportunities	Small home market
Supply to major non-Netherlands businesses	Support for exports by other governments
Supply to developing countries	Protection of national producers in their home markets
Taking greater advantage of the potential of trading companies	Limited government support on the home market for new developments
Harmonization on R&D with non-Netherlands businesses	*Limited technology transfer from research institutes to medium-sized and small businesses*
Raising the organization level	*Large number of, internationally, small enterprises with limited base for R&D costs and the necessary service network*
	Development of new products is a key factor in international competition and needs strong base
	A number of enterprises in key positions in this sector are engaged in a virtually constant struggle for survival, hence little attention for innovation
	Too little know-how in a number of high-technology fields
	Predominant mechanical engineering tradition under-oriented towards microelectronics, which is growing increasingly important in this sector
	Organization level not attuned to supplying units/modules
	Poor control of production process (delivery times)
	Many enterprises have no product development of their own but only supply capacity, which makes them vulnerable to technological competition

111

C. Sensitive sectors (Industrial sectors: textiles, leather, footwear and other light industries, and furniture manufacturing).

Opportunities

Upgrading of the product package
Taking greater advantage of the potential of trading companies
Better technology transfer from research institutes to medium-sized and small businesses
Multifibre agreement
Large number of relatively small enterprises with too small a base for market position. Cooperation could broaden this base
Diversification in sales effort
High flexibility in production process, smaller and more advanced series
Service and assistance
Reinforcement of management

Threats

Low growth as a result of stagnation in development of real family expenditure
Continuing growth of imports from OECD countries
Accession to EEC of Greece, Spain and Portugal
Small opportunity for mutual supplies (self-ordering) because of extremely small base at home
Reduction in the number of specific training courses
Sensitivity of the highly organized Dutch textile and clothing industry to competition from low-wage countries because of open character of the home market
Declining support in the engineering field from national mechanical engineering industry
Underspecialized towards high-grade quality segments
Poor control of production, and distribution logistics (delivery times, quality control)
Adaptation of production organization to marketing requirements is a problem area
Little attention to dealing with customers
Eroded financial position and poor profitability means a weak starting position

D. Food, beverages and tobacco industry.

Opportunities

Agrification (replacement of petrochemical products by agrarian ones)
Geographical location (raw materials)
Good raw materials (home market)
Concentration of export activities
Export of integrated/turn-key projects
Refinement of products
Broadening of product range
Rationalization of production process

Threats

One-sided phytosanitary and veterinary standards on the sales side
Relatively severe environmental requirements

E. Electronics industry

Opportunities	*Threats*
New market opportunities	Large and growing competition
New products	SE Asia
Reinforcement of base by intensive use of home market (eg government)	*Failed to keep up with certain key international developments*
Major companies as starting point	Support by other governments

F. Industrial services (Printing industry and publishers).

Opportunities	*Threats*
Relatively protective home market	*Under-oriented towards modern communications and informatics developments*
	Blurring of sectoral boundaries

In the Netherlands, the Advisory Committee on industrial policy considered that an approach exclusively or largely based on the traditional sectoral structure would not do sufficient justice, neither in the descriptive or in the normative sense, to the many aspects involved. On the other hand there is the practical fact that it is difficult to design policy independent of an internationally defined frame of reference capable of providing the necessary quantified data. The main limitation of the sectoral approach, however, is that not only are there differences between sectors, but there also exist large intrasectoral differences between individual firms. Sectors are often too heterogeneous to be treated as homogeneous units in the policy-shaping process. Sectors, therefore, seldom lend themselves to an integrated and/or uniform approach. Long-established sectoral organizations, quite often set-up for the purpose of wage negotiations, are in many instances not the right parties to act as intermediaries for reindustrialization and technology policies. A further crucial point is that many of the techno-economic opportunities identified were cross-sectoral in nature. The first step consists of the selection of main priority areas.

Criteria for this selection are: a link with existing industrial activity based on a comparative advantage; the existence of an innovation-oriented home market, for example in the form of a committed customer wishing to attain world class in terms of quality; and a link-up with existing expertise and knowledge, including training and research. Based on the information at its disposal, the Advisory Commission defined fourteen main priority areas by way of indication (Table 4.2).

The second step consists of selecting 'spheres of activity' for each of the main priority areas. By way of illustration, the Advisory Commission listed more than fifty techno-economic activities belonging to the fourteen main priority areas (Table 4.2). These activities were measured against the following five supplementary criteria:
- trends in market development (national and international);
- competitive position of the particular activity;
- added value aspect;
- balance of payments contribution;
- technological trends.

113

Table 4.2

Main priority areas (by way of indication)	Spheres of activity (by way of illustration)
Port areas	• traffic control systems • container handling equipment • pipeline transport • consultancy
Agrarian and food industry	• breeding and quality products • distribution systems • agricultural machinery and auction market systems • modular plant construction
Hydraulic engineering, water management and the continental shelf	• delta techniques • hydraulic engineering contracting • specialized shipbuilding • drinking water production • effluent treatment • offshore industry • maritime operations
Amsterdam airport	• (ancillary supplies to) the aircraft industry • airport/goods-handling systems • air traffic controls
Speciality chemicals	• fine chemicals • process equipment • modular construction of chemical plants • more selective processes (eg biotechnology)
Electronics and informatics	• telecommunications systems and equipment • robot application • teletext, viditel
Industrialization of business services	• computer-aided design • software industry • consultancy/engineering • turnkey projects
Maintenance and renovation	• maintenance equipment • renovation of buildings • maintenance of roads and waterways
Energy installations and equipment	• congeneration installation • energy-saving techniques and equipment • coal transhipment and transport • natural gas systems • gas-turbine maintenance
Medical technology	• measurement and control • equipment and sensors • aids for the handicapped
Waste processing, recycling and other environmental equipment	• ferrous and nonferrous metals • separation techniques for domestic refuse and agrarian waste

Defence equipment	• shipbuilding
	• vehicles
	• radar, air-defence missile guidance systems
	• optical equipment
Construction	• utility housing construction
	• wooden frame construction
	• home textiles, furniture industry
	• energy saving in the home
Office systems	• reprographic techniques
	• graphical design
	• office automation

Finally, the third phase consists of selecting projects for each of the spheres of activity. This final phase was not carried out by the Commission since it was considered that it belongs at the microlevel of the enterprise, where criteria such as expected profitability, management skills, and other consideration, will weigh heavily in determining project choice. In other words, the Commission performed the overall techno-economic constraint and opportunity analysis and identified a wide range of rather broad options (techno-economic selectivity), creating a framework for project choice at the level of the firm (project –market selectivity).

Government policies on main priority areas, be they sectoral or cross-sectoral, are neither new nor unusual as we saw in Tables 3.3 and 3.4 for Japan and France. In most countries policies towards the agricultural sector are a good example. Further examples are the Netherlands policies towards the aviation sector and the dredging sector; policies for the semiconductor industry in the USA; and policies for the pharmaceutical industry in Sweden and the offshore equipment industry in Norway. Short description of the latter two cases and the case of the agricultural sector in the Netherlands are given below.

In Sweden main priority area policy towards the pharmaceutical industry was initiated in the mid-1960s. In all industrialized countries with a pharmaceutical products industry, the private sector activities have been accompanied by extensive government regulation of new drug innovation, requiring the demonstration of the efficacy of the drug as well as its safety on the basis of well-controlled scientific tests prior to marketing approval.

In addition to such regulatory controls, many other public policies influence the innovation process in the pharmaceutical industry. Among such policies are government support for basic research in the biomedical sciences, patent and tax policies, programmes directed at the marketing and distribution of drugs and, naturally, educational programmes at the universities.

The Swedish policy well fitted this integrated approach, involving the private as well as the public sector. The approach included the stimulation of new drug development at a number of the stronger pharmaceutical companies, the strengthening of university education – including the activities of the biomedical centre at Uppsala University – and the restructuring of the regulatory agency dealing with the admission of new drugs. The effort to improve the position of the Swedish pharmaceutical industry was assisted greatly by the health service being nationalized, thereby in principle creating market power. The Swedish effort can be considered successful. Annual growth in the production of pharmaceutical products over the period 1968–72 was 6 per cent, and over the period 1972–77 a production growth of 9 per cent per year was realized. The national market share of Swedish pharmaceutical products has substantially improved and international trade in this sector, after a long period of deficit, is currently in balance.

In Norway priority area policy towards the offshore industry was initiated in 1965 at the time of the first licensing round regarding blocks of the continental shelf. This policy was reenforced in 1970 following the first major oil and gas discovery: the Ekofiskfield. Because the extent of the oil and gas discoveries greatly exceeded the relatively low fuel requirements of Norway's small population, the government followed a prudent and moderate rate of development with the prime objective of increasing Norwegian industrial involvement in the supply of offshore goods and services. Given the oil companies' practice of undertaking R&D themselves or with foreign partners, and the fact that Norwegian equipment manufacturers tended to have inadequate financial and R&D resources to accept the costs and risks involved in successful developments in this area, the government in 1979 made it conditional that oil companies applying for new acreage on the Norwegian continental shelf must place R&D contracts with Norwegian firms or with research institutes. The volume of these R&D contracts were fixed at a minimum 50 per cent of the value of the R&D associated with future field development. Subsequently, a number of oil companies have entered into large R&D contracts in Norway to meet this requirement. The oil companies were required to finance those R&D projects which would lead to substantial learning by the Norwegian partners involved, and to useful results with commercial application.

The R&D requirement marked a radical departure in worldwide petroleum licensing conditions. By late 1982 the oil companies were committed to paying some £120 million for the period 1982–86 for offshore R&D projects in Norway. A close relationship between industrial policy and technology policy has been achieved this way in the main national priority area, 'offshore'.

In the Netherlands priority area policy in the agricultural sector dates back to 1880. In that year the position of the Netherlands farmer was threatened by the then European agricultural crisis, which was caused by the development of the steam engine and the steamship resulting in the importation of cheap grain from Argentina, Canada, Russia and the

USA. The agricultural crisis led to mutual collaboration of the farmers aimed at strengthening economic power and resulted in the establishment of cooperation in procurement, sales, product processing and financing.

At an international agricultural exposition held in 1884 it became clear that the Netherlands was much behind in agricultural production technology and in the related commercial and organizational functions. In 1890 a state committee advised the Netherlands government to devise a policy to increase the level of knowledge of the farmer by stimulating agricultural education and the transfer of knowledge.

Main priority area policy has been developed since, and has received broad support. Presently a number of agricultural experimental stations, research centres, and regional extension services, all functioning in an integrated fashion with the educational system and with the Ministry of Agriculture, provide strong links between the private and public sectors.

The export of agricultural products by the Netherlands in 1981 amounted to some Dfl40 billion (10^{12})*; in the same year trade surplus amounted to about Dfl14 billion. In 1981 the Netherlands was second only to the USA in the export of agricultural products. Main priority area policy has had a major infuence on this result.

Government involvement in policies towards technical advance in main priority areas do, of course, take a number of forms. As has been previously described (in Chapter 3) governments can influence the process of advancing technical progress in industry in many ways, the four generally most important of these being (Rothwell and Zegveld, 1981): procurement; regulation; technical-scientific infrastructure; and provision of funds to diminish financial risks.

In stimulating the development of main priority areas an approach is often adopted which integrates several of the policies mentioned above and, indeed, it would be surprising if, alone, any one of these policy areas would be sufficient. Of the four forms of government intervention mentioned above, the first two can have a direct influence, either positive or negative, on technological change (Rothwell, 1979; Overmeer and Prakke, 1978); the last two forms of intervention, depending on whether they are used in a 'general' or 'directed' manner – and normally in most countries they have been used in the former mode – tend to have a more indirect influence. It should also be remarked that procurement and regulation are most often the terrain of government departments other than the one responsible for industrial and technological development.

In the rest of the chapter we shall discuss procurement and regulation. The technical and scientific infrastructure is dealt with briefly in a regional context in Chapter 7, and the financing of innovation is covered in Chapter 5.

* (European currency=10^{12};   USA currency=10^9)

PUBLIC PROCUREMENT AND
TECHNOLOGICAL INNOVATION

It is clear, when analysing public policies towards the stimulation of industrial technological change, that the overwhelming bulk of policy tools employed are on the supply side (Rothwell and Zegveld, 1981, Chapter 5). Given the emphasis on 'need factors' in the results of studies of successful innovations, and given the fact that public authorities purchase between about 30 and 50 per cent of all goods and services produced in the advanced market economies, it seems surprising that so few explicit attempts have been made to utilize public purchasing as a means to stimulate supplier technological innovations. It is even more surprising in view of the considerable evidence available showing the crucial role public (mainly defence and space) procurement played in the United States in the early development of the semiconductor, integrated circuit, computer-aided design and computer industries (Nelson, 1982; Golding, 1978; Schnee, 1978; Kleinman, 1977; for a discussion of this issue, see Rothwell and Zegveld, 1981, Chapter 7). Although the two worked in a complementary manner, it is clear that procurement was much more important in each of the above industries than the considerable level of government R&D support provided. Public procurement by the Department of Defense and NASA effectively reduced market entry risks, acting as a risk-accepting market especially for new technology based small firms (NTBFs) with no previous track record as suppliers. Military and space applications represented an effective demonstration of effectiveness for innovative new components and devices which greatly accelerated their diffusion into civilian use.

The influence that governments might have on technological progress in a particular sector depends, of course, on its market position in that sector. In the case of monopsony, the government is the sole national purchaser (eg military equipment, roads and dams, PTTs in many countries), and its potential to stimulate, or indeed to inhibit, supplier technological change in such cases is great.

In the case of oligopsony, the government is one of a few dominant purchasers (eg health care), and again has considerable potential for stimulating supplier innovations. In this instance government might, for example, reach agreement with other purchasers to purchase only goods that meet certain stringent standards of performance; indeed, governments might legislate to this effect.

In the case of polyopsony, the government is only one of many purchasers (eg building materials) and its influence on the market in general will (in the absence of performance regulations) be limited. Even

118

here, however, governments can establish demanding performance specifications which can spill over into other areas of the market.

The structure of the supply industry is also important. In the case of a monopoly supplier in a non-monopsonistic situation, the public market influence might be relatively small. On the other hand, a tight oligopoly/monopsony or closed monopoly/monopsony situation might lead to too close a relationship between the government and its supplier(s), resulting in featherbedding of the supplier industry and supplier complacency with respect to the need for innovation. In such cases, in the absence of technology stimulus from the user, the longer-term international competitiveness of the supplier industry will suffer.

While defence procurement in the US was extremely effective at stimulating civilian innovations, there appears to have been little significant spin-off from defence R&D and purchasing in the UK. In a recent report Maddock (1983) has explained this paucity of civilian benefit in terms of industrial structural factors, and in this respect has identified four categories of company in the electronics area. Type A companies (or divisions of companies) are more or less completely locked into the defence market, and their innovatory efforts are determined entirely by defence requirements. They lack the entrepreneurial skills to move into civilian markets and experience great difficulties in assessing (non-specified) civilian requirements. Where such companies are specialized and largely autonomous divisions of very large multi-product companies – more often than not the case – the military and civilian work is completely separated due to differences in approach, customer relationship and time horizons between the two markets. The two systems are culturally very different, and as a consequence, there is little internal technology transfer.

In type B companies, civilian and defence work is performed side by side, and transfer between the two was readily achieved. However, Maddock identified only a few such companies, which were specialist software houses.

Type C companies are involved mainly in producing highly sophisticated, high-technology products for civilian applications. They would sometimes become involved in military applications of their technology, but suffered problems through excessively detailed defence specifications. Military contracts, however, offer them the benefit of longer time horizons than their civilian projects, and often offer them the opportunity to acquire new technical and design skills.

Type D companies, usually small, entrepreneurial and independent, operate almost exclusively in civilian markets, producing quite unique products. In such cases their products could achieve military application where the Ministry of Defence was willing to purchase civilian items off the shelf.

Not only do the majority of procurement contracts go to firms in category A, but so too do the bulk of defence research contracts. In the case of semiconductors, for example. Dickson (1983) showed that in 1978, 79 per cent of all Ministry of Defence research contracts went to five category A firms; in 1969 the proportion was 90 per cent. It appears that this very high concentration of R&D funding has the dual effect of featherbedding the few recipient companies and locking-in the technology to military requirements. There is little technological proliferation of the kind achieved, for example, through a system of subcontracting by the principal defence contractors in the United States.

A second important factor pointed to by Dickson is that the development project specification systems is such that it can often lead to the development of devices which are so specific to defence requirements, that their potential for civilian usage is small.

Indeed, it was under a VX(M) (development project) that the Ferranti F100L microprocessor was developed, the first such device to be designed and manufactured in Europe. But it has been often noted that the lack of wider commercial success for the F100L microprocessor can be traced to MoD funding of its development since its specifications are appropriate for military applications only (Dickson, 1973, p117).

Clearly, while defence procurement (and R&D funding) can stimulate supplier innovations (although in the case of R&D funding this may not be the most economically efficient means of doing so), whether or not it stimulates innovations with civilian potential or causes firms internally to transfer technology to civilian use, depends on both the nature of the procurement system itself and on the structure and policies of the supplier firms. It seems desirable that procurement agencies spread their funds through a significant number of firms and that they specify, where possible, devices that are capable of transferring to civilian usage.

Returning to our more general discussion, in order to stimulate supplier innovations it is, of course, necessary that the public purchasing authority be technically competent. This means that purchasing agencies should be aware of the state-of-the-art technology in the particular field, as well as of its implications for the user. It also implies the need for awareness of evolving use patterns in other countries and organizations, which might be considerably more advanced in both technological and applications terms.

It is without doubt in the United States that the innovation-stimulating potential of public procurement in civilian markets was first widely recognized as a powerful tool of innovation policy. At the same time it was recognized that, outside the military field, very little was known about how to use procurement to stimulate supplier innovations. Consequently when, following a presidential directive in 1972 the US National Bureau of Standards was directed to establish the Experimental Technology Incentives Programme (ETIP) 'to determine effective ways of stimulating non-Federal investment in research and development and of improving the application of research and development results', a series of innovation-oriented procurement experiments were initiated.

ETIP began with the observation that while the federal government purchases a considerable volume of goods and services annually (estimated at about \$85 billion in 1982), it had 'proven to be an un-educated bargain-hunter concerned almost exclusively with the immediate price tag of each item it purchased':

. . . (T)he government usually purchased the cheapest products that met minimal design standards. Not surprisingly, these products were also the simplest and most basic, incorporating technology that lagged significantly behind that available to private consumers. ETIP argued that if the government specified performance needs rather than design standards and purchased products with the lowest life cycle cost (initial price *plus* operating expenses), it would not only improve the quality of the goods purchased, but also, in the long-run, save money. At the same time, this policy would encourage industrial innovation (Britan, 1977, p 56).

Three main ways were identified in which government procurement activities had potential to stimulate technological innovations and their diffusion (Herbert and Hoar, 1982). First, the most direct impact government procurement can have is by applying its buying power to create a market for products and systems beyond the state-of-the-art. There are two major categories of government purchases in this area: purchases of innovations for government's own use, as by the National Aeronautics and Space Administration (NASA) and Department of Defense, and purchases of innovations for use by society at large, as with technologies for meeting regulatory requirements imposed by such agencies as the Energy Department, the Department of Transport and the Environmental Protection Agency.

Secondly, government procurement can create a demand pull for new technologies in the process of filling its routine requirements if it expresses its needs to industry in functional or performance terms. Such an approach would permit industry to exercise initiative and creativity in responding to these needs with innovative products and approaches. The size of the government market and its continuing nature would then serve as stimuli for industry to initiate developmental work.

Thirdly, the government market also represents a sizable testing ground for innovative products. The ability to place new products in a field environment and monitor product performance can provide valuable information concerning product modifications, especially to regulatory agencies (such as the Energy Department, Transport Department, Environmental Protection Agency) congressional mandates that required product innovation to achieve national objectives.

In order to harness these three potential procurement-derived influences (market creation, demand-pull and prototype testing), ETIP concentrated on activities involving the following innovative approaches to public purchasing.

Life-Cycle Costing (LCC): determining total costs incurred over the normal lifetime of product use and substitution of these lifetime costs in place of the initial low bid as the criterion for a procurement award.

Value Incentive Clause (VIC): stipulation in procurement contracts that the manufacturer may share in cost savings to the government that result from innovative, efficient designs by the manufacturer.

Performance Specifications: stipulation of improved product performance, rather than explicit design features, in describing government needs to industry. The manufacturer is encourages to offer novel, low-cost designs so long as specified product performance standards are met.

Sliding Scale Rating: used in conjunction with performance specifications, a technique that rewards manufacturers offering superior product performance by reducing their cost bid according to an established scale for purposes of determining the effective low bid.

Two-Step Procurement: a technique whereby manufacturers are asked to submit technical proposals (to establish the feasibility of innovation) prior to cost proposals. This technique was standard in the Federal Procurement Manual but was little used by many agencies.

Prototype Purchasing: a non-competitive means of allowing manufacturers to sell a limited quantity of an innovative product on the assumption that successful testing and evaluation of the product would lead to a larger government market.

ETIP applied these six approaches to public purchasing in a variety of product groups and user circumstances, and the various experiments met with mixed success. In general, on the basis of the results of its experimental procurement programme, ETIP concluded that:

- The use of life-cycle costing in federal procurement can induce incremental technology improvements in product design as well as substantial savings in energy costs, as demonstrated in FSS purchases of energy-saving appliances;
- The use of performance rather than design specifications in federal procurement can induce technological innovation among potential suppliers; and
- The use of a value incentive clause in federal procurement contracts did not result in widespread use of the clause by suppliers or in subsequent innovation, though it could be argued that this was due to the provision of insufficient incentives.

A detailed independent evaluation of the total procurement experiment highlighted the following factors. The single most important factor affecting the ability of public procurement to influence technological change was the stage of maturity of the product and the industry. It is when the industry and product are in the early stages of their cycle of development that procurement incentives have their greatest potential impact on technological change. With mature products, the use of, for example, life-cycle costing, will result in incremental product improvements and not major product changes.

Not surprisingly, it is when government is itself the end user of the product, rather than acting as a broker or middleman, that public procurement is potentially most effective. In this instance, three factors are instrumental in improving a procurement experiment's likelihood of success: as a user, government understands its own requirements; it can communicate these requirements directly and accurately to potential suppliers; and suppliers recognize that the government's presence in the market is long-term rather than the short-term presence reflected in such cases as prototype purchasing of products intended for general market distribution.

Procurement strategies will succeed in influencing industry's decision making when they parallel firms' commercial product and marketing strategies and when they are seen to influence the developer's profits by increasing revenues from the firm's innovative activities, lowering the costs of innovative activities, and/or lowering the risk associated with innovative activity.

Procurement has an enhanced probability of influencing technological change when it is used in conjunction with other policy intruments such as regulations.

While the ETIP procurement experiments began without a thorough conceptual framework of government's impact on innovation, and while they were not altogether successful, they did represent a unique learning process. This was true not only in the USA, moreover, for a number of European procurement experiments were initiated following the work of ETIP (Rothwell and Zegveld, 1981, Chapter 7). Certainly the ETIP results contain important lessons for the establishment of innovation-oriented procurement practices in other countries.

From the point of view of reindustrialization policy, it is important to note the high potential of public procurement to stimulate innovations at the beginning of the technology cycle. This reinforces the results of the studies mentioned earlier on the role that defence procurement played in stimulating the growth of the infant semiconductor industry in the US. For example, in 1955 the US federal government enjoyed approximately a 40 per cent share of total semiconductor shipments; this grew to nearly 50 per cent in 1960 and declined to around 10 per cent during the early to mid-1970s. In the case of integrated circuits, the role of federal procurement was even more dramatic: shipments to the federal government being 100 per cent in 1962, 94 per cent in 1963 and 37 per cent even as late as 1968 (Levin, 1982).

The ETIP experiments also highlighted the need for government procurement agencies to adopt a longer-term view of their activities and, given its continued efficient performance, to remain committed to the new product during its life cycle. Uncertainties associated with lack of commitment on the part of the purchasing agency will hardly induce suppliers to become involved in major innovations. It is also important that the existing aims and strategies of supplier companies are taken into account, and this implies establishing a high level of consultation and coordination between industry and government, which may sometimes require the setting up of special linkage mechanisms such as coordinating committees.

We turn now to Europe, and to a recent analysis of the influence of public procurement practices on technological development in a new industry, namely the offshore supplies industry, in three countries in Europe (Cook and Surrey, 1982). This analysis reinforces several of the important points mentioned above. Below we shall deal with policy in only two of the three countries covered by Cook and Surrey: the United Kingdom and Norway.

Despite the considerable amount of geophysical survey work being carried out in the North Sea during the second half of the 1960s British equipment companies, largely as a result of risk aversion, were involved in only a relatively small percentage of overall supply activity (about 25 per cent by 1972). Following the major oil discoveries on 1969 onwards, the British government began taking steps to stimulate British supply activity, including offering Interest Relief Grants in 1973 and strengthening the hand of the Offshore Supplies Office (OSO) in 1975 by establishing the principle of 'full and fair opportunity' for British firms – effectively a 'buy British' policy. Also, the state-owned British National Oil Company was established in 1976 which, it was understood, would be an effective further means of encouraging participation by British equipment suppliers.

By 1980 British companies (including foreign-owned subsidiaries) enjoyed a 70 per cent share of the overall expenditure on petroleum exploration and development on the UK continental shelf, which might appear to vindicate the various measures taken by the British government. When a careful look is taken of the nature, as opposed to the volume of the British share, however, the picture is not quite so favourable:

UK shares have generally been high in activities where British industry had pre-existing capabilities and product ranges which required only moderate adaptation to meet offshore requirements . . . Imports have mainly been confined to specialist equipment embodying technology developed in the US and not available in the UK . . . Imports of drilling equipment are low because US subsidiaries now manufacture in the UK. Foreign subsidiaries constitute the main class of exceptions to the general point that pre-existing UK capabilities were an important determinant of the UK share (Cook and Surrey, 1982, p 18).

In other words, procurement policies in the UK did little deliberately to enhance the technological capabilities of British suppliers or, perhaps more important in the long-term, effectively to stimulate them to move to new and more sophisticated areas of production. 'They were concerned with the short-term business of securing orders and assisting the entry of firms rather than the longer-term objective of building capabilities in new high-technology areas.' This short-term view was the result of governmental concern over balance of payments and unemployment and, largely for this reason, the Offshore Supplies Office did not discriminate between British-owned firms and subsidiaries of foreign firms since 'the latter were likely to bring relief more quickly.'

In Norway the situation was somewhat different, there being no compelling economic reason for rapid development of the offshore oil fields. It was, however, recognized early on that 'Norwegianization' – a central theme of public policy – would necessitate

the creation of a powerful national oil company to act as the principal vehicle for government policy and state investment. Statoil, a full-owned state corporation, was created for that purpose in 1972. . . . Statoil has taken a leading role in decisions on petroleum development and the procurement of offshore goods and services. One of Statoil's important functions has been to give Norwegian firms the experience necessary to compete with foreign suppliers. Statoil has also encouraged joint ventures where necessary to give domestic firms access to foreign technology and know-how and it also contributes to industrial R&D.

The principal of 'full and fair opportunity' in Norway was strengthened in 1972 under a Royal Decree mandating the purchase of Norwegian goods and services when they were competitive. Later, greater emphasis was placed on the need to develop Norwegian know-how and skills through greater participation in international developments involving new technical concepts and solutions. This led, in 1979, (as we pointed out earlier) to an adaptation to the licensing system which included the requirement for R&D funding in Norwegian companies and research institutes:

Previous licensing rounds had required the oil companies to cooperate with, and promote learning by, Norwegian firms, including technical assistance to Statoil, Nork Hydro and Saga Petroleum. Increasingly, however, it was seen that their ability to participate in the development and commercial exploitation of *new* concepts and techniques had been hampered by the oil companies' practice of awarding R&D contracts to experienced foreign firms and by the very limited R&D resources of Norwegian firms. Since the fourth licensing round in 1979, it has been a condition that oil companies applying for new acreage should place substantial research and development contracts with Norwegian firms and research institutes. Subsequently, a number of oil companies have entered into large research and development contracts in Norway to meet the new requirements.

The new requirement marked a radical departure in petroleum licensing conditions, both in Norway and worldwide. The government required the oil companies to finance R and D projects which were expected to lead to substantial learning by Norwegian partners and to commercially applicable results. The Council for Scientific and Industrial Research (NTNF) was given the task of drawing up priorities for offshore-related R & D in this area (Cook and Surrey, 1983, p49).

As a result of the new requirement, the oil companies were committed by September 1982 to paying £120 million for offshore-related R&D projects in Norway for the period up to 1986. Partly as a result of the Norwegian experience, the Offshore Supplies Office in Britain introduced technology clauses under the eighth round of licensing in 1983. These are designed to persuade the oil companies to involve UK firms and research organizations in R&D contracts and to cooperate with them at the prototype and testing stage.

In comparing procurement policies in Britain and Norway we can see several fundamental differences. In the first case, for pressing economic and social reasons, the requirements of technology policy were not a major factor influencing procurement in the UK; technology policy requirements were subordinated to the needs of economic and social policy. This resulted in the adoption of a short-term approach in which considerations of volume (more contracts meant more jobs) overrode those of quality (a shift into new, technologically more demanding, areas of production). For the same reasons, the 'buy British' policy was nondiscriminatory in that it meant 'buy equipment manufactured in Britain', and not 'buy from wholly British-owned firms'. Thus, while manufacturing occurred in Britain, much of the associated R&D – especially for advanced specialized equipment – was performed in the United States, with little indigenous (British) accumulation of high-level technical skills and expertise. Because of the lack of accumulated technological know-how in British firms, and although the publicly funded UK effort at the level of basic research has been relatively effective, 'what has not happened is the development of a British firm with the operating and R&D experience to obtain a strong position in one of the large-scale, high-technology, high-risk areas'. While Cook and Surrey ascribe this failure largely to lack of initiative and drive among leading UK firms, lack of technological considerations in British procurement practices undoubtedly also played a part. Properly conducted, procurement could have contributed to technological and production learning in British companies from the early 1970s onwards giving them, today, a foothold in a number of technologically more demanding areas of production.

The Norwegian government, unconstrained by the pressing economic and social pressures experienced in the UK, adopted a policy of 'Norwegianization' more or less from the start. This was effectively (in contrast to the position in the UK) a long-term policy in which the accumulation of indigenous technological and production skills was a core consideration. In this way, it was reasoned, Norwegian firms could not only gain an increasing share of offshore supply contracts in the Norwegian sector, but could acquire the experience to enable them to compete elsewhere in the world.

A second key difference between the two countries was the use of Statoil in Norway to further the policy of 'Norwegianization'. The British National Oil Company played a much less coherent and effective role, especially following the threat of privatization in 1979. Statoil was an effective 'carrier' of policy, acting as an important coordinating mechanism between the supplier and user sectors. In other words, it was an effective linkage mechanism, communicating current and future technological requirements to the emerging supplier industry and associated research institutions.

In summary, we can see that public procurement can play an effective role in stimulating supplier innovations and in shifting firms into new areas of production. Its potential for stimulating the growth of infant industries appears to be particularly significant in the context of reindustrialization policy. In order to be fully effective, however, technological innovation must be an explicit consideration in the procurement contract. Procurement agencies, to be fully effective, must also adopt a long-term view of their operations and be committed to building up technological skills in supplier companies. Finally, in order that the current and future technological skills of supplier companies can be taken into account as well as their existing product market strategies, effective linkage mechanisms should be established between the supplier and user sectors.

GOVERNMENT REGULATIONS AND TECHNOLOGICAL CHANGE

During the past decade public policy makers have shown considerable interest in ascertaining the effects that government regulations can have on technological change processes in industry. This interest has grown out of grave concern expressed by many industrialists and some economists, that certain types of regulations have effectively reduced the ability of companies to innovate and, at a more aggregated level, have contributed to the 'productivity slowdown' of the past decade or so. For the United States, for example, Christiansen and Haveman (1981) calculated that environmental regulations have contributed to about 1 per cent of the observed productivity slowdown; other estimates have been considerably higher (Denison, 1979).

It is without doubt in the United States that most concern has been expressed at all levels about the negative influence of government regulations on manufacturing firms. This is well illustrated by the results of a comparative analysis of public policy recommendations by type of policy tool in six countries (Rothwell and Zegveld, 1981, Chapter 5): 49 per cent of the 96 recommendations in the United States were in the category 'legal and regulatory'. Corresponding percentages in the five other countries were: Canada, zero per cent; Japan, zero per cent; the Netherlands, 15 per cent; Sweden, 4 per cent; and the United Kingdom, zero per cent. The current US administration came to power on a strong 'deregulatory' ticket and on 6 April 1981, President Reagan introduced the annulment of thirty-four norms in the US automobile industry alone (Whiston, 1982). In addition, during its first hundred days in office, the Reagan Administration made seventy-nine separate regulatory changes 'to fulfil the president's commitment to "take government off the back of business"' (Leone and Bradley, 1981).

Analyses and empirical surveys in the United States have indicated that, by and large, the influence of regulations on firms' technological change processes, although sometimes considerable, have been greatly overestimated (Rothwell, 1979; National Academy of Sciences, 1979). Further, while regulations have had a significant – and largely deleterious – influence on the processes of technological change in some industries, in others their influence has been small. In the former category are chemicals, pharmaceuticals, basic materials processing, automobiles and textiles; in the latter category are computers, semiconductors and consumer electronics. A more recent series of studies on the influence of environmental regulations on processes of technological change in firms in Europe and Canada sponsored by the OECD, has confirmed the variable nature of regulatory influences, both between industries and between countries (OECD, 1982).

The principal results of the various studies on the regulation and technological change issues can be summarized briefly as follows. Evidence directly relating regulation to the outcome of commercial innovation projects is sparse. Regulation is only one of many factors – and rarely the most important – affecting the innovation process, and separating the impact of regulations from that of a myriad other factors is extremely difficult. The evidence that is available suggests that the impact of regulations on 'business' – as opposed to compliance – innovations is more often an indirect, rather than a direct one.

It is evident that in the US in particular there is a high level of perception by managers that regulation has had an adverse effect on innovation processes, and regulations are sometimes perceived as a barrier to innovation in areas such as pharmaceuticals and toxic chemicals production.

In terms of the impact on technological change of the nature of the regulations, performance standards are, in general, preferable to rigid specification standards as a spur to compliance innovation, since they allow for greater freedom in seeking technological solutions. In addition, forward-looking regulations based on anticipated technological feasibility can potentially act as a spur to compliance innovation.

There is considerable evidence to suggest that the costs of regulatory compliance in some industries can be high. At the same time, considerable R&D funds have been diverted to regulatory-induced testing programmes to the detriment of business innovation. In addition, evidence from the US suggests that, largely as a result of regulatory-induced costs, company funded basic research has declined (Manners et al, 1978).

One of the most widely quoted effects of regulations on innovation is their impact in delaying the market launch of new products and processes through lengthening development times and, in the case of pharmaceuticals, imposing considerable additional delays in waiting for regulatory approval. These delays can considerably reduce the effective lifetime of patents. In regulated utilities, rate-adjustment delays can also influence firms' technological change processes.

Table 4.2   Some Contradictory Policies in the United States That Affect the Operations of Industry

Policy	Contradiction
The Environmental Protection Agency is pushing hard for stringent air pollution controls.	The Energy Department is pushing companies to switch from imported oil to dirtier coal.
The National Highway Traffic Safety Administration mandates weight-adding safety equipment for cars.	The Transportation Department is insisting on lighter vehicles to conserve gasoline.
The Justice Department offers guidance to companies on complying with the Foreign Corrupt Practices Act.	The Securities and Exchange Commission will not promise immunity from prosecution for practices the Justice Department might permit.
The Energy Department tries to keep down rail rates for hauling coal to encourage plant conversions.	The Transportation Department tries to keep coal-rail rates high to bolster the ailing rail industry.
The Environment Protection Agency restricts use of pesticides.	The Agriculture Department promotes pesticides for agricultural and forestry use.
The Occupational Safety and Health Administration choses the lowest level of exposure to hazardous substances technically feasible short of bankrupting an industry.	The Environmental Protection Agency uses more flexible standards for comparing risk levels with costs.

(*Source*: *Business Week*, 30 June 1980)

Probably the most widely articulated impact of regulations on innovation is that of increasing uncertainty. This can arise from a number of sources: unclear or imprecise regulations; ambiguous regulations;

lack of coordination between different regulations and different regulatory bodies; rapidly changing regulations. Table 4.2 shows a set of apparently conflicting regulations afflicting US companies during the 1970s. This additional uncertainty imposed on already uncertain process can reduce the risk-taking propensity of regulated companies causing them to adopt an overcautious approach to new technological and market combinations.

From the viewpoint of reindustrialization policy, government regulations may facilitate or inhibit structural industrial change, and there are a number of aspects to this. Taking first start-of-cycle industries, regulation might act to reduce the speed at which new technologies enter into commercial use. There is, for example, some concern that food, drug and environmental regulations might slow down the rate of introduction of new biotechnology-based products and processes. This is illustrated in the reaction of the British food industry to a recent recommendation by a Ministry of Agriculture, Food and Fisheries advisory committee that legislation should be introduced that treats enzymes as food additives or drugs; to date, enzymes are not regulated in the UK except under the rules of 'good manufacturing practice' (Yanchinski, 1983). According to the Director of the British Food Manufacturers Industry Association, the recommended animal tests and biological screening tests for the presence of toxins – and protocols for such tests do not currently exist – will represent a considerable financial burden on firms and will adversely affect the rate of growth of enzyme-related biotechnology in the UK. The new regulations will also add to the already considerable technical uncertainties involved in the development of commercially viable new enzymes.

This issue has also been addressed in a recent report prepared by the US Office of Technology Assessment (1984).

Regulations will have a moderately important effect on the development of biotechnology and, consequently, on US competitiveness in biotechnology. Special risks may lead to limited new regulation that could direct commercial efforts away from certain areas or at least slow advancements in those areas. In addition, most of the products that could be made by biotechnology and associated processes are already subject to considerable regulation, pharmaceuticals and chemicals being the best examples. This existing regulation also will affect corporate strategies and patterns of industrial development.

The costs and time involved in complying with regulatory requirements are the price society pays for safety. However, unreasonable restrictions and unnecessary burdens may delay or prevent important products from reaching the market or may increase the business risks of developing these products. Uncertainties, for example, about what the regulatory requirements will be or which agencies have jurisdiction, will also affect the risk, time and cost of product development. Those countries that have the most favourable regulatory environment in terms of least restrictions and uncertainties will have a competitive advantage in the commercialisation of new technology (OTA, 1984, p355).

In the case of biotechnology there is another important issue, that of the differential influence of regulations on firms of different sizes. What evidence is available suggests that regulations have a relatively greater impact on small firms because of their limited resources to cope with regulatory requirements (Rothwell, 1979). As we will see in Chapter 6, however, in the USA (and also in Europe) the emerging 'new wave' biotechnology industry is largely composed of new small firms. This contrasts with Japan where it is mainly existing large firms, or groups of firms, that are diversifying into biotechnology. If regulations do affect small firms to a greater extent than their larger counterparts, this clearly might influence the competitive dynamic between the USA and Japan in biotechnological products and processes. Indeed, it might be one reason for the rapid growth in collaborative ventures between small and large firms in biotechnology in the USA. Regulatory uncertainties might also mean that firms will attempt, at least initially, to develop biotechnological substitutes for existing drugs rather than move to new areas of production for fear of high regulatory-induced costs and delays.

While overly stringent regulations might impede the growth of new industries, so too might lack of regulation. As Hill and Utterback (1979) have pointed out, the absence of regulations can pose the greatest uncertainties by leaving the rules completely undefined. Delays in reaching international agreement on laws to govern the exploitation of ocean bed resources have undoubtedly retarded the development of both a recovery industry and an equipment supply industry. Similarly, delay in reaching agreement on the legal aspects of electronic mail – which is now technically feasible – has contributed to delays in its widespread introduction, and problems in reaching agreement on various aspects of satellite broadcasting have delayed its introduction in Europe. This contrasts with the United States, where an 'open skies' policy resulted in the relatively rapid introduction of satellite system.

Turning now to end-of-cycle industries, it is clear that firms over-burdened with regulatory-induced costs and uncertainties will be less able, and perhaps less inclined, to seek new areas of production, and especially those areas that will also be subjected to stringent regulatory requirements. High regulatory-induced costs might also inhibit companies in traditional areas from seeking significant productivity increases to counter growing price competition. In 1965, for example, the US copper industry spent $1.17 million on pollution control, which represented 1.5 per cent of total capital expenditure; by 1975 this sum had risen to $162 million, which represented 36.8 per cent of total capital expenditure (Weiss, 1978). Clearly this rapid escalation in pollution control costs will have limited firms' ability to invest in high-productivity, state-of-the-art process equipment.

In terms of regeneration via innovation, perhaps the most significant factor is the diversion of R&D resources away from business innovation and towards compliance developments. This would be particularly significant in the case of fragmented industries in which an individual firms R&D resources are small. In such cases governments might assist through the establishment of collective research programmes in which regulatory requirements are tackled on an industry-wide basis.

We have already mentioned the current trend towards deregulation in the United States, and it might be worthwhile briefly mentioning two examples where this appears to have had positive impacts on technolgical innovation. In the first case, anti-trust laws in the US have in the past discouraged companies from pooling their resources in shared R&D programmes of the type common in Japan. More recently, the US Justice Department has taken a more favourable view of such undertakings, and an organization has now been established – Microelectronics Computer Technology Corporation – which is a grouping of medium-sized electronics firms. The aim of the Microelectronics Computer Technology Corporation is, via the pooling of technical and financial resources, to act in a manner similar to the government-inspired Institute for New Generation Computer Technology in Japan and develop fifth generation computers for world markets.

The second case concerns the giant American corporation AT&T which, until recently, was a regulated monopoly telecommunications equipment supplier and operator. At the same time antitrust legislation banned AT&T's involvement in international telecommunications and in the production of high-technology information systems. There were also stringent antitrust limits on AT&T's involvement in the computer area. Since deregulation and the breakup of AT&T's telephone operating interests, the company has marshalled its considerable technological strengths in Bell Laboratories to enter those areas from which it was previously debarred. For example AT&T has entered the competition to lay the first fibre-optic telecommunications table across the Atlantic, and a new subsidiary has been formed, American Bell Incorporated, to operate in consumer electronics and business information systems (*Economist*, 28 May 1983).

From the above discussion it is clear that regulation, lack of regulation and deregulation can all influence the ability and propensity of firms to undertake major programmes of technological development. The trick for governments is to devise regulations and regulatory systems that control the operations of industry in order to protect the health and safety of workers, the interests of consumers and the quality of the environment, but which at the same time maintain the appropriate competitive dynamic and do not pose so great a burden on firms that their innovatory capacities are unacceptably reduced. The question is, what are the characteristics of such regulations and the appropriate system for formulation and implementation?

In the first case, it seems in general it is not the existence of regulations per se that causes firms most difficulty, but rather their lack of clarity and unsatisfactory mode of implementation. Clearly regulatory authorities can ameliorate the first of these problems through taking greater efforts to formulate regulations in a clear and unambiguous manner. In addition, regulations should be seen to be both reasonable and necessary, and norms and standards should be based on a careful scientific analysis of the particular problem. Better coordination at the centre will also reduce problems arising from interagency ambiguities.

The results of the recent OECD studies indicate that one means of improving the regulatory system is to involve industrialists and experts in formulating the regulations. To be fully effective, industrial involvement should be initiated at an early stage in the process, and in a manner that avoids both the reality and appearance of conflict of interest. Such interaction can be mutually beneficial: industry can be made aware of the problem that led to the need for regulation and can begin to take steps towards compliance; regulatory authorities can gain much useful technical information from industry in terms both of the nature of the problem and of the technical means available or required for compliance, as well as on the time frames and costs required to introduce these means.

Other important issues arising from the OECD and other studies are as follows:

- The need for international harmonization and cooperation, both to reduce non-tariff barriers to trade, and to assist the international diffusion of new technologies and devices. Care must be taken, however, to avoid the tendency towards 'least common denominator' type agreements, which are hardly conducive to the stimulation of technological change.
- The desirability, where possible, of formulating regulations that allow maximum freedom in developing technology for compliance. In this way, new compliance technologies may be developed opening up new markets for innovative companies.
- The importance of initiating publicly backed programmes of compliance-related collective R&D to complement the efforts of individual companies, thus effectively reducing the R&D burden (diversion of R&D resources) imposed on them. At the same time, regulatory authorities should take steps to acquire, or gain access to, the relevant technical expertise.
- The desirability in some cases of public financial support for the compliance activities of small firms, especially perhaps new small firms encountering regulations for the first time.

To conclude, we can say that while regulatory compliance will always represent a financial and sometimes a technological cost to the firm, well-formulated and implemented regulations can minimize those costs. The formulation of clear and precise regulations and good coordination between different regulatory authorities can greatly reduce the uncertainties often associated with compliance. More positively, regulations can be formulated that allow for, and even encourage, compliance innovations. Finally, the establishment of the appropriate regulatory infrastructure can provide the framework necessary to the introduction and diffusion of new technology systems. Conversely, lack of such a framework can retard commercialization both nationally and internationally.

Based on insights generated in the innovation process (Chapter 2) it can be concluded that, in general, fulfilling a demand will often lead sooner to a successful innovation than starting from a developed new technical possibility. Of considerable importance here is the point that the demand generating effect of government procurement appeals well to the sales attitude in industry which is generally better developed compared with the purchasing attitude; firms generally have much stronger policies towards the market place than towards suppliers.

In the case of the main national priority areas, government will adopt an active role in order both to enlarge the scope of its activities as well as their impact on industry. The choice of the main national priority areas is of importance in this respect. Technological developments are accompanied by large uncertainties both from a technical and a market standpoint. In order to reduce these risks somewhat, a considerable level of techno-economic knowledge is required. Government will possess this knowledge largely where it has a natural role to play, where it procures or regulates. Nelson, in his recent publication *Government and Technical Progress* (1982) states: 'A policy, in which Government officizes by themselves to identify the kinds of projects that are likely to be winners in a commercial market competition, is seductive. The evidence collected [in Nelson's publication and in other studies] suggest, however, that this is a strategy to be avoided'.

Some governments, of course, have taken organizational steps to increase their technical expertise in areas where they play an active role in the choice of projects. A good example of this was the establishment of the Advisory Committee on Applied Research and Development (ACARD) in the Cabinet Office in Britain following the government's decision to adopt Rothschild's 'customer–contractor' principle to guide the funding of infrasturctural R&D. In this case, Research Requirement Boards were established at the Department of Industry under its Chief Scientist to act as a proxy for the consumer, that is the end user of the R&D results (Gibbons and Gummett, 1979). It is also the case that there is a good deal of interchange of technically skilled personnel between government technology policy departments and industry in Japan and France.

The above considerations, namely the proven effectiveness (at least in some cases) of government intervention through public sector generated demand with inherent, available knowledge at the government level, suggest that an aggressive reindustrialization and technology policy ought also to be selective in this context. In this respect it is interesting to note that in the majority of the main priority areas in the Netherlands

Advisory Committee's report there is market involvement by the public sector. The above does not mean to suggest that working via the technical and scientific infrastructure and the financing of risks should not have their place in the framework of a main priority areas policy. Indeed, they have crucial and complementary roles to play. As such, however, they should not be the determining factors in the selection of areas in which government takes the initiative.

Nevertheless, as we have suggested, the technical and scientific infrastructure plays an acknowledged role in several parts of the technological trajectory, including fundamental and applied research as well as the transfer of technology. Support for the finance both of risky R&D activities as well as for innovative investments can also lower the threshold of both costs and risks required for provoking initiatives in industry.

Next to the elements discussed as parts of a policy based on main priority areas and aiming at reindustrialization, there are two additions; namely education and training, and export promotion. Regarding education and training, it is apparent that if this is to be of a sufficient size and impact, a considerable number of workers will have to be educated and trained in skills relevant to the pertinent technologies. Moreover, not only in the generation of technological know-how will these skills be required; they must also become widely diffused throughout industry if new technology-embodying capital goods are to be taken up and used in high-quality, high-productivity production sequences (eg robots and flexible manufacturing systems). In other words such skills are crucial to the diffusion of innovations as well as to their introduction.

Government is also in an excellent position to play an important role in export promotion because governments have a broad and long-time experience with representatives abroad. This experience can be mobilized to promote exports. The government can also – through financial support to (groups of) industry – assist the presentation of industry abroad. It is interesting that firms that would otherwise not collaborate, will join in export activities. Finally, procurement of high-quality products by government nationally increases export potential; a necessary home market is created and procurement by the government increases confidence in the product abroad.

Reindustrialization and technology policy, along the lines of an approach by main priority areas, is of vital importance and must be pursued if industrial structural transformation is to be achieved. Next to making a selection of the main priority areas best fitting to the national policy as a whole, it is necessary that the policy be consistently executed on a medium to long-term time horizon.

As we have observed before, a policy based on main priority areas does not always fit with a traditional sectoral approach. This means that on the side of industry new organizational forms must be set up to voice the interest of industrial firms with public policy makers. A final point to be made concerning main priority areas policy, and one made earlier, is that the integration of the various policy elements will require that government adjust its organizational structure in order better to cope with these policies.

POLICIES TO REDUCE THE SOCIAL COST OF REINDUSTRIALIZATION AND TECHNOLOGICAL DEVELOPMENT

Contemporary reindustrialization and technology policies may be interpreted as an attempt to achieve simultaneously diverse social and economic goals which can not always be easily reconciled. On the one hand there is the general desire to at least sustain living standards. On the other hand, there are increasing pressures to discriminate between various alternative new technologies and to mitigate many of the injurious side-effects of technical change. Despite the present-day cry for deregulation, it is the socially indispensable task of those responsible for policy in this area to achieve a constructive synthesis of these objectives.

Some would argue that the conflict between objectives is so great that the pursuit of one will endanger the other. For example, it is frequently argued that the regulation of technical change on pharmaceutical products in the US has become so restrictive as to slow down the process of technical change, both its generation and its diffusion, to an unacceptably low level. A good illustrative example of this latter effect (retarded diffusion) can be found in the case of valporic acid in the United States. Valporic acid is an anticonvulsant drug that has been used in Europe for decades, but was only recently approved by the Food and Drug Administration for marketing in the US. The benefits of the drug are profound, but although valporic acid was already available in ten countries, the Food and Drug Administration required additional human subject tests, claiming that only one of the 200 odd foreign studies on valporic acid published since 1967 was fully acceptable (Gerstenfeld, 1978). Against this argument against delay there is the case of the introduction of 'Softenon' causing many hundreds of malformed babies.

The case of the weak implementation in some countries of environmental regulations of the chemical industry, and of power stations, in order to improve their competitive position, may well be placed against the devastating consequences of acid rain. The lack of regulations – or their enforcement – regarding chemical waste management is now demanding its price financially as well as in terms of confidence in governments' ability to cope with technological development.

Three further problems ought to be mentioned in relation to societal effects of technical development:

136

- uneven distribution of cost and benefits over different groups in society;
- different time horizons on which the consequences of introduced technology becomes apparent;
- organizational problems at the side of government requiring inter-departmental coordination, not always easy to achieve.

For the purpose of analysis, technology assessment studies often improve insights into the secondary effects of technology. Indeed, several countries have established active technology assessment groups. Of prime importance is the position and the organizational place of such groups in society in order to be effective. For example in the US, the Office of Technology Assessment is attached to Congress, and in Sweden the technology assessment group is connected to the Prime Minister's Office.

Establishing the right equilibrium between the different government tasks is an extremely important but complex operation. We will not deal with this aspect in great detail.

COVERT AND OVERT POLICIES:
THE UNITED STATES AND JAPAN.

While we have attempted to make the case for the adoption of coherent national reindustrialization and technology policies, it is worth posing the question whether industrial structural transformation can occur in the absence of such policies. In the case of the United States, which has long operated on laissez-faire, market-driven lines by large corporations working on an international level, the answer would appear to be 'yes'. This contrasts with the experience in Japan where long-term and consistent national policies have contributed to the remarkable industrial transformation of the past thirty-five years.

But it is pertinent to ask a further question: has the US government, in addition to exercising its advantageous position of political dominance, been involved effectively in covert (informal) rather than formal policies towards industrial and technological change? The answer to this question might be a tentative 'yes'. It is certainly a fact that the US generally led the way in the creation of the new industries of the postwar era, and there exists convincing evidence to suggest that in a number of cases – semiconductors, CAD, computers, aerospace – the US Department of Defense played an important role (Dosi, 1984; Nelson, 1982; Rosenberg, 1982; Bright, 1979). The Department of Defense played its part both on the supply side (R&D funding) and, as we have seen earlier, on the demand side (procurement). This has been summarized for the case of semiconductors by Dosi (1983):

On the supply side they involved:
(a) Stimulation towards precisely defined technological directions and areas in which to allocate R&D efforts.
(b) The incentive toward and the direct financial support of the exploration of different possible alternative paths of technical change. Especially when precise 'trajectories' are not yet well defined there is what one could define as the 'burden of the first comer' (together of course, with the rewards for the first comer).

This burden, made of the attempts of trying and testing a number of possible areas of advance (which is much greater than that required from imitating industries) has been – partly – undertaken by public institutions (military and space agencies).
(c) The speeding up of technical progress at what we could define as the 'maximum rate' compatible with the existing knowledge, technology, and experience.
(d) The subsidy to expansion of productive capacity to certain target levels considered necessary for national defence requirement.
(e) A push toward standardization of production.
(f) The lowering of entry barriers for new firms which could find a market with low 'cost of access'.

On the demand side public policies resulted in:
(g) A guarantee of a future market for any innovation corresponding to the required technological features.
(h) The expansion of demand, with associated powerful learning effects upon productivity and unit costs.
(i) (Possible) a subsidy element involved in public contracts which helped to cover fixed costs (such as R&D) that would otherwise have fallen upon civilian sales.

The policies of procurement, R&D financing and explicit indication of the required direction of technological advance, together, operated as a widespread and finalized allocative mechanism of both productive and research efforts.

More recently, the US Office of Technology Assessment has been involved in the preparation of a report which raises the question whether the US government should actively encourage the commercialization of biotechnology, and if so, whether or not this should be achieved through an explicitly stated 'formal' policy (OTA, 1984). This represents a response to the high level strategic involvement by government in biotechnological developments mainly in Japan, but also in some countries in Europe (eg the Programme Mobilisateur in France – Ministry of Research and Industry, 1982). Whether or not the US government does become involved in formulating explicit strategies towards the development of key technologies, the R&D funding and procurement activities of the Department of Defense continue at a high level. There is no reason to doubt that, as in the past, this defence-related activity will have an important influence on both the rate and the direction of technological innovation in US industry. In addition to creating a considerable source of civilian R&D funding, such activity by the Department of Defense means that the dogmatic issue of direct (formal) government involvement with industry can be circumvented.

Below we document the recent and ongoing contribution of defence-supported R&D towards civilian industry and technology in the US. We then contast this with a description of the reindustrialization and technology policy system in Japan, a country in which defence funding of R&D is minimal. It is left to the reader to judge the relative merits of these two systems, one covert, the other overt.

THE DEPARTMENT OF DEFENSE AND CIVILIAN TECHNOLOGY IN THE US

The R&D programmes of the US Department of Defense contribute significantly to the country's civilian technology and to its industrial base. In the past Department of Defense spokesmen have generally referred to this contribution in terms of dual technology and insuring an adequate industrial-production capacity to satisfy military requirements. In recent years there has begun to be reference to civilian applications per se and the importance of a competitive advantage over other countries, particularly Japan. Dr Richard DeLauer, Under Secretary of Defense for Research and Engineering, is reported to have made the following statement to representatives of the semiconductor industry in February 1983: 'The nth-generation development programme is the US answer to Japan's government-supported fifth-generation-computer programme'. The US programme to which Dr DeLauer referred is formally titled 'Strategic Computing and Survivability'.

In view of such goals it seems appropriate to compare the Department of Defense in some respects with Japan's MITI, the main disadvantage of such a role for the Department being the inefficiency resulting from the requirements for secrecy and from the primary emphasis on military applications. Defence-oriented R&D might be deemed to be a deficient means to achieve civilian innovations. The amounts of money in the Department of Defense budget for research, development, test, and evaluation (RDT&E) are, however, so large that a significant civilian industrial impact is to be expected in spite of this major disadvantage. This budget is estimated at $27.8 billion for the fiscal year 1983 and $29.6 billion for fiscal year 1984.

As an example of the impact of the Department of Defense on the scientific and technical community, it is interesting to note the employment of scientists and engineers resulting from its activities. Using its Defense Economic Impact Modelling System, the Department generated the following figures for congressional testimony in March 1983 (Table 4.3).

Table 4.3   Employment in thousands as a result of defence and other activities

	1981			1987		
	Defence	Other	Total	Defence	Other	Total
Aero-astronautic engineers	24.03	41.07	65.10	40.62	46.54	87.16
Chemical engineers	2.73	49.35	52.08	3.79	52.16	55.96
Civil engineers	12.59	143.46	156.04	15.48	166.39	181.87
Electrical engineers	45.14	261.72	306.86	61.19	298.56	359.75
Mechanical engineers	27.21	168.62	195.83	39.17	188.14	227.31
Metallurgical engineers	2.50	14.18	16.68	3.48	16.63	20.10
Engineers (other)	35.85	351.68	387.53	53.28	406.42	459.70
Atmospheric and space scientists	0.70	11.15	11.85	1.04	11.90	12.94
Biological scientists	1.24	60.88	62.12	1.52	68.88	70.40
Chemists	6.21	116.90	123.11	8.84	130.10	138.94
Geologists	0.85	31.19	32.04	1.30	37.18	38.48
Marine scientists	0.48	4.60	5.08	0.60	5.14	5.75
Physicists and astronomers	6.55	17.71	24.26	7.57	18.75	26.32
Life and physical scientists (other)	1.34	6.18	7.52	1.48	5.50	6.98
Mathematicians	3.06	6.94	10.00	3.41	7.30	10.71
Statisticians and actuaries	1.39	31.91	33.30	2.24	37.84	40.08
Computer specialists	57.15	399.76	456.91	71.29	475.75	547.04
TOTALS	229.02	1717.30	1946.31	316.30	1973.18	2289.49

There are a number of paths within the Department of Defense leading to new civilian technology and an improved industrial base, namely:

- the support of research and development leading to civilian as well as military applications;
- the support of research and development leading only to military applications but providing experience with advanced equipment of interest from a civilian standpoint;
- the allowance of funds for 'Independent Research and Development' (IR&D) in areas of interest to the Department of Defense as a cost factor in determining overhead rates for contracts;
- the purchase of large quantities of equipment incorporating advanced technology and requiring sophisticated production techniques;

- the support and the encouragement of university research;
- the implementation of an 'Action Plan for the Improvement of Industrial Responsiveness', which includes as its objectives a sufficient supply of skilled labour to meet the needs of industry and the improvement of industrial productivity.

The overall responsibility for Department of Defense research and development lies with the Undersecretary of Defense for Research and Engineering. It is interesting to note that within his organization there is an Assistant Deputy Undersecretary for Production. The latter's responsibilities include productivity and resources. In addition to the armed services, various defense agencies support research and development. The most important group from the standpoint of new technology is the Defense Advanced Research Projects Agency (ARPA). This serves as the cell for initiating new technologies. After a certain stage of development is reached, the responsibility for programmes is usually transferred to one or more of the armed services. The total budget of the Advanced Research Projects Agency, for fiscal year 1983 amounted to $691 million.

In the following sections the results are given of an effort to identify Department of Defense programmes having potential civilian applications and designed to strengthen the scientific, technical and industrial base. The investigation was complicated by the fact that numerous programmes are classified and adequate descriptions of some of the unclassified work is often lacking. The following rough estimates of funds in fiscal year 1983 for programmes likely to produce new civilian technology are as follows: microelectronics and computers $300 million; data and voice communication (including navigation) $300 million; aircraft and hovercraft $600 million; materials $100 million; miscellaneous $400 million; and research, primarily at Universities $600 million; thus making a total figure of $2300 million. Because of the difficulties alluded to earlier in the paragraph, the figures are uncertain and are more likely to be too low than too high.

Of even greater interest is the Department of Defense funding of Independent Research and Development (IR&D) by its industrial contractors, which is estimated at $1.3 billion in fiscal year 1983. Although some of this money is already included in the figure of $2300 million given above, much of it is not. When all of these factors are considered, a likely lower limit of the funding of programmes with potential civilian applications is believed to be $3 billion in fiscal year 1983. The actual figure may well be considerably higher. When this figure and the programmes to modernize university laboratories and to improve the industrial base are considered, the magnitude of civilian-related activities by the Department of Defense is indeed impressive.

In the following sections more specific information is presented on defence R&D programmes with protential civilian applications and on defence programmes to improve the US scientific, technological and industrial base.

Microelectronics and computers

Starting in fiscal year 1982, Congress appropriated $5 577 000 for an airforce programme entitled Very High Speed Integrated Circuits (VHSIC). The corresponding authorization for fiscal year 1983 is $66 004 000. The Department of Defense requested $125 000 000 for this work in fiscal year 1984. The programme has as its goal the development of high-density microelectronic chips, which would permit a large increase in signal-processing speed.

The most ambitious defence programme in the computer field is that announced early in 1983 and called 'Strategic Computing and Survivability'. The Defense Advanced Research Projects Agency has requested $50 000 000 to initiate the work in fiscal year 1984. Total funding for the programme over a five-year period has been estimated at $500 000 000. Associated work in microelectronics is expected to cost another $500 000 000 over the same period. This latter amount probably includes funds for the continuation of the VHSIC programme discussed above. The goal is the development of a new generation of computers which would be much faster than present ones and which would use artificial-intelligence software, ie fifth generation computers.

Navigation systems

The NAVSTAR Global Positioning System (NAVSTAR GPS) has obvious civilian-navigation applications. In fact the Department of Defense is developing a fee schedule based upon estimates of civilian usage with a view to recovering the programme costs over and above those for military users' equipment. NAVSTAR GPS will consist of eighteen satellites and various ground stations. It is designed to provide the following information under all weather and visibility conditions: time with an accuracy of five nanoseconds; three-dimensional-spatial positioning worldwide with a probable spherical error of 16 m; and velocity with an accuracy of 0.1 m/sec. Near the beginning of 1982 the estimated costs of research, development, test, and evaluation for NAVSTAR GPS were as follows: space segment $512 million; control segment $199 million; user segment $431 million; making a total of $1142 million. It is expected that the system will be operational by 1988. If widely used, it will generate a significant market for civilian-user equipment.

Data and voice communications

The NAVSTAR GPS work described above is part of a larger programme known as Communications, Command, Control, and Intelligence (C3I). The C3I programme involves advanced data and voice-communication systems for military purposes with strong emphasis on satallites. It includes an important element for the development of an improved meteorological data-gathering system. In spite of much work specific to military applications, a significant portion of the R&D has potential civilian applications.

Aircraft and hovercraft

Large amounts are being spent on research and development in the field of aircraft. There has also been significant funding for a hovercraft programme (US Marine Corps), which is now entering the production phase. The craft is designed to have a maximum speed of 50 knots and a payload of at least 60 tons. As in the case of the C3I programme an important portion of the work has potential civilian interest. Even in the case of programmes for specific military aircraft, at least a small portion of the work is of interest for civilian aviation. In the case of the more general programmes, probably most of the work is of civilian interest. If the total of such programmes is considered, it appears likely that the funding of investigations with potential civilian applications is at least $500 million to $600 million in fiscal year 1983. This figure does not include research and development on avionics or on aircraft materials.

Materials

There is an important R&D effort aimed at improved materials and materials-processing techniques. Areas of particular emphasis include: nondestructive-testing methods, composites with high strength/weight ratios, high-temperature and high-strength materials, rapid-solidification technology as a means to improve mechanical properties and reduce production costs (eg, gas-turbine blades). Appropriations for R&D programmes on materials for the armed forces and the Advanced Research Projects Agency for fiscal year 1983 are estimated at some $126 million.

Miscellaneous

Other R&D programmes with civilian potential are given below. The figures in parentheses at the end of each description give the total appropriations for each technological category congressional fiscal year 1983.
- Biotechnology. The work includes development of drugs and vaccines by the Army and of antifouling substances by the Navy. The Air Force programme on aerospace biotechnology accounts for about two-thirds of the total funding ($67 500 000).
- Clothing and Shelter. The Army has a small programme in this field ($6 000 000).
- Cold-regions engineering. There is a small Army programme dealing with this subject ($6 000 000).

- Human factors, training, training devices, etc. There are a variety of programmes with funding by all three of the armed services ($138 100 000).
- Energy. The Army and the Navy have several energy programmes. Among them are the Navy's Energy-and-Environmental Protection Programme ($6 500 000), the Navy's RACER programme for the development of a Rankine bottoming cycle for heat recovery (estimated at $21 000 000 in fiscal year 1983), the Army's Fuels-and-Lubricants Programme ($1 900 000) and two Army programmes ($4 800 000) on electric-power sources.
- Environmental protection. There are small programmes on environmental technology within all three of the services ($27 400 000).
- Fibre-optics. The Air Force has a small fibre-optics programme. There are probably others ($2 900 000).
- Food. The Army has a food-technology programme for all of the armed services ($5 600 000).
- Lasers. All three services and Advanced Research Projects Agency have laser programmes. Applications include weapons, range finding and communications. The weapons work in this area may produce results of civilian value. For example, the high-energy lasers may be applicable to nuclear-fusion technology ($250 000 000).
- Manufacturing and product reliability/availability/maintainability. There is a Navy programme covering manufacturing technology ($3 300 000) and an Air Force product programme ($9 700 000). There are probably numerous other similar programmes associated with specific weapons systems.
- Nuclear. The Navy has five R&D programmes in the nuclear field ($82 400 000).
- Ocean engineering. The Navy has two ocean-engineering programmes ($15 500 000).
- Oceanographic instrumentation. The Navy has a small R&D programme on oceanographic instrumentation ($3 000 000).
- Radar. There are several radar programmes under the aegis of the Air Force and the Navy. Some of the work is undoubtedly of civilian interest ($120 600 000).
- Ships and ship propulsion. There are five Navy programmes in addition to those for specific vessels, which are not included here ($76 200 000).
- Space shuttle. The Air Force provides a great deal of support for the space-shuttle programme of the National Aeronautics and Space Administration ($355 700 000).
- Vehicles. There are three Army programmes. In addition there are major weapons-system programmes (eg, the M-1 tank) not included here ($32 600 000).

Support for universities

All three military services and some of the defence agencies, primarily the Defense Advanced Research Projects Agency, have programmes entitled 'Defense-Research Sciences'. With a few minor exceptions, the activities discussed in the previous section are not included in these programmes. They therefore represent a large source of additional research funding, primarily for universities. The appropriations for them are shown below (Table 4.4)

Table 4.4   Appropriations for defence-research sciences (in $million)

	FY 1981	FY1982	FY1983
Air Force	125.2	136.5	155.0
Army	125.0	157.0	182.0
Navy	225.0	255.0	283.0
Defence agencies	100.7	100.0(est)	101.0
Totals	575.9	648.5	721.0

Because of the basic nature of the work which is supported, most of it probably has long-term potential civilian applications. Eighty per cent is probably a reasonable figure for the share of this type of activity. It is thus estimated that something of the order of $550 million to $600 million is presently supporting research, primarily at the universities, of interest from a civilian standpoint.

In addition the Lincoln Laboratory (electronic systems) is operated for the Air Force by the Massachusetts Institute of Technology. Although much of this laboratory's work is only of interest for weapons systems, some of it certainly has civilian potential. Appropriations for advance-technology development at the Lincoln Laboratory amount to $23 079 000 in fiscal year 1983.

Other activities to strengthen the universities are as follows. Beginning with fiscal year 1983, the military services requested $30 000 000 per year over a five-year period to assist in the modernization of university equipment. Industry is encouraged to cooperate with universities by considering this factor in the evaluation of independent research and development (IR&D) when awarding contracts to industrial firms (the independent R&D programme is discussed in the following section). A fellowship programme for scientific and engineering students has been instituted. In the case of the reserve officer training (ROTC) programmes of the Air Force and the Navy, 80 per cent and 70 per cent respectively, of the ROTC scholarship holders are required to enroll in scientific or engineering curricula. A cooperative programme provides opportunities for students to work at Department of Defense Laboratories on a part-time basis. The Intergovernmental Personnel Act, which is utilized by the Department of Defense as well as other government departments, permits university and government personnel exchanges for periods up to two years.

Improving the industrial base

As in the case of the universities, the funding discussed earlier in this section entitled 'Research and Development Programs with Potential Civilian Applications' serves to improve the position of American industry. An additional incentive provided by the Department of Defense is the support of independent research and development on the part of its contractors. Some or all of the costs of independent R&D, with the exception of general and administrative expenses, are allowed in determining overhead rates under certain conditions, namely:

- The independent R&D must bear some relationship to a military function or operation.
- If the company receives payments of $4 000 000 or less from the Department of Defense in a given year, the negotiation of an advance agreement for independent R&D is not necessary. In the case of individual profit centres which contract directly, the limit is $500 000 for each. The costs are then allowed according to a formula based upon the historical average of all independent R&D performed by the company or the profit centre to its total sales.
- For companies or profit centres receiving payments exceeding the limits just mentioned, an advance agreement must be negotiated with an Armed Services Technical Evaluation Committee. This committee evaluates the independent R&D in terms of its value and establishes the level of support.

It is to be assumed that most companies plan their Department of Defense-supported independent R&D projects in such a way that the results are of dual value. Therefore a large fraction of the funding is probably of interest from a civilian as well as a military standpoint. In testimony before a Congressional Committee on the budget for fiscal year 1981, the Undersecretary of Defense for Research and Engineering estimated that annual corporate costs of approximately $2 billion for independent R&D were offset by Department of Defense reimbursements of $700 000 000. If these reimbursements have increased in the same ratio as the Department of Defense budget for research, development, test, and evaluation, they should amount to approximately $1.3 billion in fiscal year 1983. Congress has become concerned about the independent R&D costs (also about bid-and-proposal costs, which may be included in overhead) and has directed that they be shown as a line item beginning with the budget for fiscal year 1985. For fiscal year 1984 Department of Defense must submit proposed ceilings for the costs which are to be approved by Congress.

Finally the Department of Defense is directly working actively to increase the productivity and the product quality of its industrial contractors under its Action Plan for the Improvement of Industrial Responsiveness. Programmes of particular importance for this purpose are as follows. The Manufacturing Technology Programme is designed to improve industrial productivity and responsiveness. The activities under this programme, which are funded primarily as part of procurement contracts, are expected to produce 'factory floor applications of productivity enhancing technology'. The Technology Modernization Programme is handled on a joint-venture basis with industry. Based upon a negotiated agreement, which is linked to procurement contracts, Department of Defense invests 'in enabling manufacturing technologies and industry invests in capitalization for modernization'. The funding for the programmes could not be determined. When account is taken of the programme descriptions and the possibilities for depreciation charges in contract overhead, the amounts are probably considerable.

The information presented above for the US points at the very important indirect and direct influences of defence R&D spending towards civilian industrial development. Set against the considerable levels of civilian R&D funded by the Department of Defense are the potential opportunity costs to civilian market-related developments as a result of the vast sums of cash and large volumes of human capital resources devoted to military developments (Kaldor, 1980 has discussed the issue of defence-related opportunity costs in the UK). There is little doubt that defence is today's growth sector in the US. Indeed, top-level military spokesmen now claim that defence R&D and procurement expenditures are the dynamo of the US economy; these same spokesmen now openly claim to be consciously fulfilling a MITI-like role in coordinating and funding a significant percentage of total US R&D activity. In 1982 'defence' R&D accounted for 56.9 per cent of total government-funded R&D; in fascal year 1983 this increased to 61 per cent. In the same year 'defence and space' R&D accounted for 70.9 per cent of total government-funded R&D. In 1983 government R&D expenditure in the US is expected for about 50 per cent of total national expenditure on R&D (estimated at $83.6 billion).

But, as we suggested above, there may be significant opportunity costs associated with this high level of military R&D. Thus while in the 1980s total US government R&D funding increased (+ 2.7 per cent in 1980/81; + 0.6 per cent in 1981/82; + 5.2 per cent in 1982/83), the civilian allocation fell (− 6.2 per cent in 1980/81; − 10 per cent in 1981/82; − 5.3 per cent in 1982/83). 'Overall growth in the eighties was due exclusively to a large increase in defense funding which outweighed the drop in civilian oriented allocation' (OECD, 1983).

A recent investigation ('Pentagon Inc' *Frontline America*, Channel 4 television UK, 10 August 1983) of some of the influences of defence R&D spending and procurement on the civilian sector in the US highlighted a number of important problem areas. There is evidence to suggest that the military industrial complex is depriving the civilian market-oriented sector of many of the country's top brains in such crucial areas as computing and electronics. Large amounts of human capital are being 'locked in' to rather esoteric projects that do not have

147

significant apparent civilian spin-off potential. Finally, defence procurement is featherbedding some suppliers (eg in the clothing area) due to inadequate quality control procedures and lack of accountability. In short, it is being suggested that military R&D spending is seriously distorting the broad thrust of American technological development along paths dictated by military requirements and away from the current and future needs of world markets for civilian goods. This contasts sharply with trends in Japan. On the other hand there is the possibility that military R&D might be establishing some of the technological trajectories of the future. In addition, there will surely be considerable civilian spin-offs and an increase in the accumulation of national expertise in areas of advanced technology and manufacturing know-how. Whether these benefits will outweigh the costs, or vice versa, remains to be seen.

PUBLIC POLICY AND INDUSTRIAL TRANSFORMATION IN JAPAN

So far in this book we have attempted to justify the need for national reindustrialization and technology policies and to provide a framework – that of technology-dependent cycles – as a basis for discussing such policies throughout the book. We will end the chapter by describing the elements of one nation's technology policy which, during the past twenty or more years, has borne copious fruit; the country is, of course, Japan.

Following the World War II, the decision was made in Japan deliberately to restructure its industry better to match the evolving market and technological requirements of the second half of the twentieth century:

A corollary of Japan's determination to lift her productive capacity to a higher plane of technical and commercial competence was her awareness of the need to adapt her industrial composition to changes in markets and techniques. Structural adaptability was recognized as a condition of the continuous growth in GNP. Moreover, Japan did not simply respond to exogenous forces; she was remarkably successful in anticipating change. In the early 1950s her chief export industries still consisted of labour-intensive trades, where her low wages made her an effective competitor with her western rivals, and her superior management and organization kept at bay challenges from the developing countries. But, as her policy showed, she fully realized these advantages were transient, and she soon began to set up a new capacity in several large-scale, capital intensive trades, notably steel, shipbuilding and chemical fertilizers. By the early 1960s, when these trades were well established, she turned her attention to a number of engineering industries, especially radio, television sets and motor vehicles, as well as to petrochemical products. By the end of the 1960s her motor car, electronics and watch and clock industries ranked with the world's leaders, while her eminence in steel, motor cycles and shipbuilding remained unassailed. The check to her industrial growth after 1973 was followed by a recovery (in 1978) which was associated especially with the further development of her motor, machinery, instrument and electronic manufactures (Allen, 1981, p69 and 70).

This transformation of Japanese industry (from end-of-cycle to start-of-cycle sectors) can be depicted in Figure 4.1, which is a chart used by the Japanese Economic Planning Agency to explain Japan's economic development. It well illustrates Japanese movement towards higher value added, more knowledge-intensive industries. The point is, this transformation is the result of a coordinated (public and private) national strategy, in which technology policy has played a key role. The main features of the public policies that have contributed to this industrial transformation have been summed up in a recent document from the National Economic Development Council in the UK (1982).

Figure 4.1   The evolution of industrial structure

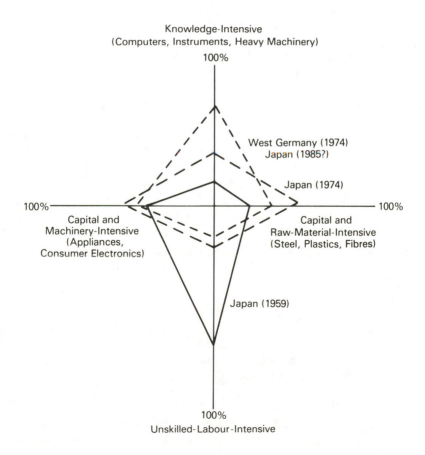

Industrial policy Japan has implemented a single-minded, continuous and consistent industrial policy. It is an active and selective approach, based on close and continuous dialogue between government and industry. It has aimed to ensure international competitiveness in specific industries through supporting economies of scale and to identify where future comparative advantage will lie or must be created. Trade policy is subjugated to industrial policy.

Financial systems Public features of this are:
- strong tax incentives to lenders and borrowers;
- the fiscal investment and loans programme which channels 'soft' loans to selected industries,
- the steering role which the Bank of Japan adopts, in the light of MITI plans, when supplying funds to commercial banks.

Engineering education Japan makes a massive investment in engineering education which results in over four times as many engineers per head of the population as in the UK. Salary, status and career prospects are all considerable for engineers, who occupy many of the top posts in industry and in government agencies concerned with industry.

The Japanese response to the shocks of the 1970s were also identified in the NEDC document:

Macroeconomic policy After the 1973 oil crisis, imports and inflation were cut quickly by deflation, followed by a policy of fiscal expansion in 1975 to restore growth, profits, investment and productivity growth.

Energy conservation Although already much more economical [than the UK] in the use of energy before 1973 Japanese industry has since matched energy savings achieved in the UK and has therefore retained its advantage.

Competitiveness Renewed rapid productivity growth of 7 per cent per annum since 1975, coupled with deceleration of earnings increases from 20 per cent to 6 per cent have improved competitiveness still further, permitting rising real incomes.

Structural adjustment Industrial policy has aimed at rapid restructuring away from energy and labour-intensive sectors towards knowledge-intensive ones. Intervention to ensure effective research and support for growth industries, and rapid rationalization of declining ones has put Japan in a very strong position for the 1980s.

Innovation Having been the world's leading importer of technology Japan is now engaged on a large scale R&D effort. This involves very large numbers of trained personnel, large scale funding, both public and private, clear guidelines on priority areas of innovation and national coordination and support from the highest authority.

The transformation of Japanese industry, as suggested above, was not simply the result of adopting the right public policies. The private banks played an important role also, but of course it was the efforts of private companies which were the dynamo of the transformation. Nevertheless, there is little doubt that the establishment by public bodies, in close consultation with industry, of long-term national strategies and aims played an important part. Government set national objectives, established guidelines, provided the appropriate support and played the key coordinating role. In short, public policy in Japan established a suitable framework in which the industrial transformation could take place. Moreover, as the Japanese case illustrated, having the right macroeconomic policies is crucial also. The treatment of such policies is, however, beyond the scope of this work. Undoubtedly some combination of Keynesian demand management, monetarist and supply-side policies will continue to dominate most industrialized countries macroeconomic management. Several mainly initial and partial attempts are being undertaken, however, in most industrialized countries, that relate these macroeconomic components to an overall development and growth strategy. Interrelated reindustrialization and technological innovation policies can well bridge the gap.

FORECASTING THE FUTURE IN JAPAN

One of the most significant differences between the roles played by the US Department of Defense and MITI in Japan in the respective industrial transformations that have taken place in the two countries, is that in the US the Department of Defense was involved – deliberately or not – in creating new branches of industry, while in Japan MITI was involved in a process of catching up with the US in these branches once they were well established. In other words, the US Department of Defense was associated with initiating new technological trajectories, while MITI's concern was with assisting Japanese companies to move rapidly along these trajectories after they were rather well defined. Japanese companies, of course, succeeded in this spectacularly well, adding, in the process, many novel features of their own.

While the Japanese ability to adopt and adapt foreign technology successfully can not be in doubt, a great deal of concern is currently being expressed in Japan concerning the ability of Japanese researchers and managers to achieve creative leaps forward. This concern has been summed up succinctly as follows:

like quality engineering yesterday, creativity is the holy grail in Japan today. Its industries having caught up with the West's technological innovation, the

Japanese worry that their scientific seeds for future growth may produce a weedy crop (*The Economist*, 6 August 1983, p39).

Despite this concern, the process of forecasting and planning for Japanese industrial restructuring to accommodate the techno-economic combinations of the future is continuing apace, and this process is well exemplified in a document produced in 1981 by Ueno of the Nomura Research Institute as part of the 'Research on the Strategic Plan for 21st Century Tokyo Metropolitan Area' (Ueno, 1981). Ueno has identified what he terms 'new frontier technology industries', and a selection taken from his very comprehensive compilation is listed in Table 4.5. Table 4.6 provides a reduced list of frontier industries with projected market sizes compiled by Ueno from forecasts undertaken by a variety of Japanese agencies.

Ueno further points out that while each of these industries will separately enjoy considerable growth, each industry will have a considerable impact on the other industries. He foresees their pattern of development as follows:

1. With the development of new technology, new products are developed and create new markets (video-disks, word-processors, etc).
2. With the development of new technology, existing products will be replaced and their functions improved (optical communications system, electronic watch, etc).
3. With the development of new technology, new functions will be added to existing markets and the market expanded (mini-computers, micro-computers, numerically-controlled machine tools, machining centers, industrial robots, etc).
4. With the development of new technology, related fields such as parts and raw materials will be expanded (LSIs, ultra-LSIs, etc).
5. With the development of new technology, peripheral equipment and software services will be expanded (computers, various new energies, etc).

Ueno then sums up:

The characteristic of the new technology industries in the future will be that they are compounded and are mutually interrelated. A breakthrough in one basic technology will produce new multiple, linked industries. New fields and growth industries towards the 21st century will be diverse and varied. Consequently, the place where medium-sized firms and small firms which are venture businesses can be active will expand. Among large firms, there will be increases in the cases of small and medium-sized organizations which are spun out as affiliated companies.

This raises a final crucial point, that of technical interrelatedness. Developments in one branch of industry might well be held up due to lack of progress elsewhere, creating severe technological bottlenecks, (Rosenberg, 1982). It is a prime function of reindustrialization and innovation policies to overcome such bottlenecks and to capitalize on potential intertechnological synergies where they exist. This implies the need for well-coordinated, coherent policies of technology choice.

Table 4.5 Frontier technology industries

| | Energy | ELECTRONICS | |
		Computer and Communication	Semiconductor and electronic material
Frontier technology industries in the 1980s			
For consumers	Solar house Solar battery	TV telephone, video disc Home facsimile CATV, digital studio system Two-way home TV system, automotive electronics Home computer	Microcomputer kit
For business	Geothermal power generation Oil shale, tar sand Heavy oil dissolution Coal-petroleum mixed fuel LNG latent heat power generation	Office computer, point-of-sales system Car telephone, EFTS Word processor Japanese character reading system, voice recognition system Data bank, electronic file	Optical fibre Magnetic bubble domain memory Very large-scale integrated circuits Amorphous semiconductor Sensor element
For public uses	Coal liquefaction New nuclear converter Nuclear fuel cycle Garbage power generation Solar power generation	Communications satellite Remote sensor Optical fibre	Optical fibre for communications Superconducting material
Frontier technology industries in the 1990s			
For consumers	Home heat accumulator Home fuel cell	Character-multiplex telecasting Stop-action telecasting Home data bank	
For business	Deep-water petroleum development Fuel cell power generation Gasohol Biomass Hydrogen engine	Voice-operating typewriter Automatic porgramming system Super-computer	Josephson element Multi-layered LSI Optical semiconductor
For public uses	Fast breeder reactor MID power generation Nuclear fusion Super-conductive power transmission	Administrative organs' data service system Electronic mailing	

Frontier technology industries in the 1980s

	Mechanical electronics	*ELECTRONICS* Resources	Materials
For consumers	Very large picture TV Fully automated cooker Wall-hung TV Home appliances central control system Electronic transistor		Artificial jewel Synthetic paper
For business	Automotive electronics Industrial robot, automatic designing system Heat pump, heat pipe Laser-beam machine tool Unmanned fabrication line	Resource exploration technology Low-grade ore refining Waste recovery system C1 chemistry	Carbon fibre, lightweight super-solid material Fixed oxygen New ceramics High-performance compound plastic Artificial wood
For public uses	Man-made satellite High-performance jet engine Space shuttle	Seawater desalination Continental shelf development Long-distance pipe line	

Frontier technology industries in the 1990s

	Mechanical electronics	*ELECTRONICS* Resources	Materials
For consumers	3-dimensional TV Home robot Very small video camera		Bond-sewing materials Artificial precious metal
For business	Deep-water operation vessel, seabed operation robot Unmanned navigation system Stirling engine Ceramic engine	Refining by microorganism	Amorphous metal
For public uses	Automatic metering system Laser surveying system	Manganese module collection Resources collection from seawater	

(*Source:* Ueno, (NRI), 1981)

Table 4.6 Market sizes of promising industries

Area	Industry	Unit	1978	1985	1990	Average increase rate/year		Source
						1985/78 %	1990/78 %	
						(%)	(%)	
Electronics Mechanical electronics	Industrial robot (demand)	Y billion	(1979) 42.4	240– 300	450– 600	33.5 38.6	21.7– 24.4	NRI
	NC machine tool (domestic demand)	Y billion	(1979) 105.9	581		32.8		NRI
	Word processor	Y billion	(1980) 0.5	20	100	69.4	55.5	Japan Business Machine Hal Association: Estimation
	Electronic transistor, learning machine and other business machines							
Electronic appliances for people	VIR (No. of shipment)	1000	–	40	100	–	–	Japan Electronic Industry Development Association
	Video disc (No. of shipments)	1000	13.7	71.5	70.1	26.6	14.6	
Electronics-applied equipment and parts	Computer and peripheral (production)	Y billion	910.2	2396	4271	14.8	13.7	
	Measuring instrument	Y billion	224 (1979)	458.4	709.6 (1989)	10.8	10.0 (1989/79)	NRI
	Semiconductor, IC	Y billion	343.2		3040	18.8– 23.8 (1983/78)	17.7	
	Semiconductor element	Y billion	253.9	120– 160 (1983)			12.0	
	Product Incorporating IC	Y billion	6100		19000			
	Automotiva electronics	Y billion	36.0					
Communications equipment	Electronic telephone switching system (production)	Y billion	86.8	211.6 (1983)	(1983)	19.5 (1983/78)		Research Centre. Nikko Securities
	Facsimile	Y billion	45.0	150	500	27.0 (1983/78)	27.2	Economic Research Institute Machine Promotion Association
	for business	Y billion	40.5	140		28.5		
	for other purposes	Y billion	4.5 (1979)	10		17.1		
	Optical fibre system	Y billion	5.0	200		84.9		

(*Source*: Ueno (NRI) 1981)

REFERENCES

Allen G 1981 Industrial Policy and Innovation in Japan. In Carter C (ed.) *Industrial Policy and Innovation*, London, Heinemann

Bright J R 1979 Technological Forecasting as an Influence on Technological Innovation: Past Examples and Future Expectations. In Baker M J (ed) *Industrial Innovation*. MacMillan

Briton G M 1977 *An Evaluation of ETIP for the National Academy of Sciences*. National Bureau of Standards, Washington DC 20234

Christiansen G B and Haveman R H 1981 The Contribution of Environmental Regulations to the Slowdown of Productivity Growth. *Journal of Environmental Economics and Management* 8:381–90

Cook L and Surrey J 1982 *Government Policy for the Offshore Supplies Industry*. Science Policy Research Unit, Occasional Paper Series No. 21, October.

Denison E F 1979 *Accounting for Slower Growth: The United States in the 1970s*. Brookings Institution, Washington DC

Dickson K 1983 The Influence of MoD Funding on Semiconductor Research and Development in the UK. *Research Policy* **12** (2) April

Dosi G 1984 *Technical Change and Industrial Transformation: The Theory and Application to the Semiconductor Industry*, MacMillan

Golding A M 1978 The Influence of Government Procurement on the Development of the Semiconductor Industry in the US and Britain. Paper presented to Six Countries Programme Workshop on Government Procurement Policies and Industrial Innovation, Dublin, Eire

Herbert R and Hoar R W 1982 *Government and Innovation: Experimenting with Change*. Final Report of ETIP, National Bureau of Standards, Washington DC, NBS-GCR-ETIP 82–100

Hill C T and Utterback J M 1979 *Technological Innovation for a Dynamic Economy*. Pergamon Press

Kaldor M 1980 Technical Change in the Defence Industry. In K. Pavitt (ed) *Technical Innovation and British Economic Performance*. MacMillan

Kelineman H S 1977 *The US Government Role in the Integrated Circuit Innovation*. OECD, Paris

Leone R A and Bradley S P 1981 Towards an Effective Industrial Policy. *Harvard Business Review* November-December

Levin R C 1982 The Semiconductor Industry. In Nelson R R (ed) *Government and Technical Progress*. Pergamon Press

Maddock I 1983 *Civil Exploitation of Defence Technology*. Report to the Electronics EDC, NEDC, London, February

Manners G E Nason H K and Steger J A 1978 *Support of Basic Research by Industry*. National Science Foundation, Washington DC, NSF-C76-21517

National Academy of Science 1980 *Antitrust, Uncertainty and Technological Innovation* Washington DC

NEDC 1983 *Transferable Factors in Japanese Economic Success* NEDC (82):50

Nelson R (ed) 1982 *Government and Technical Progress*. Pergamon Press

NICIP 1981 A New Spirit for Industry. Report by the Netherlands Advisory Commission on Industrial Policy, The Hague, Netherlands

OECD 1982 *Environmental Policy and Technical Change*. Environment Directorate, OECD, Paris

OTA 1984 *Commercial Biotechnology: An International Analysis*. Office of Technology Assessment, Congress of the United States, Washington DC 20510

Overmeer W and Prakke F 1978 Government Procurement Policies and Industrial Innovation. TNO-Delft, The Netherlands

Rosenberg N 1982 *Inside the Black Box*. Cambridge University Press

Rothwell R and Zegveld W 1981 *Industrial Innovation and Public Policy* Frances Pinter

Rothwell R 1979 *Industrial Innovation and Government Regulation*. Report to the Six Countries Programme on Innovation, TNO, PO Box 215, 2600 AE Delft, The Netherlands

SCGP 1980 Place and Future of Netherlands Industry. Report by the Netherlands, Scientific Council for Government Policy, The Hague, The Netherlands

Schnee J E 1978 Government Programmes and the Growth of High-Technology Industries. *Research Policy* 7:2–24

SPRU-TNO 1977 The Current International Climate and Policies for Technical Innovation. Six Countries Programme on Innovation, TNO-Delft, The Netherlands

Ueno Y 1981 New Industrial Development in Japan, Nomura Research Institute, Tokyo

Van Erven-Dorens P J 1984 The Netherlands Offshore Industry: Developments and Prospects. Industrial Council for Oceanology, Delft, The Netherlands

Weiss M 1978 *The Impact of Environmental Control Expenditures on the US Copper, Lead and Zinc Mining and Smelting Industries*. National Economic Research Associates Inc, Washington DC

Whiston T G 1982 *Environmental Regulations and the European Automobile Industry: Compliance Costs, Corporate Consequence and Productivity Issues*. Synthesis report to OECD, Paris

Yanchinski S 1983 Row Looms Over New Rules on Enzymes. *New Scientists* 20 October

CHAPTER FIVE

Financing Technological and Industrial Change

There are a number of important and traditional arguments both in favour of and against the public funding of industrial R&D. On the one hand there are those who argue that the requirements for radical innovation are so great that individual companies will not embark on these activities unless at least a proportion of the cost and the risk is underwritten by the public sector. On the other hand there are those who argue that public subsidies for R&D and innovation are inherently inefficient; they lead to the 'feather-bedding' of companies' R&D activities and the misallocation of public funds to areas of high technical sophistication but low commercial potential. A good illustrative example often brought forward in this context is the Anglo-French Concord supersonic aircraft project.

Both groups would probably accept, however, the need for public funding of basic or undirected research. This is seen as a public good, the results of at least a proportion of which will eventually diffuse into commercial use across perhaps a broad spectrum of industries. Good examples of this today would be the funding of research in areas such as semiconductor physics and bio-engineering. In the case of basic research, moreover, it is clear that the bulk of publicly funded work will take place in nonindustrial institutions such as universities and government funded research establishments. Recent approaches in Japan also include government funding of basic research in industry whereby the results become available to all industries participating in the programme.

A special case is generally made for the public funding of industrial R&D in areas that are clearly desirable for the public good, such as health care, education, the development of norms and standards, energy self-sufficiency and national security, but which might not be expected to yield a direct profit to private companies, and therefore in which companies would not be willing to invest. A special case is also often made for the public funding of R&D in small firms. These, so the argument goes, are important for social policy, as well as for technology policy, and they therefore merit public support (Rothwell and Zegveld, 1982).

Perhaps one of the main objections to allocations based on the issue of public versus private benefits of R&D, is the evidence suggesting that the social rates of return on innovations that were introduced purely on the basis of private profit potential often greatly outweigh the private rates of return (Mansfield, 1981). If we accept this objection, then perhaps the only sensible general conclusion to be reached is that, ultimately, all R&D is a social good. It does not automatically follow from this, of course, that all R&D should be publicly funded. In the framework of this book, however, technology in relation to reindustrialization well deserves, as we have shown in Chapter 4, public sector stimulation and funding. From our discussion and description of the innovation process in Chapter 2, it should be clear that R&D is only one component, albeit a core one, in the overall process of innovation. Because of the interactive nature of the innovation process and associated difficulties in accounting, or poor accounting procedures, it is often difficult to break down total expenditures on innovation according to the different 'stages' of the innovation process. This is especially the case with smaller companies that often do not have strict functional (departmental) separation, or do not account for the different functions separately. Nevertheless, a number of researchers have attempted innovation expenditure breakdowns, and the results of several such excercises are summarized in Table 5.1, taken from studies in Israel, Canada and the USA (Kamin et al, 1982).

Table 5.1   Comparison of innovation cost distributions (%)

TI Phase	Charpie Panel	Mansfield	Statistics Canada	Israel
R&D[a]	15 – 30	46.2	59	47
Tooling and manufacturing facilities[b]	40 – 60	36.9	31	18
Manufacturing start-up	5 – 15	9.1	6	15
Marketing start-up	10 – 25	7.7	2	20

a) Charpie Panel: Research/advanced development/basic invention engineering and designing the product.

   Mansfield: Applied research, preparation of project requirements and basic specifications, prototype or pilot plant design construction and testing.

b) Statistics Canada: R&D, product and design engineering.

   Israeli study: Not including capital investment.

(*Source*: Kamin et al, 1982)

While for a variety of reasons precise comparisons between countries are difficult, and while the figures do vary a great deal from industry to industry, one interesting fact emerges from all the studies: that is, the post-R&D costs constitute a very significant proportion of total innovation costs. This suggests that governments might consider shifting from funding only R&D to the funding of innovations.

Table 5.2 gives the innovation costs breakdown for nearly 300 innovations introduced by Canadian companies between 1960 and 1978 according to size of innovating company, and for product and process innovations separately (de Melto et al, 1980). It shows that, in the case of product innovations, for the smallest companies (employment of 100 or less), R&D and marketing start-up costs are relatively high, while manufacturing start-up costs are relatively low. In the case of process innovations, development costs are relatively high in small firms, while manufacturing start-up costs are relatively high in the largest sized firms. These data indicate that total R&D costs are generally high in small firms. Given the inability of such firms to spread these costs over a portfolio of projects, this must represent a significant burden to them, which might be taken as a good case for government intervention in this area.

Table 5.2   Average of ratios of spending per stage to total expenditures per innovation by type of innovation and firm size, all industries

	0–100 (N=78)	101–500 (N=66)	Over 500 (N=21)
	— —(%)— —		
Product Innovations			
Basic research	8.0	8.1	2.4
Applied research	15.9	8.8	9.2
Development	41.4	47.3	44.0
Manufacturing start-up	23.6	27.1	41.4
Marketing start-up	11.1	8.7	3.0
Total	100.0	100.0	100.0
	— —(%)— —		
Process Innovations	(N=17)	(N=22)	(N=22)
Basic research	6.4	3.6	1.8
Applied research	11.2	10.0	20.1
Development	45.8	31.0	19.1
Manufacturing start-up	34.4	53.2	57.9
Marketing start-up	2.2	2.2	1.1
Total	100.0	100.0	100.0

(*Source*: Economic Council of Canada Discussion Paper No. 176, 'Preliminary Report: Innovation and technological change in five Canadian Industries' (Ottawa, 1980), by Dennis P De Metto, Kathryn E McMullen and Russel M Willis)

The same study also found differences between firms of different sizes in the time taken from the initiation of a project to its commercialization (lead time). In the small firms, the median lead time was one and a half years; in the larger firms (employment above 5000) this

Figure 5.1   Trends in GERD as a % of GDP in the 1960s and 1970s

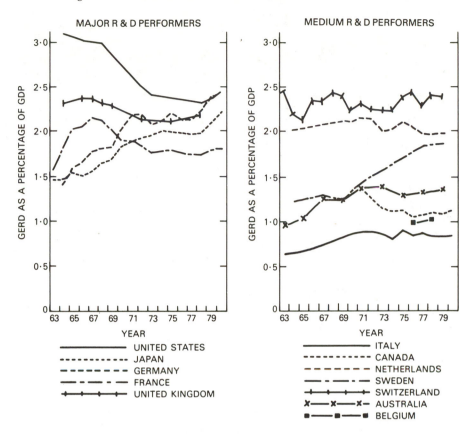

(Source: OECD, *Science and Technology Indicators*, 1982).

rose to two and a half years. Moreover, for small firms there was no significant difference in lead time between product and process innovations. In the case of large firms, the average product lead time was two and a half years while the average process lead time was three and a half years. Apart from the nature of the innovations small firms presumably are under greater pressure than their larger counterparts to achieve quick financial returns on their innovatory investments.

Below we shall present data on levels and patterns of R&D expenditure in a number of advanced market economies. In keeping with the central theme of this book, that of technological and economic cycles, we shall also discuss national systems of industrial funding in terms of funding for existing industries and funding for new firms, ie 'Schumpeterian' funding. In other words, we shall draw a distinction between systems for the support of activities in existing corporations, and those for the support of new technology based firms (NTBF) that appear to play a major role in the initiation of techno-economic regimes.

Table 5.3a   Total national R&D efforts 1979

		United States	Japan	Germany	France	United[a] Kingdom
GERD	million $	56 560.5	18 284.7	12 530.6	7 964.4	7 961.1
R&D personel	thousand FTE	1 334 0[b]	605.5[d]	363.2	230.8	310.0[b]
RSE	thousand FTE	621.0	367.0[d]	122.0	72.9	104.4
GERD/GDP	percentage	2.38	2.11	2.40	1.81	2.20
Civil GERD/ GDP(b)	percentage	1.81	2.10	2.30	1.54	1.67
R&D Personnel/ Labour force	ʹ/●●	12.7[b]	10.8	13.7	10.0	11.7[b]
RSE/Labour force	ʹ/●●	5.9	6.6[d]	4.6	3.2	4.0
GERD pc population	$	256	158	204	149	142
Civil GERD pc population	$	194	197	196	126	108
GERD per RSE	thousand $	91	50	103	109	76
GERD per R&D personnel	thousand $	42.4[b]	30.2	34.5	34.5	25.7[b]
	where, GDP pc = 1	3.9	4.0	4.0	4.1	3.6
Support ratio per RSE	percentage	1.1[b]	0.6	2.0	2.2	2.0[b]

(a) 1978
(b) OECD estimate
(d) Overestimated. Not in full-time equivalent.

NATIONAL PATTERNS OF R&D FUNDING

Figure 5.1 shows the trends in gross national expenditure on research and development (GERD) as a percentage of gross Domestic product (GDP) for five major R&D-performing countries and seven medium R&D-performing countries between 1963 and 1979. Taking first the major R&D performers, in the United States, the UK and France, gross national expenditure on R&D as a percentage of gross domestic product generally fell between the mid-1960s and about 1977, when it began to increase. Japan and West Germany, in contrast, generally increased gross national expenditure on R&D as a percentage of gross domestic product throughout the whole period, with rather rapid increases after 1977. In the case of the medium R&D-performing countries the percentage was, with some fluctuations, fairly constant throughout the 1970s, except in Sweden where it experienced consistent growth.

Simply taking the evolution of gross expenditure on R&D as a percentage of gross domestic product does, of course, have certain disadvantage when making international comparisons, perhaps the major disadvantages being that it does not take into account differences

Figure 5.2   Gross expenditure on R&D (GERD) as a percentage of gross domestic product by major source

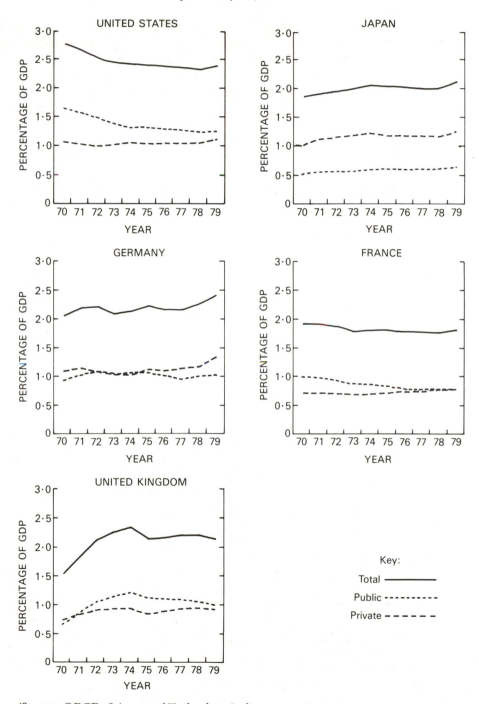

(Source: OECD, *Science and Technology Indicators* 1982).

in levels of domestic growth. For example, while gross expenditure on R&D as a percentage of the gross domestic product in the Netherlands moved around the 1.9 per cent level during the 1970s, the growth in the Dutch economy during this period was significantly lower than the OECD average, indicating a lower than average absolute growth in national R&D outlays. Japan and West Germany, in contrast, experienced relatively high growth rates in their gross domestic products during the same period. Table 5.3a indicates total national R&D efforts in the five major R&D-performing countries in 1979. It illustrates the massive total commitment to R&D in the United States in terms of expenditure, R&D personnel and research scientists and engineers (RSE), with Japan coming a strong second. Table 5.3b shows average annual growth rates in both categories in the five countries. It shows relatively high growth rates in Germany and Japan, with an especially high Japanese rate of growth in gross expenditure on R&D.

Table 5.3b   Average Annual Growth Rates

	United States	Japan	Germany	France	United Kingdom
	1970–79	1970–79	1970–79	1970–79	1972–78
GERD	1.7	6.4	4.7	3.3	2.8
RSE	2.1^c	4.7	4.4	2.5	2.1
Total R&D personnel	..	2.2	3.4	1.0	..

(c) 1971 to 1979.

(Source: OECD, *Science and Technology Indicators*, 1982).

Turning now to the major sources of R&D funding, public or private, Figure 5.2 shows the evolution of gross expenditure on R&D as a percentage of gross domestic product by major source for the five important R&D-performing countries during the 1970s. The most interesting feature of the graphs are the consistantly high percentage of R&D funds provided by private industry in Japan, and to a lesser but growing extent in West Germany, and the convergence between private and public sources in the US, the UK and France.

Table 5.4 shows the business expenditure on R&D (BERD) in a number of countries in 1979 as a percentage of gross expenditure on R&D and by source of funding. In the case of the major R&D-performing nations it can be seen that particularly in Japan but also in West Germany, industry funds the bulk of its own research and development, and that in Japan direct government R&D funding in industry is extremely small.

Tables 5.5a and 5.5b illustrate some characteristics of government-financed R&D activities in a number of advanced market economies. In Table 5.5a, the data are for 1964–66 and 1977–79. In Table 5.5b, the

Table 5.4   Contribution of industry to total national R&D expenditure 1979
(BERD as a percentage of GERD)

	United States	Japan	Germany	France	Kingdom
Financed by:					
Industry	45.4	57.0	54.8	42.4	41.0
Government	22.1	0.8	12.6	12.9	19.0
Abroad	0.0	0.0	1.5	4.1	6.0
Total BERD	67.4	57.8	69.1	59.5	66.0
Percentage GDP	1.6	1.2	1.7	1.1	1.4

(a) 1978

Contribution of industry to total national R&D expenditure 1979
(BERD as a percentage of GERD)

	Italy	Canada	Netherlands	Sweden[a]	Switzerland	Australia	Belgium
Financed by:							
Industry	54.5	35.8	45.7	59.9	72.7	20.0	65.6
Government	2.5	3.6	3.0	8.9	2.5	2.5	3.4
Abroad	1.2	2.8	2.8	0.9	–	0.8	0.7
Total BERD	58.2	42.2	51.5	69.7	75.2	23.3	69.7
Percentage GDP	0.50	0.41	1.02	1.31	1.51	0.24	0.5

(a) Natural scientists and engineers only.

(Source: OECD, *Science and Technology Indicators*, 1982).

(largely provisional) data are for 1980, 1981 and 1982. Table 5.5a shows great variation in the percentage of total national R&D financed by government (high in the UK, Canada and the USA; medium level in France, West Germany, Italy, the Netherlands and Sweden; low in Switzerland and Japan) and in the percentage of industrial R&D financed by government (high in the UK, Sweden and the USA; medium level in France; low in West Germany, Italy and Canada; very low in Switzerland and Japan).

If we look at the objectives of government financed R&D, we again see some major differences. In the UK and the United States, for example, public resources devoted to defence, space and energy (largely defence) are extremely high. Particularly in the USA, public resources directly devoted to industrial development are extremely low. Especially in Japan and the Netherlands, and to a lesser extent in West Germany, Italy and Sweden, the percentages of the government resources directed towards the advancement of knowledge are considerable. The more recent data in Table 5.5b indicate that those differences have persisted, with exceptionally high levels of public funding of defence R&D in the United States and the UK, and relatively large resources going towards the advancement of knowledge in Japan and

Table 5.5a Some characteristics of government-financed R&D activities

Country	Year	Percentage of all R&D financed by government	Percentage of industrial R&D financed by government	Percentage of all government-financed R&D Performed in industry	Percentage of all government-financed R&D for the following objectives:		
					Defence, space and energy	Industrial development	Advance of knowledge
United Kingdom	1964	54.1	33.8				
	1978	48.1	29.3	39.0	61.7	6.1	21.7
France	1964	61.2					
	1966		40.5				
	1977		25.2				
	1979	42.2		30.5	47.6	10.2	23.6
German FR	1964	44.2	17.4				
	1977	44.2					
	1978		17.6	23.3	29.1	7.2	47.2
Italy	1963	43.7	1.8				
	1977	47.8	11.0	n.a.	35.5	9.8	41.0
Netherlands	1969	43.5					
	1978	47.5	5.0	5.2	11.2	4.9	55.9
Sweden	1964	45.2	32.8				
	1979	37.9	32.8	23.5	31.2	5.6	39.3
Switzerland	1963	9.4	1.8				
	1964						
	1978	23.0	2.9	8.9	32.8	2.5	38.9
Canada	1963	61.0					
	1964		17.1				
	1978		12.8				
	1979	54.9		11.7	18.4	15.5	20.0
USA	1964	68.5	57.1				
	1978	51.9	33.6	42.7	73.1	0.3	na
Japan	1971	28.9					
	1978		1.4				
	1979	29.8		2.7	19.0	5.8	53.1

(*Source*: OECD Documents DSTI/SPR/81.28 and 82.05. Taken from: House of Lords, 1983)

Table 5.5b   Percentage of government R&D expenditure
on defence, the advancement of knowledge and
industrial growth, 1981–83

	1980			1981			1982		
	D	AK	IG	D	AK	IG	D	AK	IG
United States	47.3	3.9	0.3	51.8	3.8	0.3	56.9	3.6	0.3
Japan	2.3	52.5	5.8	-	-	-	-	-	-
Germany FR	10	43.1	10	8.8	42.3	10.9	8.5	40.7	12
France	36.5	22.2	9.3	37.2	24.6	8.8	35.1	23.5	12.5
United Kingdom	54.1	22.5	6.6	52.0	22.4	7.7	52.2	23.7	7.0
Italy	2.7	35.7	17.4	6.5	32.4	18.6	6.7	40.3	13.5
Canada	6.8	21.8	12.8	6.6	21.3	13.2	-	-	-
Netherlands	3.1	55.2	5.7	3.0	54.0	7.6	3.0	52.7	10.4
Sweden	15.6	39.4	7.7	16.0	39.5	4.8	19.2	38.5	4.5

D - defence
AK - advancement of knowledge
IG - industrial growth
(*Source*: OECD (1983), Basic Statistical Series, Vol.A., *The Objectives of Government R&D Funding*, (1974–85), Paris)

Note: The figures for 1981 and 1982 are largely provisional.

the Netherlands. As we have indicated elsewhere (Rothwell and Zegveld, 1981) large public expenditures on defence-related R&D, and indeed on defence spending generally, appear to carry with them high opportunity costs associated with the diversion of resources away from developments associated with economic growth, productivity increase and industrial competitiveness in civilian markets. In Chapter 4 we have, however, illustrated that defence R&D expenditures in the US are increasingly serving an industrial development function.

The effects of high defence R&D spending are clearly demonstrated in Table 5.6 which shows average rates of economic growth and average share of output devoted to military spending and to investment between 1954 and 1973, and productivity growth rates between 1950 and 1976, for Japan, West Germany, France, Italy, the USA and the UK. These

Table 5.6   Military expenditure and economic growth, 1954–73

Country	Av economic growth	Av share of output devoted to:		Productivity growth* 1950–1976
		Military spending	Investment	
	%	%	%	%
Japan	10.1	1.1	33.4	7.5
West Germany	6.1	3.8	24.2	5.8
France	5.6	5.5	22.5	4.9
Italy	5.3	3.6	22.3	5.3
USA	3.9	8.3	16.4	2.3
UK	2.9	6.1	16.4	2.8

* Growth in GDP/person/annum

(*Data Source1:* OECD and SIPRI. Taken from: Tank, 1983)

data strongly suggest the existence of opportunity costs, expressed by the inverse relationship between economic and productivity growth rates and rates of military expenditure in general, and we might expect more direct effects in the case of R&D expenditure in particular. The exception to this pattern is France. Tank (1983) has suggested that this is the result of a fiercely nationalistic French procurement policy and an almost unrestrained arms export drive, which have minimized the deleterious effects of high defence expenditure.

We turn now to the institutional patterns of performance of national R&D activities, and data for the advanced market economies are presented in Figure 5.3. These data indicate some shift of R&D resources from the scientific and technological infrastructure into industry between the early 1960s and late 1970s in the UK, France, West Germany, Canada, the USA and Japan, which might suggest a shift in emphasis towards applied research and development activity. In the Netherlands, Sweden and Switzerland, in contrast, there was some shift of resources from industry to the higher education sector, and in general there appears to have been some overall movement of resources from government laboratories to the higher education sector.

More recently, the shift of public R&D funds from the public to the private sector appears to have intensified. In the UK, for example, in 1977/78 53 per cent of technology support from the Department of Industry went to government laboratories and research associations, while 39 per cent went to industry; in 1980/81 the percentages were 42 and 52 respectively. The Netherlands technology policy report presented by the Minister of Economic Affairs to Parliament in February 1984, also calls for such shifts.

FISCAL MEASURES FOR R&D

A general tendency towards government promotion of R&D in industry, in addition to special R&D financing programmes (these have been described in detail elsewhere (Rothwell and Zegveld, 1981 and 1982; OECD, 1979) and will not be dealt with here) is by means of fiscal instruments. In many countries this has taken the form of tax credits. Below some of these fiscal measures promoting R&D in different countries are mentioned briefly.

In the USA the Economic Recovery Tax Act of 1981 provides three R&D tax incentives:
1. a tax credit amounting to 25 per cent of the increase in R&D expenditure in a given year in relation to the average expenditure in the last three years;
2. a new capital cost recovery system for R&D equipment; and
3. an increased deduction for manufacturers' donations of new R&D equipment to universities.

Figure 5.3   Institutional patterns of performance of R&D activities

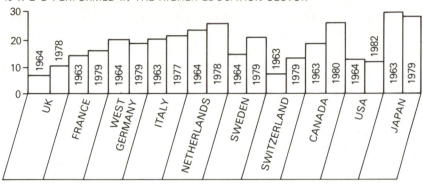

% R & D PERFORMED IN THE HIGHER EDUCATION SECTOR

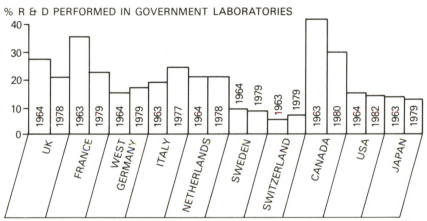

% R & D PERFORMED IN GOVERNMENT LABORATORIES

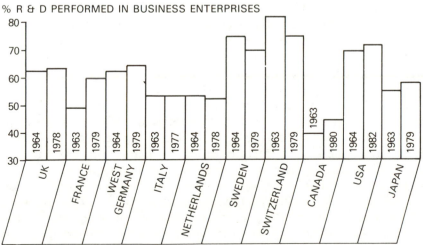

% R & D PERFORMED IN BUSINESS ENTERPRISES

(*Source*: OECD Documents DSTI/SPR/81.28 and 82.05. Taken from: House of Lords, 1983)

Research at the National Science Foundation (Collins, 1981) assessed the R&D tax credit as being an improved tax treatment for growing R&D budgets and to encourage firms to maintain growth in R&D spending despite the recession. The Tax Equity and Fiscal Responsibility Act (1982) supplies a tax credit of 10 per cent on equipment with an economic life of longer than seven years. Another US fiscal arrangement to support private firms in their R&D activities can be found within the framework of the 'Independent Research and Development' arrangement of the US Department of Defense (see Chapter 4).

In Japan a R&D tax credit is provided for 20 per cent of the increase in R&D costs in any 'base accounting period'. This tax credit is limited to 10 per cent of the corporation tax (before any credits). The Canadian tax credit, working over the period 1978–87, amounts to 50 per cent of the increase in R&D costs (including investment in fixed assets) related to the average R&D costs of the past three years. The purpose of the Swedish tax credit arrangement is explicitly stated as the improvement of external competitiveness. It consists of a general tax credit of 10 per cent of the R&D costs (making R&D 110 per cent deductible) and of 20 per cent of the increase in R&D costs compared with the previous year. Since 1982, France has a R&D tax credit system amounting to 25 per cent and in the Netherlands, such an arrangement is currently under consideration, as was announced in the recent government technology policy paper.

GOVERNMENT DIRECTION OF R&D ACTIVITY

While in most countries governments fund a substantial proportion of national R&D activity, the degree to which these funds are directed by government into certain industries or areas of technology, ie the degree of selectivity, varies considerably between nations. It is, perhaps, in Japan that the level of selectivity is greatest in both the public and private sectors, which collaborate closely in major national projects in such areas as amorphous semiconductors and fifth generation computers. Projects are selected following an opinion sampling exercise to obtain a consensus, in which MITI plays an important coordinating role. Resources are then focused onto the selected technologies in both national laboratories and the R&D laboratories of major companies, and the projects are supported through both public and private funds. Other countries (and the European Community) are now copying this approach.

There is also a high level of selectivity exercised by the French government, which presently controls over 50 per cent of national industrial R&D and research workers. The recently enacted 'Programme Law', designed to provide encouragement and incentives to industry to increase its R&D commitments, defines a number of 'mobilization programmes' for R&D, which apply to both the public and private sectors. The government has also selected five major indus-trial areas to be preferentially supported from public funds: steel, chemicals, electronics, health and materials. A significant feature of the French system is the concept of 'filière', which applies to the chain of production from, for example, raw materials to the commercialization of final products.

In the German Federal Republic, where the bulk of industrial R&D is carried out in industry with its own funds, it is industry that largely establishes its own R&D priorities. The Federal Ministry for Tech-nology (BMFT) generally acknowledges that it should only become involved in projects with certain special features, such as especially high scientific and technological risk; very large financial requirement; long development horizon; lack of short- term market acceptance but high public benefits. The choice of rather broad areas for support is made by BMFT, but in consultation with industry and professional associations through an elaborate advisory system, and, of course, parliament.

In the United States governments traditionally have had an aversion towards attempting to pick winners, relying on market dynamics to dictate efficient patterns of R&D allocation. In reality, however, de-fence and space R&D support and procurement activity inevitably have biased a large proportion of the national R&D effort along certain specific paths and have very effectively stimulated the growth of new technology-based industries. In a significant departure from established practice, the Carter Administration suggested the provision of public support for selected generic technologies. This was abandoned by the Reagan Administration which instead has attempted to facilitate the establishment of generic cooperative research activities by industry itself, the first of these being the cooperative effort in microcircuitry by the Semiconductor Industry Association in California. In practice, in the US (as well as in Europe) market dynamics have forced the administration to devote considerable resources to bailing out problem industries (eg the automobile and shoe industries) rather than to supporting high-technology industries (apart from working through aerospace and defence budgets).

In the UK, in the past, there have been some attempts to support developments in specific high-technology industries (eg computers and nuclear energy), but since the mid-1970s the British government has adopted a market-forces policy that is largely nonselective. Just as in the United States, however, the high level of public R&D support for defence-related projects has inevitably focused resources on specific areas of technology. In addition, and again following pattern of the US (and other countries), a large portion of public funds has gone towards supporting ailing industries, most notably automobile and steel pro-duction. More recently, the British government has become overtly selective and, following the Alvey Report on a programme for advanced information technology (see Chapter 9), has released plans for the selective support of major collaborative projects in this area. This is likely to be followed by a second programme in the area of advanced materials technology.

STOCK MARKETS, BANKS AND INDUSTRIAL FINANCING

In the major industrialized market economies there are, broadly speaking, two main methods of funding industrial activity: stock markets (capital market instruments) and other financial institutions, largely banks (non-capital market instruments). Using data on the sources of external funds of large quoted companies in six countries between 1960 and 1971, Rybczynski (1974), for example, showed that Japanese corporations raised more than 80 per cent of their funds from non-capital market sources.

In the UK and the USA, in contrast, large firms obtained between 40 and 50 per cent of their funds from long-term capital markets. Continental countries fell somewhere between these extremes, obtaining from 25 to 40 per cent of external finance from long-term capital markets. Moreover, over the period covered, these differences not only persisted, but they intensified.

A crucial question is, of course, to what extent do these different modes of financing exert an influence on industrial expansion and innovation. Rybczynski provided some important hints by looking at a number of ratios indicating the relationship between the various types of funds used by companies and the types of assets they were used to aquire, and among the different types of finance themselves. The ratios employed were: own funds to fixed assets; permanent funds to fixed assets; own funds to medium- and long-term debt; current assets to current liabilities.

The first ratio, own funds/fixed assets, indicates the extent to which funds provided by the owners or large quoted companies, who in the ultimate analysis assume the risk, have been used for the purchase of productive capacity, i.e. plant, machinery, etc.; the second ratio, 'permanent' funds/fixed assets, shows the degree to which 'permanent' productive capacity has been acquired with the proprietors' funds as well as those borrowed on long-term and which do not have to be renewed in the short-term; the third ratio, own-funds/medium- and long-term debts, throws light on the relative importance of the risk-assuming proprietors' contribution to that of long-term lenders who endeavour to limit the risk they are prepared to take; the last ratio, current assets/current liabilities, is indicative of the way providers of short-term funds look at the use made of finance they supply and which is employed to hold quickly-realisable assets.

All four ratios tend to be higher for the two countries with the 'market-orientated' pattern of private company finance (i.e. the USA and the UK) than for the countries with the 'bank-orientated' approach prevailing on the Continent of Europe and above all in Japan. Higher ratios in market-orientated countries tend to suggest – subject to reservations arising from the accounting methods employed – a more conservative, i.e. more cautious, approach towards company finance. (Rybczynski, 1974, p65).

The results of a study by Lorenz (1979) would appear to support this view to the extent that 'a more cautious approach' is equivalent to 'a shorter-term approach'. Comparing industrial financing in the UK and West Germany Lorenz concluded that:

Whereas German banks are geared to the long-term, British stockholders take an almost entirely short-term view of company prospects, focussed on the next few profit declarations and dividend payouts. In their eyes, a successful company is one whose profits and dividends are likely to increase over the next six months, year or (at most) two years (Lorenz, 1979, p11).

This conclusion has serious implications for the ability of British companies to initiate and sustain major long-term programmes of technological development. As we have suggested, such programmes are of particular importance today when major corporations increasingly need to seek regeneration through technological change. Given declining rates of industrial profitability, for example, in the UK, it seems unlikely that the bulk of British industry can fund such programmes using internal resources, which further underlines the seriousness of the apparent lack of long-term external finance in Britain.

Reflecting on stockbrokers attitudes in Britain, Lorenz underlines this point:

Since they take such a short-term view, and share society's ignorance of the needs of manufacturing, it is not surprising that stockbrokers breathed a loud sigh of relief in 1978 when EMI decided to slash its R & D spending, but maintain its dividend at the previous year's level. Virtually no-one questioned whether the company's long-term future might be damaged by this allocation of resources, and the thinking which lay behind it (Lorenz, 1979, p11 and 12).

Table 5.7 shows the average amounts raised for domestic corporations (1970–78) in different financial markets as a percentage of gross domestic product for five of the major advanced market economies, as well as the time horizons of external loans. If we leave out stocks and bonds and consider what is mainly bank lending, then the proportion of short-term to medium-to-long-term loans is as follows: France, 0.71; Japan, 0.28; West Germany, 0.22; United Kingdom, 0.82; United States 0.85. We can thus see that in those countries where, historically, capital market instruments have dominated industrial finance (Britain and the United States) over 40 per cent of bank loans between 1970–78 were short-term; in those countries where non-capital market instruments historically have played the dominant role (West Germany and Japan) about 80 per cent of bank loans were medium-to long-term.

Table 5.7   Average amounts raised for domestic corporation in financial markets

Country	1970–78 averages % of GDP				
	Bonds	Stocks & shares	S/T loans	Medium & l/t loans	Total medium & l/t loans
France	0.61	1.04	2.45	3.40	5.05
Japan	0.63	0.86	2.90	10.20	11.69
West Germany	0.15	0.35	1.25	5.54	6.04
United Kingdom	0.22	0.59	3.06	2.52	3.33
USA	1.26	1.12	1.63	1.90	4.26

(*Sources*: OECD Financial Statistics and Japan Statistical Yearbooks 1973–80 Taken from: House of Lords, 1983)

Table 5.8   Outstanding bank loans of industrial and commercial companies

	% of GDP			
	1973	1974	1975	1976
Japan (a) Corporate	97.05	96.25	97.86	96.14
(b) Non-corporate	30.00	30.80	32.69	33.07
West Germany	38.03	37.97	37.55	37.17
United Kingdom	21.53	26.60	20.92	21.36
USA	11.96	12.97	11.51	10.52

(*Sources*: Calculated from (i) *Japan Statistical Yearbook 1977, 1978*, Tables 234, 241.) (ii) *Germany*, OECD, July 1978, Table 4, (iii) Economic Trends, HMSO, March 1976, Table 62. (iv) Federal Reserve Bulletin, January 1978 and July 1980, Tables 1.22 and 1.23. Taken from House of Lords 1983)

Table 5.8 shows outstanding bank loans of industrial and commercial companies in Japan, West Germany, the United Kingdom and the United States between 1973 and 1976. These data again illustrate the relative importance of non-capital market funding in the former two countries. Moreover, taken together with different effective rates of interest in the different countries and the time horizons of the loans, Edwards (1983), in his submission to a recent House of Lords enquiry, has illustrated how the average repayment rate associated with business debt varies dramatically from country to country.

(a) The average repayment rate in Britain seems to be about 38 per cent of bank loans, assuming *all* overdrafts are rolled over, and if all term debt is repaid as due.
(b) The average repayment rate in Germany appears to be about 22 per cent of bank loans, as the average loan has a period of about six years and an interest rate of about 8 per cent.
(c) In general, only an interest rate of about 7 per cent seems to be repaid on Japanese loans.

The annual repayment burden of corporate debt in Japan, Germany and Britain therefore is:

Japan: $96\% \times 7\% = 6.72\%$ of GDP
Germany: $38\% \times 22\% = 8.36\%$ of GDP
UK: $21\% \times 38\% = 7.98\%$ of GDP

(House of Lords, 1983, p 99)

The figure given for Japan assumes a very long-term effective loan period. In fact, even shorter-term loans in Japan are usually refinanced 'on the understanding that the capital will not be repaid at the end of the term of the loan, but will be refinanced at its maturity date at the then prevailing rate of interest'. (Carrington and Edwards, 1979, p110). In other words, in Japan, most borrowing has been in the form of rollover loans.

We can thus see, comparing Britain to Japan, that the annual re-payment burden is one per cent greater in Britain despite the very much greater percentage of GDP borrowed by business in Japan. Given these figures it is hardly surprising that British business borrows less than Japanese business. Further, in order to repay the high annual cash-flow cost of borrowing in Britain, it would not be surprising if British businesses emphasized investments in shorter-term projects having high rates of return. As stated above, programmes of industrial regeneration require management to adopt a long-term view which emphasizes in-novation and market penetration and growth, rather than short-term return on investment. The implementation of such programmes, moreover, requires access to 'patient money'. Given the availability of long-term bank loans in Japan – sometimes coupled (especially in the case of public finance) to preferential rates of interest – and a, relatively, very high debt-to-equity ratio, it seems hardly surprising that Japanese industry has succeeded in funding major programmes of industrial restructuring, including R&D, or that the Japanese economy has en-joyed such a high growth rate during the past thirty years or so.

In an earlier quote from Lorenz, it was implied that British stockbrokers are to a degree ignorant of the needs of manufacturing industry. At the same time British banks, while happy to provide financial services to industry, prefer to adopt an arms-length approach to direct involvement and equity participation. In Germany, in contrast, banks are very much involved in the firms they finance:

There [West Germany], the prime source of industrial finance is bank debt, with equity (shares) playing a very secondary role. In other words, German companies have a high debt/equity ratio. Moreover, most of the shares are controlled (and many owned) by the banks (Lorenz, 1979, p11).

Given these differences, it is not perhaps surprising that banks appear to adopt a longer-term view of industrial financing in West Germany than do their counterparts in the UK. In addition, we would expect German bankers, because of their involvement, to have more sympathy with, and to understand better, the problems, needs and aims of German companies. Thus, in order fully to understand the nature of the influences of bank finance on industrial companies in different countries, and in particular on their propensity to take a longer-term view of investment, including investment in technological development, it is necessary to understand the nature of the relationship between banks and industry in these countries. Below we shall describe briefly the relationships between banks and industry in the UK, the USA, West Germany and Japan (for a detailed comparative analysis, see Carrington and Edwards, 1979).

Allen (1981) has described in detail the evolution of the present-day banking system in Japan. In 1978 there were 121 commercial banks (13 city banks, 63 regional banks, 54 foreign banks and the foreign exchange bank), 10 long-term credit banks and 1077 financial institutions for small business. There are also two government banks, the Japan Development Bank and the Export-Import Bank of Japan, as well as a number of other government financial institutions. Allen also described the operations of the Japanese banking system:

So much for the structure of the banking system: we must now analyse its operations. These, it must be emphasised, were governed by the purpose to which economic policy was directed from the time that Japan regained her autonomy, viz. rapid economic growth to be achieved by industrial expansion. Since this expansion was linked with the development of technology intensive, capital-intensive industries, priority had to be assigned to investment in equipment. The consistent pursuit of this policy meant that the share of GNP devoted to investment (gross fixed investment plus increases in stocks) was far higher throughout the post-war period than in any other industrial country – 35 per cent in 1960 and 38 per cent in 1971–73. An exceptionally large proportion of the new capital was embodied in industrial plant (Allen, 1981, p51).

An important feature of banking in Japan pointed to by Allen and others, is that the city banks, which play the most significant role in industrial finance, have sometimes been in an 'overloan' position; in other words, the ratio of city bank loans to city bank deposits has exceeded 100 per cent. This means, in effect, that it is not only savings, but also circulating credit, that is financing investment in Japan. According to Carrington and Edwards (1979):

Japanese businesses therefore obtain funds from a number of sources: government money (indirectly canalized through Bank of Japan loans to city banks), the savings of private individuals, long-term capital loans directly via government banks, and call money borrowed by city banks from local and often rural savings banks. The Bank of Japan deliberately assists long-term capital formation by permitting city banks to loan more than 100% of their deposits; the city banks had overloan, or loan to deposits plus debenture ratios, of 107 in 1957, 105 in 1962 and 104 in 1964; the overloan position during 1956–68 was never less than 90%, and reached 100% in 1957. The Bank of Japan guarantee – that no major bank would be allowed to collapse because of advancing funds for industrial investment – has obviously released large capital flows which prudence would have kept as reserves (Carrington and Edwards, 1979 p13 and 14).

A number of authors (Allen, 1979; Carrington and Edwards, 1979; Lockwood, 1968) have pointed to the close relationship that exists between the major business groupings in Japan and the commercial banks. While by law a bank cannot hold more than 10 per cent of the shares of any company, the major business groupings often have a large bank as part of the grouping, and bankers often sit on the boards of companies. In other words, the industrial and financial systems in Japan are highly integrated, working towards a set of common aims; rapid industrial and economic growth. The Japanese government, via MITI and the flow of funds through the Japan Development Bank, plays important coordinating and 'enabling' roles with respect to this common aim. Finally, the strong integration between industrial groupings and banking institutions in Japan has resulted in a system that reorganizes businesses to eliminate inefficiency and transfers resources to more productive use, rather than allowing faltering businesses to go to the wall (Gibbs, 1980).

In France, where the big three banks were nationalized in 1945, and where government traditionally has adopted a system of indicative planning via a series of national plans whose aims are backed by a system of public agency investment credits, bank financing for industry – mainly large companies – has to a significant extent been channelled into investment programmes associated with the implementation of the national plans. At the same time there appears to have been a system of close relationships between family firms and local bankers.

Since the nationalization of the French banking system in 1982 under Mitterand's socialist government, public control of the banks has greatly increased. Now, more than ever before, they are deeply involved in government policies of industrial restructuring. This involves debt restructuring for ailing industries and, via the interministerial committee CIRI, finding 'partners' for failing companies (Marsh, 1983). At the same time, the French government has made strong efforts to involve the banks to a greater extent in funding new business start-ups.

During 1983, turnover in French equities increased by over 30 per cent, and a new over-the-counter market for shares in small, unquoted companies was introduced. According to Marsh (1983), one reason for the rapid rise in bank market issues in Paris in 1982/3 is that '... first the industrial companies and the banks themselves are being encouraged to issue non-voting loan stock to raise from the market urgently needed capital', capital being short because of a very high level of government debt. Whether or not nationalization of the French banks results in a more efficient allocation of resources to industrial development, or whether it channels a large proportion of available capital into ailing industries for social policy reasons (maintenance of jobs), remains to be seen. According to Marsh (1983), the current administration appears lately to have adopted a more pragmatic approach to industrial policy, which might provide a pointer to possible future trends in patterns of industrial financing.

In Britain and the United States, while banks provide a variety of financial services to industry, the financial and industrial systems are quite distinct. In neither country do indicative national plans exist that selectively and directly channel the resources of the private banks into particular areas of industry or technology. In both countries the banks generally offer only short-term investment credit to industry, although, as Carrington and Edwards (1979) have pointed out, because banks in the United States largely are organized on a state or regional basis, there are more links between major city banks and the local industrial community than there are in the UK. It is hardly surprising, then, that in both countries stock markets play the major role in supplying long-term capital investment to industrial companies.

In West Germany, as in Japan, there is a high degree of integration between the industrial community and the banks, and this is especially strong at the local, or *Land*, level. Bank nominees sit on company boards and play an active role in formulating and supervising the implementation of company policy. The banks are also deeply involved in funding and advising on programmes of industrial restructuring. According to Carrington and Edwards, '. . . the power of banks in business is considerable because the banks are not only the major providers of industrial loan capital but also wield the voting powers of most equity shareholding'. German banks are loath to see companies fail and instead will advise on, and help finance, measures necessary to regain company viability.

However, as Jones (1983) has pointed out, there can also be dangers in too close a relationship between industry and banking, because over time, it can lead to introspection and complacency on the part of both partners with associated lack of perception of external threats. Such a situation arose with the German machine tool industry, which consistently ignored warnings concerning the growing threat posed by Japanese competitors. It was only following dissemination of detailed information by the German Engineers' Association (VDI) that major German manufacturers and the associated banks sat up and took notice. Significantly, the close relationship between companies and banks then proved its worth through the quick provision of finance to fund firms' belated but rapid structural and technological responses to the Japanese competitive threat.

To summarize, we can do no better than to quote Carrington and Edwards:

If the five countries had to be ranked in descending order of integration of banking with business, then the order would be (i) Japan (highly integrated) (ii) West Germany (well integrated) (iii) France (fairly integrated) (iv) the USA (close links in some cases) and (v) the UK (relatively unintegrated, with clear separation between banks and business). One indication of this level of integration is the relative ease with which businessmen become bankers, or indeed bankers are businessmen, where there is close integration, and vice versa. In the UK and the USA banks provide a service to their customers; in

Japan and West Germany, the role of the banking system is predominantly to assist industry (Carrington and Edwards, 1979, p151 and 152).

Finally, the relative lack of long-term bank finance for industry in Britain and the USA might at least partially explain the relatively high levels of public funding of industrial R&D in these two countries. In other words, the public purse is providing a high percentage of the 'patient' and high-risk finance that is not available from private sources. It can be concluded that the various government financing schemes that have been instituted were introduced to correct imperfections in the banking system rather than to adapt this system to the needs of innovative industry. In the following section we will describe some changes in the banking system for the supply of venture capital.

FINANCE FOR SMALL FIRMS: VENTURE CAPITAL

In the previous two sections we described some national patterns of expenditure on R&D and discussed industrial financing systems in a number of countries. As we have pointed out in Chapter 3, the bulk of public R&D support has gone mainly to assist development activities in large companies. Most of these funds have been concentrated on large, prestigious projects in a few sectors of industry (aerospace, computers, defence, nuclear energy); of the remainder, a significant proportion has gone in support of marginal projects of the sort that the large companies would not fund wholly out of their own resources because of the high technical risk and relatively low market potential. (Keck, 1977; Walker, 1976; Zysman, 1975; Little, 1974). In the case of private sector industrial support, in most countries loans and equity participation have also been concentrated in large companies. Thus, finance for the technological development activities and growth of small firms generally has been sparse during most of the postwar era.

Since the mid-1970s public policies in the advanced market economies have increasingly begun to attempt to redress the balance more in favour of small firms. This has been the result of a growing belief in small firms' greater than average capacity for innovation, for employment creation and as a tool of policy for regional industrial renewal. A number of governments have, as a consequence, earmarked funds specifically to support the R&D activities of small and medium-sized firms (SMFs), and a number of these schemes are summarized in Table 5.9. In addition, in 1980, the British government introduced a loan guarantee scheme for small firms under which banks are guaranteed 80 per cent of loans up to £75 000 to approved companies. By the end of 1983, over £400 million had been lent to more than 12 000 companies.

Table 5.9   Government subsidies to small and medium sized firms' R&D activities

Names of schemes (upper limit of public contribution)	Approximate budgets (fiscal year)	Percentage of funds for SMEs (upper size of firms)
Australia		
Commencement grants	-	−100%
Project grants	A$ M.2.5(76/77)	-
Austria		
Forschungsförderungsfonds der gerwerblichen wirschaft	sch M.314(78)	-
Belgium		
Aid to prototypes (50–80%)	F.B. M.4.5(77)	15% (500 p)
IRSIA's subsidies (50%)	F.B. M.1600(77)	27% (500 p)
Interest's premium on bank loans for R&D	-	-
Canada		
IRAP (payment of firms' R&D salaries)	C$ M.20(78/79)	
Mini IRAP (payment of salaries in outside contractors	C$ M.0.5(78/79)	100%
Enterprise Development Program (70%)	C$ M.26(77/79)	100%
Defense Industry Productivity Program subsidies and loans (70%)	C$ M.45(78/79)	-
Program for industry/laboratory projects	C$ M.4	33 out 47 beneficiary firms
Denmark		
Product development support (40%)	D.Kr. M.50(80)	63%
National Agency of Technology's	−D.Kr. M.70(80)	
Project support to industry and institutes	M.30 special appropr. for SMEs	

France		
'Actions concertées'	FF.M. 381(77)	10%
Innovation aid		
(Aide au Development (50%))	−FF.M. (319 + 27.5)(77)	(15% + 63%)
(Aide au Prédévélopment)		
Innovation Premium (for contract placed outside)	FF.M. 1(79)	10%
Guarantee on bank loans for innovation	−	−
(lettre d'agrément)		
Finland		
Ministry of Trade and Industry's subsidies		
for product development		
—grants	Mk.M. 25.0(78)	39%(100 p)
—loans	Mk.M. 21.5(78)	36%(100 p)
SITRA's loans	Mk.M. 26.4(78)	38%(100 p)
Regional funds (KERA)	Mk.M. 15. (78)	100%
Germany		
Subsidies to cost of R&D personnel (40%)	budgeted DM.M.300(79)	100%(1000 p)
Subsidies to R&D contracts placed outside (30%)	budgeted MD.M.8(78)	100%
Direct of R&D projects: BMFT's priorities. BMWI's	estimation: DM.M.150	
Initial Innov. Prog. Technical Dev. in Berlin	for SMEs(1000 p)	
Ireland		
IDA grants for R&D facilities (35%)		
IDA grants for product and process development	£Ir. M. 0.62	mostly in SMEs
(IDA grants for new enterprises)	(£Ir. M. 39.4)	
Italy		
IMI's Fund for Applied Research	L.M. 250(1968–77)	28%(300 p)
Japan		
SMEA's technical development subsidies	Y.M. 995(79)	100%(300 p)
SBFC's loans for industrialization of new	−	
techniques		

Program	Amount	Share
Netherlands		
Development credits (70%)	F1.M.60(78)	44%
Increase of development credits for SMES (for large firms)	F1.M.2(80) 3.8(81)	
Subsidies for contracted research placed outside (30%)	(F1.M.7.9(80) 47.3(81)) F1.M.2(budgeted 79)	
Guidance scheme for SMEs innovation projects	F1.M.7.9(80) 12.6(81)	
(Assistance to tech. and com. feasibility studies and support to agencies providing advice and know-how)		
New Zealand		
Projects and commencement grants	-	Mostly for SMEs
Norway		
Innovations Plan (NTNF subsidies + Industriefondet) loans (85%)	No.Kr. M.150	10%(200 p)
Portugal		
Subsidies to prototype and industrialization development (75%)	-	Mostly for SMEs
Switzerland		
Countercyclical program subsidizing R&D contracts placed outside	S.F. M.24	Mainly for SME's
United Kingdom		
PPDS's reimbursable subsidies (50%)	-	-
Department of Industry (requirement boards and sponsorship divisions)	-	-
CASE Awards	-	(100%)
United States		
NS? Small Business Innovation Program	~S .5 Million (Progressive extension to other agencies up to $M. 150)	100%

In 1975 SMEs received 7.8% ($ M.665) of total government business awards for R&D
(*Source*: OECD, 1981)

VENTURE CAPITAL

In several places in this book we emphasize the role of new technology-based firms (NTBFs) in reindustrialization. In particular we describe how NTBFs were instrumental in the rapid growth of a number of start-of-cycle industries in the United States in the 1950s and 1960s, and in the rapid market diffusion of new product groups (Chapter 6). New dynamic, high-technology small firms appear to be playing an important role today in the emergence of the 'new wave' biotechnology industry in the United States. In contrast to the United States, in Europe and Japan NTBFs have played a much less significant role in the industrial shift to new, higher technology product groups. A report for the Anglo-German Foundation in 1977, for example, confirmed that while NTBFs have played a major role in the US economy, their role in the UK and West Germany has been only small (Little, 1977). In the mid-1970s there were several thousand NTBFs in the US employing in excess of two million. In the UK the number of NTBFs then in existence was only about 200 with total sales of about £200 million; in West Germany the number of NTBFs was even less.

One reason for the low level of NTFB formation in Europe and Japan undoubtedly can be found in cultural differences between these countries and the United States. Specifically, 'job-hopping', a notable feature in US industry, is relatively less prevalent in Europe – and hardly ever occurs in Japan – and the propensity of workers to spin-off to form their own firms is correspondingly lower. The propensity of academics to spin-off to form entrepreneurial new firms is also considerably lower in Europe and Japan. A second, and extremely important factor, has been the relative paucity of high-risk venture capital in Europe and Japan, which contrasts markedly with the United States where venture capital has for many years been relatively abundant. However, since 1980 the situation in the UK has changed dramatically. There are now some 80* sources of equity for unquoted companies and an estimated £315 million was available for investments in the unquoted sector in 1983.

Just as governments have begun increasingly to provide special funds to support the R&D activities of existing SMFs, so also have they taken steps to increase the flow of venture capital to stimulate the establishment and growth of NTBFs. Venture capital schemes have taken a number of forms, both wholly public and public/private mixes, and a number of these schemes are summarized in Table 5.10. In addition to the initiatives shown in the Table, several years ago the British government introduced a tax relief scheme (the Business Start Up Scheme) whereby individuals can invest in new start ups without payment of tax on the capital invested. The Business Start Up Scheme became the Business Expansion Scheme following the 1983 budget. It is designed to

* This includes 30 funds operating under Business Expansion Scheme rules.

Table 5.10 Public sector venture capital

		Mechanism	Operational rules	Indicative volume
CANADA	Loans	Federal Business Development Bank	Fixed term loans	1972 5889 loans $262.3 millions 1978 9908 loans $479 millions
		Enterprise Development Program	Guarantees up to 90% of loans received from private banks	1978 67 loans $100.7 millions
	Loans guarantee	Small Business Loans Act	Guarantees up to $75 000	1970 1367 loans $13.2 millions 1978 5158 loans $82.1 millions
	Equity	Federal Business Development Bank	New programme, flexible rules	1978 69 new investment value $11.7 millions
FRANCE	Loans	Caisse Nationale des Marchés de l'Etat	Medium-term loan Loan guarantee	1976 FF. 2.5 million
		Sociétés de développement régional(15)Equity	Long-and medium-term loan/guarantee	
	Equity	Venture capital companies (2 companies, Sofinova, Soginnove)	Variable	Approximately 20 investments totalling some FF. 15 million/year for the 2 companies
		Sociétiés de développement régional	Up to 35% equity	Less than FF. 20 millions/year
GERMANY	Loans	Kredit anstalt für Wiederaufbau (KFW)	Long-term loans Entrepreneur establishment programme	1978 DM 975 millions
		Länder banks	Long-term 'soft' loans	1978 DM 500 millions
	Loans guarantee	Länder banks	Guarantees given to SME's own banks	
		KFW		
	Equity	Deutsche Wagnisfinanzierungs Gesellschaft	Minimum participation DM 400 000	*Up to 1978 DM 50 millions invested*
N'DLND	Loans	Development Credit Scheme (Ministry of Economic Affairs)	15 years, interest at 5 500 – no start-ups Usually 25–50% equity (entrepreneur can buy-back at predetermined price)	1971 HFI 15.7 millions 1978 HFI 58 million
		Industry Guarantee Fund	Up to 50% equity	Has made over 100 investments altogether
		Spearpoint + technologically advanced projects		1977 12 new investments 1977 HFI—43.7 million on 15 projects

	Institution	Terms	Data
Equity	Regional Development Funds (WON, LOE, GON)	Up to 100% equity (average 61%)	1978 Total equity stock up 4Fl. 110 million
Loans	State craft and industry loan fund AF1 + ABF	15 year loans, 90% of security offered Premium over commercial rates	1970 512 new loans 1978 1766 new loans
SWEDEN			
Loans guarantee	AB Industie Kredit(AB1) AB Företags Kredit(ABF) State craft and industry loan fund		
Equity Företags kapital AB Swedish industry	Minority holdings (20–45%)	Low level of activity total holdings about SKr. 100 millions	
UK			
Loans	Industrial Commercial Finance Corporation(ICFC) Development agencies	15 years fixed interest Minimum £5000 Concessionary rates 5–10 year life	
Equity	ICPC National Research Development Corporation National Enterprises Board	Minority equity state Joint-ventures about 50% equity— £5000 minimum Minimum £100 000	1978 £50 million in 120 companies at about £4.5 millions per annum
USA			
Loans	Small Business Administration	Variable	1970 8719 loans $528 millions 1978 27 626 loans $3100 millions Increasing
plus Loan guarantee Equity	Local Development Corporations Economic Development administration (SBICs)	Loans up to $1 million, guarantees up to 90% of $3 million Variable package of equity + convertible loan	1970 1514 participations 110 millions

(*Source:* OECD, 1981)

inject development capital in unquoted businesses across all sectors of industry. It allows individual investors to claim tax relief on equity investments of up to £40 000 committed for a minimum of five years in unquoted companies. About 50 per cent (£40 million) of the funds committed have been through professionally managed funds established specifically for this purpose. The scheme appears to have significantly biased UK venture capital investments towards start ups. Also, an unlisted securities market was established for equity investment in smaller unquoted companies in 1980. By August 1982 the unlisted securities market had seventy-six member firms (Jarrett and Wright, 1982), which has now risen to over 250.

In Japan, where large corporations have played the major role in the structural industrial changes of the past thirty years, the government has recently become more concerned at the paucity of venture capital and lack of NTBF start-ups. In 1981/82, for example, there were only nine venture capital firms in Japan with outstanding venture capital of $50 million. While there is now an 'over the counter' market in Japan, in 1982 there was only a total of 123 issues; in the US, in contrast, the number of issues on the longer-standing over-the-counter market was 3691. In order to stimulate the venture capital market in Japan, in 1982, according to Twaalfhoven and Hattori (1982), MITI announced plans to:

- relax the legal conditions for joining the over-the-counter market (these were: minimum capital required, Y 100 million; minimum net assets, Y 200 million);
- introduce an automated listing of over-the-counter stocks in 1983;
- set aside an initial Y 2000 million venture capital to be managed by the Small Business Finance Corporation;
- expand the investment insurance system so that the government will cover 50 per cent of the loss of venture capital resulting from the bankruptcy of a venture company;
- set up a new investment and loan company.

That these plans will make more venture capital available in Japan is already evident by the large number of new Japanese and foreign venture capital companies that are being set up this year. Whether these plans will also bring forward the independent entrepreneurs which can translate this capital into new ventures is to be awaited (Twaalfhoven and Hattori, 1982, p46).

In addition to public initiatives, the private banks in a number of countries have begun to establish special units to provide venture capital and other support services for new and young small firms. Examples are the Venture Capital and Business Advisory Services of the Nederlandsche Middenstand Bank (de Haan, 1982); the INNOVA Wiener Innovationsgesellschaft mbH (Arnegger, 1982); the Business Development Unit, Internationale Effecten - en Credietbank NV (Gransberg, 1982); and the Small Business Unit, Barclays Bank (Lovett, 1982). In the case of Barclays Small Business Unit:

The scheme is intended to provide start-up finance for new limited companies, or finance for established companies wishing to launch a new project or product. Business-start loans as they are called, have certain radical features. The primary one is that charges are calculated as a percentage of the borrower's sales rather than by the payment of interest. By doing so the cost of credit is linked directly to the performance of the company or the product. There is no repayment of capital for five years and there are, therefore, considerable cash flow advantages to companies in the early stages of their development (Lovett, 1982, p75).

During its first year or so of operation, Barclay's Small Business Unit lent over £10 million to more than 300 small firms.

Finally, a number of large companies have also entered the venture capital business. For example in the UK Pilkington Brothers and BP have initiated venture capital schemes.

VENTURE CAPITAL IN THE UNITED STATES

Since it is in the United States that venture capital has been most abundant and has operated most effectively, we shall describe several of the important features of the US venture capital industry. In the first case, the size of the industry is relatively small in relation to overall investments and was estimated, in 1981, to be less than $600 million, which was less than one thousandth of pension fund assets (Pratt, 1982). Pratt has estimated that at 15 September 1981, the total capital, at cost, committed to organized venture investment was $5 000 000 million. A second important feature of the industry is its diversity, and it includes public as well as a variety of private sources of capital. Capital commitments to independent private venture capital firms in 1979, 1980 and 1981 (first six months) are shown in Table 5.11 by source of funds.

Table 5.11 Capital commitments ($ million) to independent private firms only: 1978, 1980, 1981

	Capital commitments($ million)			% of Total commitments		
	1979	1980	1981 (6 mths)	1979	1980	1981
Pension Fund	53	197	120	31	30	29
Insurance Cos.	7	88	92	4	13	22
Individuals/ Families	39	102	71	23	16	17
Corporations	28	127	69	16	19	17
Endowments/ Foundations	17	92	46	10	14	11
Foreign	26	55	12	15	8	3
Total	170	661	410	100%	100%	100%

(*Source: Venture Capital Journal.* Taken from: Pratt, 1982)

Table 5.12   Venture capital industry estimated fundings and disbursements in million US $

Year	New private capital committed to venture capital firms	estimated disbursements to portfolio companies	Public underwritings of companies with a net worth of $5 million or less	
			number	amount
1980(estim.)	900	1 000	(135)	822
1 789				
1979	319	1 000	(46)	183
1978	570	550	(21)	129
— — — — — — — — — — — — — Capital gains tax decrease — — — — — — — — — —				
1977	39	400	(22)	75
1976	50	300	(29)	145
1975	10	250	(4)	16
466				
1974	57	350	(9)	16
1973	56	450	(69)	160
1972	62	425	(409)	896
1971	95	410	(248)	551
1970	97	350	(198)	375
— — — — — — — — — — — — Capital gains tax increase — — — — — — — — — —				
1969	171	450	(698)	1367

Total capital committed to the organized venture capital industry
Estimate at 15 September 1981

in million US$

Independent private venture capital firms	$2 100 000
Small business investment companies	$1 500 000
Corporate subsidiaries (Financial and non-financial)	$1 400 000
TOTAL	$5 000 000

This pool remained static from 1969 through 1977 at some $2 500 000 to $3 000 000 million (with new fundings more or less equal to withdrawals).
(*Source*: Venture Economics Division, Capital Publishing Corporation. Taken from: Pratt, 1982)

According to Clark (1983), a top estimate of the number of venture capital firms in the United States is 900, but many of these would have only an occasional participation in the market. Clark suggests that there are 125 'first tier' firms (all members of the Venture Capital Association) and between 150 and 200 'second tier' firms. Of the 125 first-tier firms, about 30 dominate the markets and funding by one of those firms, according to Clark, is tantamount to a stamp of quality approval.

Table 5.12 provides a time-series profile of the US venture capital industry (1969–80) in terms of fundings, disbursments and annual number of public underwritings of small companies. An interesting feature of the Table is the decline on all counts between 1969 and 1978. While the 'oil crisis' of the early to mid-1970s undoubtedly had a hand in the rapid falls of 1974 and 1975 since it badly shook the confidence of investors and would-be entrepreneurs alike, Morse (1976) has identified two additional factors. These were an increase in capital gains tax and new regulations governing the use of pension funds. When capital gains tax was reduced, and the restrictions on the use of pension funds for investments in entrepreneurial small firms were relaxed, capital flows into venture capital firms increased dramatically. This example of the interaction between public policy and private investment is important, since it illustrates how policies in one area can significantly influence techno-economic activity elsewhere, and thus indicates the need for total policy coherence.

Bullock (1983) has discussed the factors leading to the formation of the venture capital industry in the US. He describes a process of mutual learning and skill accumulation during the 1950s between technical entrepreneurs – initially university based – and banks and other capital institutions. In explaining this mutual learning process, Bullock developed a model that describes the transition of university entrepreneurs from a 'soft' to a 'hard' mode. The soft mode consists of the establishment of a technical consultancy, effectively a software (knowledge transfer) operation. This gradually evolves to the stage where the entrepreneurs begin to sell one-off, custombuilt items of equipment (the transfer of hardware). Finally it reaches a stage at which a new (spin-off) company is established – a fully 'hard' company – selling standardized products to a general market. During this 'hardening' process, the entrepreneurs had recourse to local sources of finance and established close relationships with them. At the same time, local bank managers learned a great deal about technical entrepreneurship and technical entrepreneurs. This culminated in the emergence of the professional venture capital industry in the early 1960s, which grew out of the original networks in Massachussetts and Northern California.

The emergence of venture capital therefore depends upon prior developments of the entrepreneurial networks and the accumulation of management experience in handling the considerable risks involved in hard research-based companies. Indeed, it was only after working closely with the entrepreneurial networks for a number of years, that the first wave of professional venture capitalists emerged in Massachussetts from amongst banking officers who had been involved in lending to soft companies during the 1940s and 1950s, and in California from members of the local financial community that had built up close links with the research based companies gathered around Stanford University (Bullock, 1983, p3).

Because of the accumulation of knowledge during the past twenty years or so, venture capitalists in the United States are now generally well able to assess the prospects of would-be entrepreneurs. According to Bullock, sophisticated assessment techniques are rarely used, and many venture capitalists claim that the key factors are a good understanding of the market and, most importantly, a correct assessment of the would-be entrepreneurs. Market assessments are based largely on the new company's business plan, and there is a great deal of accumulated experience available to the entrepreneurs to assist them in formulating such a plan.

The situation in Europe is less satisfactory in these respects. In the case of the more recent venture capital initiatives undertaken by European banks, there is a general lack of expertise within the banks to enable them properly to assess technical and market prospects of new technology-based ventures. At the same time, the would-be entrepreneurs – often with a technical as opposed to a business background – experience difficulties in formulating an overall business plan.

In a recent study Whiston (1983) has highlighted a number of these problems with reference to the bank financing of new computer software companies in the UK. Whiston's results are, however, relevant to other countries in Europe and to the financing of NTBFs generally. He has identified essentially three categories of problem, two relating to the banks, and one to the specific conditions encountered by small firms or individuals: these are assessment problems, communication problems and small firm problems.

First, taking assessment problems, for the purposes of allocation decisions, the banks need to assess:

1(a) The way in which a particular 'area' of science, technology or related industrial sector is developing. For traditional areas say textiles, chemicals, machine-tools or whatever, branch-managers located in relevant industrial areas have built up networks of consultants etc., who have provided this facility.

However, in immature, rapidly developing areas such as microelectronics, optical fibre technology, laser technology, computing-systems applications, biotechnology etc., assessment of these fields becomes much more difficult.

1(b) In assessing a particular applicant there are two main facets, first the technical aspect of his product or service and second, the business acumen/marketing ability/business viability aspect. The former is more easily done the greater the knowledge obtained at level 1(a) described previously.

The second aspect, assessing the 'business/marketing' aspect, is perhaps more easily done by the banks – or so they would consider. But it is here that considerable communication and problems of misjudgement can occur. (The financiers placing over-reliance on accounting procedure or mentality and failing to recognise the importance of an application as a stimulant to industrial or commercial development; or the applicant over-emphasising the importance of the technicalities of his new product or service to the detriment of market assessment) (Whiston, 1983, p2.12).

Communication problems arise because of the differing perspectives of the banker and the applicant:

Consider first the 'differing perspectives' aspect. The banks, not surprisingly, will usually emphasise the marketing, the cash-flow, managerial and market and sales forecasting aspects of the potential development. However the applicant often approaches the problem from the standpoint of the uniqueness of his product or service. Thus we have not so much a clash of interest (though this can occur) rather than a mismatch of priorities. The clash of interest can occur in that although an individual may have serious commercial intentions his prime interest is in product development – in technological initiative.

Irrespective of the 'differing perspective' aspect however, many communication problems in relation to high technology, developing small firms, radical innovations and computing or systems-engineering would seem to occur at the *branch-manager level*; where a manager may not have the appropriate experience to assess, or understand the applicants product, ideas or intentions. Much then depends upon the internal communication and assessment procedure the bank has developed.

The third communication difficulty derives from the inability due to the lack of resources, of marketing competence or managerial spare-capacity of an applicant to satisfy the 'assessment procedure'; it is as if the applicant is sandwiched between the need to provide an overall case for his assessment and the constraints of his own circumstances – either personal or company-wise (Whiston, 1983, p2.12 and 2.13).

Whiston has listed a number of problems characteristic of many small firms (or individuals) seeking venture funds, which result in them entering a 'catch 22' situation. For example, in order to prepare a realistic business plan to satisfy bankers concerning market prospects, the small firm requires marketing expertise which – especially in the case of start-ups – they often lack: at the same time, due to constraints, they cannot buy-in such skills or release staff for the appropriate training. Further, new start-ups lack the business track record bankers often wish to inspect before committing funds, and hence are unable to obtain financial backing; in the absence of financial backing they are unable to establish the requisite track record.

These 'Catch-22' situations (eg limited staff-size which does not allow for release for training in (say) marketing skills, or the lack of time to undertake proper market appraisal surveys etc.) can necessarily compromise an application for funding. Similarly at an 'individual' level a technologist or 'technocrat' (who may well find that he has to face rigid attitudinal constraints for some institutions, merely for having been labelled as a 'technocrat') may well lack appropriate business and marketing experience, which compromises his application as far as the bank is concerned. However without the backing he is often unable to obtain the experience required to obtain the backing . . . Such situations can and do occur as has been pointed out by several of the banking staff who were interviewed. But it is important not to over play such an argument . . . many developments and financial support systems *do* emerge.

What needs to be recognised, though, is that the day-to-day load and difficulties of many small companies very often does not allow for optimum presentation of their case for funding. If their needs and the difficulties under which they function (which may vary from overloaded management, limited marketing resources, cash-flow problems, over-run problems, lack of man-power reserve, etc.) are recognised as not necessarily permanent features but functions of a critical growth-stage, then the application for financial support and an allied prescription for improving these structural deficiencies can be satisfied. As we will note later much depends upon the *perception and under-standing* of the bank manager who is approached and the internal procedures for judging applications in a particular bank or financial agency (Whiston, 1983, p2.14).

A number of British banks have taken steps to improve their assessment capabilities through developing specialist inhouse units, through forming joint operations with experienced venture capitalists and/or management consultants, or through utilizing external con-sultants. A government scheme was also initiated several years ago which involves business training for those wishing to set up their own independent businesses. Between them, these initiatives should help towards overcoming a number of the bank/applicant problems identified by Whiston and discussed briefly above. What these problems do suggest, of course, is that would-be entrepreneurs require more than simply access to risk capital. They require access also to a whole range of skills required in 'growing' a new business; accountancy, personnel management, business planning, marketing and so on. The implication is that public policy should be concerned with providing a range of services – or underwriting the cost of access to such services – to start-up firms and not solely with stimulating the supply of venture capital (albeit the total supply is still inadequate in most European countries, but not in the UK where there was an excess of about £80 million on the independent venture capital market in 1983).

Finally, the American experience suggests that it takes time to accumulate the knowledge necessary for the operation of a successful venture capital system. This means that banks, other financial in-stitutions and governments that have recently entered the venture capital field will need sufficient patience to allow for this knowledge accumulation to occur. It involves the acceptance of high risks in normally risk averse institutions, as well as other fundamental attitudinal and cultural changes. Such changes cannot occur overnight. In the context of reindustrialization, however, they are clearly essential.

To summarize, we can say that in the case of countries undergoing industrial renewal via a technological catching up process (eg Japan in the 1950s and the 1960s), a financial system characterized by private and public banking institutions working in close collaboration with in-dustry, and adopting a long-term view of industrial financing, and in which investment efficiency is enhanced through channelling funds, in a coordinated manner, into specific areas of technology and industry, is the most appropriate funding mechanism. In the case of newly emerging and rapidly changing technologies, where both the structure of industry and its markets are in a fluid stage of development, the former characterized by the emergence of many new, technology-based small firms (eg the United States during the 1950s and early 1960s), the most appropriate means of finance is a venture capital system characterized by diversity of form and a propensity for risk-taking.

REFERENCES

Allen G C 1981 *The Japanese Economy*. International Economic Series, Weidenfeld and Nicholson

Arnegger K 1982 Experience of INNOVA Wiener Innovationsgesellschaft mbH. In Gibb and Neumann (eds) *Financing More Innovation at Less Risk*, EEC, INFOBRIEF, Luxembourg, SARL

Bullock M 1983 *Academic Enterprise, Industrial Innovation, and the Development of High Technology Financing in the United States*. Brand Brothers and Company

Carrington J C and Edwards G T 1979 *Financing Industrial Development*. MacMillan

Clark R 1983 A View of US Venture Capital, (Mimeo) Technical Change Centre

Collins E L 1981 *Corporation Income Tax Treatment of Investment and Innovation Activities in Six Countries*. National Science Foundation, PRA Research Report 81–1, Washington DC

de Hann M A 1982 Cooperation Between Bank and Enterprise. In Gibb and Neumann (eds) *Financing More Innovation at Less Risk*. EEC, INFOBRIEF, Luxembourg SARL

de Melto D P McMullen K E and Wills R M 1980 Preliminary Report: Innovation and Technical Change in Five Canadian Industries, Economic Council of Canada, Discussion Paper No. 176 Ottawa

Edwards G T 1983 Written submission to House of Lords Enquiry on Engineering Research and Development, Vol III – Written Evidence, London, Hansard HMSO, February

Gibbs R 1980 *Industrial Policy in More Successful Countries: Japan*. Discussion Paper 7, NEDO, London

Gransberg H C A 1982 New Trends in Venture Financing. In Gibb and Neumann (eds) *Financing More Innovation at Less Risk*. EEC, INFOBRIEF, Luxembourg, SARL

House of Lords Parliamentary Debate (Hansard) 1983 *Engineering Research and Development*. Vol I REPORT, London, HMSO, February

Jones D T 1983 Motor Cars: A Maturing Industry? In Shepherd, Duchene and Saunders (eds) *Europe's Industries*. Frances Pinter

Kamin J Y Bijaoui I and Horesh R 1982 Some Determinants of the Cost Distributions in the Process of Technological Innovation. *Research Policy* 11(2), North-Holland Publishing Company, Amsterdam

Keck O 1977 *Fast Breeder Reactor Development in W. Germany: An Analysis of Government Policy*. Doctoral dissertation, University of Sussex

Little A D 1977 *New Technology-Based Firms in the United Kingdom and the Federal Republic of Germany* Wilton House Publications

Little B 1974 The Role of Government in Assisting New Product Development. School of Business Administration, University of Ontario, Working Paper No. 114, London, Canada

Lockwood W M 1968 *The Economic Development of Japan.* Princeton University Press

Lorenz C 1979 *Investing in Success: How to Profit from Design and Innovation.* Anglo-German Foundation for the Study of Industrial Society

Lovett I N 1982 New Ways of Financing Technology and Product Development. In Gibb and Neumann (eds) *Financing More Innovation at Less Risk.* EEC, INFOBRIEF, Luxembourg, SARL

Mansfield E 1981 Analysis of Industrial Innovation. IIASA Conference on Innovation Management, Laxenburg, Austria, 22–25 June

March P 1983 French Banking and Finance, II. *Financial Times* 2 December

Morse R S 1976 *The Role of New Technical Enterprises in the US Economy.* Report to the Commerce Technical Advisory Board to the Secretary of Commerce, Washington DC, January

OECD 1978 *Policies for the Stimulation of Industrial Innovation.* OECD, Paris

OECD 1981 *Government Policies on Stimulating Innovation in Small and Medium-Sized Firms.* (Draft commentary), DSTI/SPR/8020, Paris, June

Pratt S E 1982 The United States Venture Capital Investment Marketplace. In Gibb and Neumann (eds) *Financing More Innovation at Less Risk.* EEC, INFOBRIEF, Luxembourg, SARL

Rothwell R and Zegveld W 1981 *Industrial Innovation and Public Policy.* Frances Pinter

Rothwell R and Zegveld W 1982 *Innovation and the Small and Medium Sized Firm.* Frances Pinter

Rybczynski R M 1974 Business Finance in the EEC, USA and Japan. *Three Banks Review.* (103) September: 58–72

Tank A 1983 Why Defence is Killing Industry. *Technology* 7 November

Twaalfhoven F and Hattori T 1982 *The Supporting Role of Small Japanese Enterprises.* Indivers Research, Schiphol, The Netherlands

Walker W 1976 *Direct Government Aid for Industrial Innovation in the UK.* Report to Policy Studies Group, TNO, Delft, The Netherlands

Whiston T G 1983 Employment Generation: Financing Problems of New, Small and Developing Computer Software (and Related Applications) Companies. (Mimeo) University of Sussex, Science Policy Research Unit, January

Zysman J 1975 Between the Market and the State: Dilemmas of French Policy for the Electronics Industry. *Research Policy* 3:312

CHAPTER SIX

The Role of Technology-Based Small Firms in the Emergence of New Technologies*

It is clear from recent policy statements on technological and economic change that, generally speaking, governments in the advanced market economies increasingly have laid greater emphasis on measure to support small and medium sized manufacturing firms (in Europe, for the purposes of government policy, generally taken as firms with employment between 1 and 499) (Rothwell and Zegveld, 1981). This is based on the belief that small and medium sized firms (SMFs) are a potent vehicle for the creation of new jobs, for regional economic regeneration and for enhancing national rates of technological innovation.

The debate concerning firm size and innovation is of long standing, some commentators arguing that large size and monopoly power are prerequisites for economic progress via technological change, others that because of behavioural and organizational factors small firms are better adapted to the creation of major innovations. Some of the advantages and disadvantages variously ascribed to large and small firms in innovation are listed in Table 6.1, which suggests, a priori, that comparative advantage in innovation is unequivocally associated neither with large nor small scale.

It is possible to classify innovations according to three aspects: product change, technology change and market change. If we are able to define, for analytical purposes, what is 'present' and what is 'new', then each innovation can be placed in one segment of the cube in Figure 6.1. Policies for reindustrialization (start-of-cycle industries) will generally be aimed at the segments shaded (new market, new product, new technology). Policies of industrial regeneration (end-of-cycle industries) generally will require the development of major new products, often incorporating new technology and applied to existing product/market areas, ie regenerating market demand through major innovation.

* This chapter is based largely on: R. Rothwell (1984), 'The Role of Small Firms in the Emergence of New Technologies', *OMEGA*, Vol. 12, No. 1

Table 6.1   Advantages and disadvantages* of small and large firms in innovation

	Small Firms	Large Firms
Marketing	Ability to react quickly to keep abreast of fast changing market requirements. (Market start-up abroad can be prohibitively costly.)	Comprehensive distribution and servicing facilities. High degree of market power with existing products.
Management	Lack of bureaucracy. Dynamic, entrepreneurial managers react quickly to take advantage of new opportunities and are willing to accept risk.	Professional managers able to control complex organizations and establish corporate strategies. (Can suffer an excess of bureaucracy. Often controlled by accountants who can be risk-averse. Managers can become mere 'administrators' who lack dynamism with respect to new long-term opportunities.)
Internal communication	Efficient and unformal internal communication networks. Affords a fast response to internal problem solving; provides ability to reorganize rapidly to adapt to change in the external environment.	(Internal communications often cumbersome; this can lead to slow reaction to external threats and opportunities.)
Qualified Technical Manpower	(Often lack suitably qualified technical specialists. Often unable to support a formal R&D effort on an appreciable scale.)	Ability to attract highly skilled technical specialists. Can support the establishment of a large R&D laboratory.
External Communication	(Often lack the time or resources to identify and use important external sources of scientific and technological expertise.)	Able to 'plug-in' to external sources of scientific and technological expertise. Can afford library and information services. Can subcontract R&D to specialist centres of expertise. Can buy crucial technical information and technology.
Finance	(Can experience great difficulty in attracting capital, especially risk capital. Innovation can represent a disproportionately large financial risk. Inability to spread risk over a portfolio of projects.)	Ability to borrow on capital market. Ability to spread risk over a portfolio of projects. Better able to fund diversification into new technologies and new markets.
Economies of Scale and the Systems Approach	(In some areas scale economies form substantial entry barrier to small firms. Inability to offer integrated product lines or systems.)	Ability to gain scale economies in R&D, production and marketing. Ability to offer a range of complementary products. Ability to bid for large turnkey projects.

Growth	(Can experience difficulty in acquiring external capital necessary for rapid growth. Entrepreneurial managers sometimes unable to cope with increasingly complex organizations.)	Ability to finance expansion of production base. Ability to fund growth via diversification and acquisition.
Patents	(Can experience problems in coping with the patent system. Cannot afford time or costs involved in patent litigation.)	Ability to employ patent specialists. Can afford to litigate to defend patents against infringement.
Government Regulations	(Often cannot cope with complex regulations. Unit costs of compliance for small firms often high).	Ability to fund legal services to cope with complex regulatory requirements. Can spread regulatory costs. Able to fund R&D necessary for compliance.

* *Note* The statements in brackets represent areas of potential *disadvantage*. Abstracted from Rothwell and Zegveld, 1982.

(*Source*: Rothwell, 1983)

Figure 6.1 Classification of Innovations

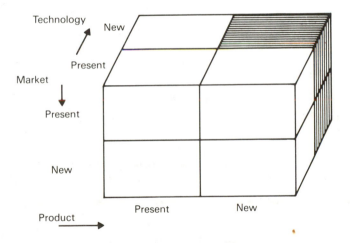

Each form of innovation has its own implications for the organizational structure most appropriate to its implementation. The most radical forms of innovation, the creation of new products using new technologies, (the shaded segments of Fig. 6.1) often require new organizational structures in the form, for example, of a new division within an existing organization, a subsidiary company of a large firm or a completely new, usually small independent business organization. Data from the UK on some 2300 important innovations introduced by – though not necessarily developed by – British companies during the

197

period 1945 to 1980 have thrown some light on the issue of the distribution of innovations over firm- and unit-size categories (Townsend et al, 1981).

Data on some thirty-five sectors of industry show that, at an aggregate level, SMFs' share of innovations in the UK has, during the period 1945 to 1980, consistently averaged about 20 per cent of the total (Table 6.2). At the same time the share enjoyed by firms in the largest size category (greater than 10 000 employees) increased progressively from 36 per cent during 1945–49 to 59 per cent during 1975–80. Moreover, the data also showed that the larger firms increasingly have innovated via smaller units (subsidiary, division, etc.) and that independent firms increasingly were displaced by subsidiaries of larger firms as the major source of innovations (Table 6.3).

Table 6.2   Percentage of innovations in each firm size category for each five-year period

No. of employees	1945–49 %	1950–54 %	1955–59 %	1960–64 %	1965–69 %	1970–74 %	1975–80 %	TOTAL %
1–199	16.0	13.0	11.0	11.0	13.0	15.0	17.0	14.0
200–499	9.0	9.0	5.0	6.0	7.0	9.0	7.0	7.0
500–999	3.0	2.0	7.0	3.0	3.0	4.0	3.0	4.0
1 000–9 999	36.0	36.0	25.0	27.0	23.0	17.0	14.0	23.0
10 000 and over	36.0	44.0	30.0	51.0	52.0	55.1	59.0	32.0
TOTAL	100.0	100.0	100.0	100.0	100.0	100.0	100.0	100.0
No. of innovations	94	191	274	408	497	401	461	2326

(*Source*: Wyatt, 1982)

Table 6.3   Percentage of innovations in each unit size category for each five–year period

No. of employees	1945–49 %	1950–54 %	1955–59 %	1960–64 %	1965–69 %	1970–74 %	1975–80 %	TOTAL %
1–199	30.0	23.0	17.0	14.0	21.0	27.0	32.0	23.0
200–499	11.0	18.0	14.0	14.0	16.0	16.0	14.0	13.0
500–999	9.0	6.0	13.5	12.0	11.0	13.0	16.0	12.0
1 000–9 999	48.0	41.0	38.0	43.0	40.0	34.0	30.0	38.0
10 000 and over	13.0	12.0	16.0	17.0	12.0	10.0	8.0	13.0
TOTAL	100.0	100.0	100.0	100.0	100.0	100.0	100.0	100.0
No. of innovations	94	191	274	408	497	401	461	2326

(*Source*: Wyatt, 1982)

An at least partial explanation is that performing innovative activities in smaller units of larger firms combines the advantages of smaller and larger firms listed in Table 6.1.

Simply counting innovations, of course, tells us nothing about the relative innovative efficiency of small and large firms (nor about the degree of 'radicalness' of the different innovations) measured as innovations per unit of employment or innovations per unit of output. Nor does it inform us of relative R&D efficiency, that is the innovations per unit of R&D expenditure. In relation to the former measure, Wyatt (1982) has suggested on the basis of innovation data from the Science Policy Research Unit that, in general, the innovative efficiency of the very largest firms consistently has been higher than that of their smaller counterparts during the whole of the 1945–80 period. Regarding R&D efficiency, Wyatt found that:

'small firms' (employment between 100 and 500 employees) share of innovations is considerably greater than their share of R&D expenditure for all 35 industry sectors. This is sometimes interpreted as small firms' greater efficiency in R&D activities. Another explanation is that there is a lower degree of functional specialisation in small firms, so that a higher proportion of innovative activities occurs outside of what is defined as R&D activities (Wyatt, 1982).

At a more disaggregated level, relative innovative efficiency varied between sectors and in some sectors such as mining machinery, textile machinery, electronic capital goods and scientific instruments, small firms enjoyed innovative efficiencies greater than unity. In terms of share in total sectoral innovations, in some sectors such as pharmaceuticals, SMFs played a very small or zero role; in other sectors, for example scientific instruments, SMFs played a consistently significant role. Not surprisingly where R&D requirements are very large and capital costs very high, high entry costs prohibit the participation of small firms; where technical, capital and marketing start-up costs are relatively low, entry by small firms is entirely possible.

An interesting case is electronic computers. Between 1945 and 1969 innovative activity (and output) was dominated by large firms producing predominantly mainframe computers. This involved high capital costs, a large R&D effort and the establishment of comprehensive production and servicing facilities. During the period 1970–80, however, SMFs have emerged as a significant force and accounted for 40 per cent of all important innovations introduced in the UK. This reflects the introduction of high density integrated circuits and the microprocessor which made possible the entry of new small firms producing mini- and microcomputers. These are skill-intensive, require considerably less capital investment than previous models and have opened up a large variety of new market niches suitable for exploitation by technical entrepreneurs. Thus, while one type of technological change, that requiring high development costs and large investment for commercial realization, can pose a barrier to entry by small firms, other types of technological change can provide them with many new opportunities.

The development of the electronic-computer sector ran parallel with the development of an associated software sector. A Dutch study

(Overmeer and Prakke, 1980) looked at the factors behind the rapid growth in the number of software houses in the service sector in the Netherlands during the 1970s. Initially, in 1969, a decoupling in the prices of hardware and software took place. Mainframe computer firms standardized their software programs, whereas the needs of the users became more specific, creating many opportunities for the growth of new software houses. Secondly, minicomputer manufacturers concentrated on the production of hardware. Because of a lack of knowledge concerning the software requirements of the diversity of users, especially in the service sector, a new market for software houses arose. Finally, the development of the microcomputer, with its divergent applications, was responsible for the rise of system houses directed to applications in specific areas.

In the software sector too, the more important process- and product-innovations are performed in the larger software houses having the necessary skills and financial capacity. Small, new software houses concentrate on the adaptations of existing programs to the specific needs of relatively small groups of clients. Their role is mainly the diffusion of computer technology throughout the marketplace.

Two important points emerge from the above discussion. The first is that the debate concerning firm size and innovation should proceed on a sector-by-sector basis. The second is that a dynamic approach clearly is necessary: the relative contribution of firms of different sizes to innovation in a particular industry might depend on the age of that industry; the *type* of innovation typically produced by large and small sized firms at different stages in the industry cycle might vary also, ie product or process innovations. This evolutionary dynamic was described in our discussion of industry and product/process cycles in Chapter 1.

It was, of course, Schumpeter (1939) who made the major initial contribution to the discussion of industrial dynamics. He emphasized that while entrepreneurs play a significant role in the establishment of new industrial branches, during the latter phases of development innovation requires large firms because of the high costs involved and considerable market power if innovation is to be worthwhile.

According to Freeman et al (1982), there are essentially two Schumpetarian models of innovation; 'entrepreneurial' innovation and 'managed' innovation. In the first case new basic technologies emerge that are coupled in an unspecified way to new scientific developments and which are largely exogenous to existing companies and market structures. Risk-taking entrepreneurs grasp the techno-economic opportunities thus offered and, via radical innovation, foster the growth of new industries and the emergence of major new product groups. It is during this phase of the industry cycle that dynamic new small, but fast growing firms play the key role as innovators. (See chapter 1)

As the technology and the markets mature and average firm size increases, inventive activity becomes progressively internalised in the form of large inhouse R&D laboratories (which remain coupled to external sources of science and technology). As Freeman et al put it:

In Schumpeter (model) II therefore there is a strong positive feedback loop from successful innovation to increased R&D activities setting up a 'virtuous' self-reinforcing circle leading to renewed impulses to increased market concentration. Schumpeter now sees inventive activities as increasingly under the control of large firms and reinforcing their competitive position. The 'coupling' between science, technology, innovative investment and the market, once loose and subject to long time delays, is now much more intimate and continuous.

Finally as the industry and its technology mature, the possibilities for major product innovations diminish. At the same time market requirements become increasingly well specified and competing products are little differentiated technically. As a result, price becomes a more significant factor in competition, and development efforts become more and more directed towards process efficiency improvement (cost reduction). If this pattern of evolution is valid, then while the initial small entrepreneurial firms are concerned primarily with new product innovation and major product improvement, the subsequent large established firms become increasingly involved in process innovation and minor product improvements.

Recognition that smaller firms as well as larger firms have their advantages and disadvantages with respect to innovation has led to growing interest in the so-called 'new venture approaches' that are aimed explicitly at combining the advantages in innovation enjoyed by firms of different sizes (Rothwell and Zegveld, 1982). At the same time, as we suggested earlier, radical innovation might require a separate organization operating independently from the existing activities in a firm.

One of these new venture approaches is the so-called spin-off technique, which is sponsored by an already existing (large) company. In the spin-off approach the exploitation of ideas which have arisen largely in the R&D section of a major firm, but which are not suitable, or are irrelevant, for exploitation by the firm internally, occur through the formation of an independent new company in which the 'parent' has a stake. In other instances, workers might spin-off and form their own new company independently of the parent.

A study of fifteen such spin-off cases in the Netherlands (van der Meer and Van Tilburg, 1983) investigated, for each case, the history of the spin-off and of its entrepreneur, as well as the attitude towards it of the parent company. The cases were taken from different sectors, varying from electronic computers to the breeding of salmon trout in seawater floats, most of them being innovative in character.

The study showed that there are a variety of reasons why new ideas were not translated into commercial goods or services by the firm internally. In a number of cases the new idea did not fit into the strategy or objectives of the firm or into its divisional structure. Another reason for the exploitation of new ideas by spin-offs is the often small scale of the activities. In a few cases, spin-off represented an important opportunity for saving a developed idea which would otherwise remain unexploited because of bankruptcy of the firm in which the original R&D took place. Where founders of a spin-off worked in the sales department of such a firm, they often exploited an identified gap in the market. It is interesting to note that in some cases spin-offs were supported by, or cooperated with, the firms which they had left. More generally, there is evidence from several countries which illustrates this phenomenon of cooperation and support, not only concerning spin-offs, but also other small firms. A study of new technology based firms (NTBFs) in Sweden (Utterback, 1982), for example, concluded that larger firms in Sweden backed all kinds of NTBFs largely through the provision of technology and skilled labour.

Moreover, these larger firms often acted as early markets for the NTBFs, and prepayments were among the most important sources of finance for half of the NTBFs in the sample. The question can thus be posed as to the degree to which stimulating the rise of small – especially new technology based – firms is generally in the interests of large existing firms. In the Dutch study mentioned above, a number of the cases illustrated that both the spin-off and the parent firm benefited through cooperation or from support by the latter. In several cases the large firm and the small spin-off firm together were able to offer a complete range of products and/or services. An illustrative example is the case of Philips and B&B Elekronika BV, a spin-off from the former, which specialized in the production and installation of electronic matrix scoreboards and related products. These activities were of too small a scale to be of interest to Philips, but B&B was able to produce a qualitatively equivalent product at lower cost. The support of Philips consisted of the provision of technical information and the transfer of appropriate labour to the spin-off. The most important support, however, consisted of obtaining orders from Philips and assitance with B&B's export activities. Philips included the B&B products in quotations to its customers, thus enabling it to offer complete installations for projects such as football stadiums, etc.

Another kind of mutual advantage was found to be the rendering of supplementary services by the spin-off with respect to the products of the parent firm, one example being in the area of traffic control systems. Philips, a large producer of traffic control systems, considered their installation a necessary but not particularly advantageous undertaking and a firm spun off from Philips to specialize in the installation of traffic control systems and related activities. It is clear that in the first years of its existence, Philips was the most important customer of the new firm. The benefit for both companies was clear: the spin-off obtained orders for its services and Philips had no further worries about installation activities.

Both the above examples illustrate that the operations of a spin-off may indeed be of benefit to the parent firm. In the latter example the complementarities between the small and the large firm were based on the flexibility of the spin-off in offering customerized services, while the large firm's organization was more suited to the production of standardized goods. In the first example there was an indication of technical and market complementarities between both firms.

A second type of complementarity can exist between the dynamics of related (sub-) sectors of the type discussed in Chapter 2; for example between electronic computers and the associated software sector. Earlier in this chapter we discussed the rise of small software firms in the Netherlands, operating in specialist market niches which arose because development in hardware greatly reduced capital requirements thus opening up many new areas of application (for microcomputers). Capital start-up costs in the associated software sector were small and the new software firms obtained their comparative advantage through accumulated specific applications expertise. A condition for the development of the software sector was a technically well-developed computer hardware supply industry.

Corresponding complementarities also exist between the audiovisual hardware and software sectors. Quality improvements and weight reduction in videorecorders and cameras, for example, contributed to the rapid growth in the video market which resulted in the associated rapid growth in the software sector. In addition to technological developments, institutional and legal changes have contributed to the expansion of the Dutch audiovisual software sector, in which there are now some 200 small new firms.

A Dutch study (Wissema et al, 1982) has indicated a tripling of the market for the audiovisual software sector during the next decade. This is based on expansion in the general field of entertainment and information, and in instruction, education and documentation, which latter three areas will open up many new opportunities for small specialist software houses. However, in order to achieve this growth potential, it is clear that infrastructural developments will be required as well as adaptation to existing government regulations.

Given the central importance of technological innovation to policies of reindustrialization, it is essential that the appropriate industrial structures are found both for the regeneration of existing sectors and for the creation of new techno-economic combinations. This will involve policies that capitalize on cross-sectoral complementarities and interdependencies. It will also involve policies that recognize the complementarities that can exist between firms of greatly differing sizes. These complementarities are, of course, dynamic, and the relative roles that large and small firms play, both separately and cooperatively, are likely to vary over the industry cycle. Below we shall attempt to illustrate the dynamic complementarities that can exist between large and small firms, especially NTBFs, during the early phases of industrial evolution, and the role the latter can play in the diffusion of radical new product groups. Understanding this dynamic is important to reindustrialization policy.

THE EVOLUTION OF THE US SEMICONDUCTOR INDUSTRY

An approximate example of Schumpeterian industrial evolution, and one which illustrates the importance of complementarities between large and small firms, can be found in the evolution of the US semiconductor industry. The following description is taken largely from Rothwell and Zegveld (1982).

The beginnings of the semiconductor industry can be traced to the invention of the transistor effect in Bell Telephone Laboratories in 1947 by Bardeen and Brattain. Although their findings paved the way for the invention of the bipolar junction transistor, the real breakthrough came in 1952 when Shockley, the research team leader, described a field effect transistor with a central electrode consisting of a reverse-biased junction. Shockley subsequently left Bell Laboratories and several years later he established his own company in his native Palo Alto, backed by finance from the Clevite Corporation. Shockley attracted a number of leading physicists and engineers into his company but, in 1957, eight of his brightest people left to form their own company. This marked the beginning of the rapid growth of NTBFs in the Palo Alto area, which subsequently gave it its name of Silicon Valley. While a number of other centres of semiconductor production were emerging concurrently, notably at Dallas, Texas (Texas Instruments) and Phoenix Arizona (Motorola), nevertheless it is true that Silicon Valley has been exceptional in world terms in the amount of semiconductor production and technological innovation that has occurred in such a concentrated area.

The eight ex-Shockley workers succeeded in obtaining backing from the Fairchild Camera Corporation, which had been actively seeking diversification, and, in September 1957, Fairchild Semiconductor was founded in Mountain View, California. In 1959, Fairchild Camera Corporation exercised an option to buy a majority interest in Fairchild Semiconductor. The latter grew rapidly from sales of $0.5 million in 1960 to $27 million in 1967 to $520 million in 1978.

During the next few years there was considerable spin-off from Fairchild Semiconductor of both people and technology, and many companies were formed by people formerly with, or associated with, Fairchild. This process has been described by Mason (1979):

... The first spin-off was in 1959, when Baldwin, not from the original Shockley team, left Fairchild to form Rheem Semiconductor, *collecting on the way people from Hughes Aircraft.* In 1961, four of the originals left to form Amelco and one of these, Hoeni, left in 1964 to form Union Carbide Electronics; moving on in 1967 to form Intersil. Of ... interest ... was another event in 1961, when Signetics was formed. This was formed by four people who were a significant part of the Fairchild Semiconductor team. ... *They managed to get venture capital backing from the Dow-Corning group for this move.*

At the same time that NTBFs were being spawned in Silicon Valley, Bell Laboratories (a subsidiary of AT&T), continued with its vigorous inventive and innovative activity, although all AT&T's output (via Western Electric) was produced for its own use in order to avoid anti-trust litigation. Bell Laboratories, along with other major companies

Table 6.4   Major product and process innovations in the US semiconductor industry

Innovation	Principal company responsible	Date
Point contract transistor	Bell Telephone Laboratories	1951
Grown junction transistor	Bell Telephone Laboratories	1951
Alloy junction transistor	General Electric Co. RCA Corp	1952
Surface barrier transistor	Philco Corp	1954
Silicon junction transistor	Texas Instruments Inc	1954
Diffused transistor	Bell Telephone Laboratories, Texas Instruments, Inc.	1956
Silicon controlled rectifier	General Electric Co	1956
Tunnel diode	Sony (Japan)	1957
Planat transistor	Fairchild Camera and Instrument Corp	1960
Ephezial transistor	Bell Telephone Laboratories	1960
Integrated circuit	Texas Instrument, Inc., Fairchild Camera and Instrument Corp	1961
MOS transistor	Fairchild Camera and Instrument Corp	1962
DTL integrated circuit	Signetics Corp	1962
ECL integrated circuit	Pacific (TRW)	1962
Gunn diode	International Business Machines Corp	1963
Beam lead	Bell Telephone Laboratories	1964
TTL integrated circuit	Pacific (TRW)	1964
Light-emitting diode	Texas Instruments, Inc	1964
MOSFET (MOS field effect)	Bell Telephone Laboratories, Philips (Holland)	1968
Collector diffusion Isolation	Bell Telephone Laboratories	1969
Schottky TTL	Texas Instruments Co	1969
Charge-coupled device	Bell Telephone Laboratories, Fairchild Camera	1969
Complementary MOS	RCA Corp	1969
Silicon-on-sapphire	RCA Corp	1970
Ion implementation	Bell Telephone Laboratories	1971

(*Source*: D. W. Webbink, The Semiconductor Industry; Structure Conduct and Performance, unpublished Staff Report to the US Federal Trade Commission, January, 1977.)

have, between them, accounted for a high percentage of all major innovations in semiconductor technology, which is illustrated in Table 6.4 for the two decades up to 1971. Interestingly, since 1976, major Japanese companies have made an increasing contribution to technological advance in semiconductors: Sharp's automatic bonding on 'exotic' subtrates in 1977; Mitsubishi's vertical injection logic and V-MOS in 1978; Fujitsu's 64-K bit in 1978 (Dosi, 1981).

Despite the initial dominance of large companies in basic invention in the semiconductor field, NTBFs played a key role in commercial exploitation, especially during the earlier stages in the US semiconductor industry's development. What in fact occurred during the evolution of the US semiconductor industry was a classical example of the dynamic complementarities that can exist between large and small firms. Existing large firms provided much of the basic, state-of-the-art technology, venture capital and technically skilled personnel which were essential to the start-up of new technology based firms; the NTBFs provided the risk-taking entrepreneurial drive and rapid market exploitation. It was a synenergistic relationship.

From the late 1960s onwards the output of the US semiconductor industry began increasingly to be concentrated in the top ten or so companies. Production economies of scale grew in importance (and plant size increased), as did production learning, and firms began actively to seek rapid movement down the production learning curve. The importance of price in competition increased as the unit cost of semiconductor component production decreased. According to Sciberras (1977), the prime motive for rapid cost reductions was to deter new entrants by creating significant scale barriers to entry in addition to technological entry barriers. This might at least partially explain why semiconductor technology was exploited in Europe mainly by large existing electronics companies: Europe entered the race at a late date, by which time existing scale and technological barriers largely precluded entry by new small firms.

Earlier we implied the possibility of a move from a focus largely on product innovation to one largely on process innovation as industry and its technology mature. Figure 6.2 plots the cumulative number of patents issued in the US in the areas of 'semiconductor internal structure technology' and 'semiconductor preparation technology' between 1963 and 1974. It indicates that the balance of inventive activity has indeed shifted from product (internal structure technology) to process (semiconductor preparation technology), which might be taken as support for the validity of our argument.

Thus, in the development of the US semiconductor industry, we see an example of Schumpetarian industrial evolution from the 'entrepreneurial' model of the newly emerging industry, to the 'managed' model of the mature international oligopoly of today. Nowadays, the main opportunities for new entrants appear to be not in semiconductor

Figure 6.2   Number of patents issued in the US in semiconductor structure technology, and semiconductor preparation technology

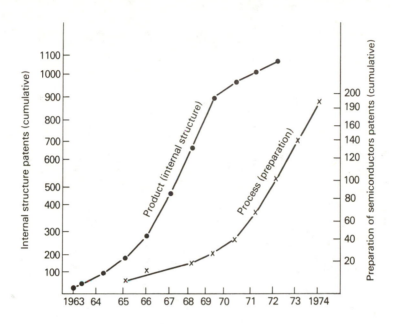

(*Source*: Taken from Rothwell and Zegveld, 1982)

production itself, but rather in the application of semiconductor devices to the production of new products, notably in the general area of information technology, currently mooted as the 'new' industry of the next decade. Indeed, as Table 6.5 indicates, in the US it is mainly young firms in the information technology field that are currently enjoying the fastest rates of growth in sales, with accompanying high employment growth rates. This represents no mean feat during a period of world recession. At the same time existing large companies such as IBM and Exxon are moving into the information technology field, the latter through the acquisition of innovative companies in this area.

Table 6.5   Firms with annual average growth rates in the USA (sales 1976–80) of more than 40 per cent

Firm	Sector	1976–80 Average annual growth			1980		
		Sales (in %)	Profits (in %)	Empl. (in %)	Sales (million $)	R&D/ Sales ratio (in %)	Profits traders ratio (in %)
Tandem Computers	Information processing: computers	247.4	284.5	n.a	109	8.1	10.1
Oray Research	Information processing: computers	197.0	126.8	71.8	61	14.3	18.0
Apple Computer*	Information processing: computers	144.7*	n.a.	11.2	117	6.2	10.5
Floating Point Systems	Information processing: computers	120.5	67.0	n.a.	42	10.9	9.5
Intermedics	Electronics	111.5	113.4	53.5	105	4.6	10.5
Triad Systems	Information processing: peripherals services	89.5	110.3	n.a	57	6.6	8.0
Prime Computers	Information processing: computers	88.1	132.0	73.8	268	7.6	11.6
Rolm	Telecommunications	79.0	101.4	69.7	201	6.7	8.5
Lanson & Sessions	Miscellaneous manufacturing	65.3	n.a.	26.8	235	6.6	–1.3
Auto-Trol Technology	Information processing: peripherals services	64.1	96.9	n.a.	31	12.1	7.0
Data Terminal Systems	Information processing: peripheral services	64.0	n.a.	49.5	118	5.1	–2.5
Computervision	Information processing: peripherals services	59.0	116.3	44.7	224	9.9	10.5
Paradyne	Electronics	37.9	132.8	31.8	76	8.4	10.5
Siltec	Electronics	56.5	64.0	n.a.	57	3.6	5.5
Advanced Micro Devices	Semiconductors	36.2	91.0	48.6	226	12.3	10.2

Sovin	Information processing: office equipment	33.7	90.2	33.5	357	2.9	7.0
American Management Syst.	Information processing: peripherals services	33.3	37.2	n.a.	39	7.1	3.4
CPT	Information processing: office equipment	49.4	35.5	37.9	59	3.4	10.2
Wang Laboratories	Information processing: office equipment	48.5	72.1	n.a.	343	6.7	9.6
Storage Technology	Information processing: peripherals, services	48.2	38.0	n.a.	604	6.5	7.3
Comshare	Information processing: peripherals, services	47.6	51.6	38.9	78	6.3	9.1
Datapoint	Information processing: peripherals, services	47.3	61.0	36.6	50	8.7	10.3
Verbatim	Information processing: peripherals, services	47.3	28.5	45.6	319	3.8	2.0
US Surgical Instruments	Instruments	46.9	52.8	34.1	86	3.3	9.3
Sega Enterprises	Miscellaneous manufacturing	46.8	33.5	9.3	140	1.2	8.6
TIE/Communications	Electronics	44.9	94.3	n.a.	60	2.5	5.0
Kretes	Instruments	44.0	44.3	n.a.	56	7.5	3.6
Intel	Semiconductors	43.9	43.4	27.5	835	11.3	11.3
Datacard	Information processing: peripherals, services	42.6	55.5	n.a.	66	2.6	10.6
Gerber Scientific	Instruments	61.5	83.9	32.1	74	7.1	8.1
Data General	Information processing: computers	41.0	33.0	31.0	654	10.0	8.4
Computer Consoles	Information processing: peripherals, services	40.7	33.8	16.1	44	10.5	11.4
Analogic	Electronics	40.3	67.7	n.a.	67	8.9	9.0
Miller (Herman)	Miscellaneous manufacturing	40.3	40.0	35.1	230	2.5	9.2
Pengo Industries	Machinery	40.1	22.8	n.a.	78	1.9	3.8

*For Apple Computer Inc. which only became publicly held in 1980, the growth in sales relates only to the period 1979–80.
Source: Calculated from Business World, June 6 1961.
(*Source:* Freeman, Soete and Clark, 1982)

THE EVOLUTION OF THE COMPUTER-AIDED DESIGN INDUSTRY

A second example of industrial evolution that indicates an important role for NTBFs can be found in the case of the computer-aided design (CAD) industry. The data below are drawn from the work of Kaplinsky (1981, 1982), who has identified four main phases in the development of the CAD industry: pre-1969 (industry origins); 1969–1974 (dynamic new firms); 1974–80 (the trend to concentration); post-1980 (maturity).

During the first phase development was concentrated in established large companies in the defence, aerospace and aeronautical industries in collaboration with mainframe computer manufacturers, and in the late 1960s General Motors entered the field with the development of its 'Design Augmented by Computers' programme.

In summary, therefore, during this early period there was hardly any 'market' for CAD, with most developments occuring to assist own-use by large, technically advanced engineering corporations in the US and (to a lesser extent) in the UK (Kaplinsky, 1981).

The second phase was characterized by the emergence of new small spin-off firms in the US (from both CAD producers and electronics companies) which played the primary role in the rapid diffusion of CAD devices into the electronics industry. Several of these firms grew extremely rapidly to become, along with IBM, today's market leaders. In Europe, in contrast, the major existing electronics firms developed CAD equipment for their own use.

In summary, therefore, this second period of industry development saw the emergence of new, independent firms and the rapid diffusion of the technology out of the defence, aerospace and automobile sectors to the electronics sectors (Kaplinsky, 1981).

The third phase saw the rapid diffusion in use of CAD across manufacturing, a process in which the 'newcomers' played a key role. During this period of extremely rapid market growth, the industry became increasingly concentrated, 93 per cent of US market share in 1980 being held by eight companies and notably Computervision with 33.2 per cent of the total. At the same time patterns of ownership began to change and there were a series of takeovers by major corporations of several of the fast-growing newcomers.

To summarise, therefore, this third phase of industry development was associated with the growing size of CAD firms, the growing organic trend towards concentration within the sector, and a tendency for formerly independent CAD firms to be swallowed by existing trans-national corporations (Kaplinsky, 1981).

At the beginning of the current phase in development, the market was dominated by turnkey suppliers supplying either mainframe systems (user entry costs of about $500 000) or minicomputer systems (user entry costs of about $200 000). From 1980 onwards, as the user base has broadened, a market niche has emerged for dedicated systems. These are based not on a comprehensive and flexible package of software applications, but on limited software packages for specific applications. A number of microcomputer based companies, founded by spin-offs from existing CAD suppliers, and using 'mature' application programs developed by these suppliers, have begun to emerge, offering systems for as little as $30 000 each.

To summarise, therefore, this most recent stage of industry development has seen two divergent trends – a continued tendency to concentration and an opposing tendency for the entry of new small firms selling limited capability dedicated systems (Kaplinsky, 1981).

In the UK, it has been estimated that US firms held a 62 per cent share of all CAD systems installed up to mid-1981 (Arnold, 1982). Of the remaining 38 per cent share of installations, 17 per cent were held by subsidiaries of large electronic companies established in the late 1960s, 12 per cent by spin-off companies, 5 per cent by a public body (essentially a software house) and 4 per cent by other companies.

DISCUSSION

From the above brief descriptions of the evolution of two high-technology industries we can draw out a number of significant factors:
- Established large US corporations played a crucial initiating role in invention and innovation both in semiconductors and CAD technology. In both instances the early inventive and innovative activity was geared towards 'own use'.
- In the case of semiconductors, much of the dynamic growth and market diffusion came about as a result of the formation and rapid expansion of NTBFs.
- In the CAD industry, NTBFs similarily played the key role in the rapid diffusion of CAD systems to electronics and other areas.
- In both cases, the technological entrepreneurs often came from established corporations, bringing a great deal of technological and applications know-how with them.
- In both cases established corporations and venture capital institutions played an important part in funding the start-up and growth of NTBFs.
- In both cases the industries rather quickly became highly concentrated and subject to external takeover.
- In both cases, as the industries matured, scale economies became increasingly important in the mainstream activities and strong

211

oligopolies were formed, leaving only specialist market niches for new and small suppliers. In the case of CAD, the most significant scale economy has been accumulated software expertise: it is the size of the knowledge base that is a very much more significant barrier to entry than manufacturing capacity.

It is clear from our description of the evolution of the semiconductor and CAD industries that it is indeed necessary to consider the interactions between small and large firms if we are fully to understand the evolutionary dynamic. In both instances existing large corporations played the major initial role in invention, producing new devices largely for inhouse use only. The major role in the initial rapid market diffussion of these new devices, however, was played by new, small but fast-growing companies founded by technological entrepreneurs. Moreover, the technical know-how, the venture capital and the entrepreneurs themselves very often derived from the established corporations, as well as, in the case of the latter two, from major companies operating in other areas. A spin-off firm appeared to be the most suitable organizational form for types of innovation where (the application of) new technologies are involved. Thus we see a system of dynamic complemetarity between the large and the small: both had their unique contribution to make; both were necessary, the former to the initiation of the new technological paradigm, the latter to rapid market diffusion and general commercial exploitation.

What our discussions suggest is that established technology-based large corporations can be extremely effective in creating new technological possibilities; they are highly inventive. While they are adept at utilizing the results of their inventiveness inhouse (new technology for existing applications), they are less well adapted to the rapid exploitation of their inventions in new markets (new technology for new applications). This conforms to what we remarked at the outset of this chapter: more radical innovations require new organizational forms. It appears that new firms, initially, are better adapted to exploit new technological market regimes, breaking out from existing regimes within which established corporations, for historical, cultural and institutional reasons, might be rather strongly bound. Referring back to Table 6.1, it appears that during the early phases in the evolution of a new industry the behavioural advantages of small scale are crucial; as the industry evolves, technological possibilities become better defined, market needs become increasingly well specified, and the advantages of large scale begin to dominate. Comparative advantage shifts to the larger firms and the industry develops towards a mature oligopoly, a situation characteristic of the semiconductor and CAD industries today.

The question now, of course, concerns the future and whether we can detect indications of technological entrepreneurship in areas of great growth potential for the coming decades. We have already dealt with CAD and role of NTBFs in its rapid growth phase, but it is worth adding that markets of up to $12 billion for CAD systems have been predicted for 1990 (Kaplinsky, 1982). In the general area of information processing, as Table 6.5 indicated, out of thirty-six companies that enjoyed an annual growth rate in sales in the US between 1976 and 1980 of greater than 40 per cent, twenty three (or 63 per cent) were in the information processing area. Between them these relatively young firms had combined sales in 1980 of approximately $4000 million.

More recent reports, however, suggest that many of these 'newcomers' in the minicomputer area are currently suffering from severe price competition from very large corporations that entered the race later, but which enjoy huge advantages of scale in production, distribution and marketing (notably IBM). If this trend continues, then the possibilities for entry by NTBFs might be rapidly diminishing, with only specialist market niches being left open for participation by SMFs. On the other hand, cheap and efficient minicomputers offer many opportunities for existing SMFs to improve their operations through facilitating better purchasing, stock, production and marketing control procedures. The increasing ability to 'plug in' in large data bases should also ease the current problems of many SMFs of all types in seeking technical and market information.

Turning finally to biotechnology, the economic potential of this infant industry is immense, and many new firms have been established within this area – most notably in the US – during recent years, frequently being closely linked to university-based research (in this instance the state-of-the-art knowledge is vested in the academic system). It is interesting that, when it became generally realized that biotechnology was still in its research intensive phase (the com-mercialization of biotechnological products on a large scale being a thing of the late 1980s onwards), private venture capitalists began to have second thoughts concerning their investments in the newcomers. Increasingly, established large corporations stepped in to fill the venture capital gap. In fact we can today see synergistic interactions occuring between a number of large and small firms. Dow Chemicals and Monsanto, for example, while pursuing their own research and develop-ment programmes, are investing also in smaller companies; Biotechnology General, an entrepreneurial newcomer in the US, is negotiating for venture capital with three large firms to help finance the development of three new agricultural products; Bio Isolates of Swansea is now setting up a joint venture with Dunlop; Grand Metropolitan has invested more than £4 million in Biogen, a new Swiss-based biotechnology company; and so on. (Several further examples are given in Table 6.6).

Whether or not any of the new small biotechnology firms become the giants of the future or whether they act as a technical resource for existing large firms is, today, less important than whether their role in stimulating widespread interest and greatly increased investment in

213

Table 6.6   Some collaborative ventures between new biotechnology firms and established US and foreign companies[a]

New biotechnology firm – Established company	New biotechnology firm – Established company
Biogen N.V. (Netherlands Antilles)[b] —*Meiji Seika Kaisha, Ltd* (Japan) has licence and development agreement with Biogen NV for the scale-up of a still unnamed agricultural chemical which Meiji could bring to market by 1984–85. —*International Minerals Corp.* has exclusive marketing rights to Biogen's rDNA-produced swine and bovine growth hormones. Biogen will receive royalties. —*Shionogi & Co Ltd* (Japan) will conduct clinical trials and pursue the commercial development in Japan of Biogen's gamma interferon for human therapeutic use. —*Merck* is developing Biogen's hepatitis B vaccine. —*Shionogi* (Japan) has a licence from Biogen to develop and market Biogen's human serum albumin in Japan and Taiwan. —*Shionogi* (Japan) has a licence and development agreement with Biogen to develop interleukin-2. Shionogi will conduct Japanese clinical trials. —*INCO* has a contract with Biogen to do studies of the feasibility of bioextraction of nonferrous metals from low-grade ores and other sources of minerals. —*Fujisawa Pharmaceutical Co* (Japan) has an agreement to develop and produce Biogen's tissue plasminogen activator in Japan, Taiwan, and South Korea. —*Monsanto* will fund Biogen's developments of a technique to produce and purify tissue plasminogen activator. —*KabiVitrum* (Sweden) is collaborating with Biogen in the development of commercial products based on Factor VIII. Biogen intends to market the products in the United States and Canada, and KabiVitrum will have the right to market such products in certain other countries.	**Cetus:** —*Roussel Uclaf* (France) has a contract with Cetus under which Cetus produces vitamin B12. Cetus is receiving royalties. —*TechAmerica* has a contract with Cetus under which Cetus will develop a rDNA antigen to be used as a vaccine against calf bovine diarrhoea. TechAmerica will perform clinical research, manufacture, and market. —*Norden Labs, Inc* has a contract with Cetus under which Norden will produce and market rDNA colibacillosis vaccine. Cetus receives royalties. —*Cooper* will market a MAb from Cetus Immune that is used in tissue typing for organ transplants. —*Shell Oil Co* gave a research contract to Cetus under which Cetus will develop human beta-l (fibroblast) interferon. **Chiron:** *Merck* possesses option for exclusive worldwide licence for the use, manufacture, and sale of Chiron's hepatitis B vaccine. **Collaborative Genetics:** —*Akzo NV* (Netherlands) gave Collaborative Genetics a research contract to develop genetically manipulated microorganisms to produce bovine growth hormone. —*Green Cross* (Japan) has licensed from Collaborative and Warner-Lambert the process by which urokinase is microbially produced. —*Dow* has given a research contract to Collaborative under which Collaborative will produce rennin via genetically manipulated microorganisms. **Cytogen:** —*American Cyanamid* has an agreement with Cytogen to develop a MAb that will deliver a chemotherapeutic agent to cancer cells.

—*Green Cross* (Japan) has a licence from Biogen to manufacture hepatitis B vaccine. Green Cross has exclusive licence to market in Japan.

—*Suntory, Ltd* (Japan) has an agreement with Biogen under which Biogen will develop rDNA microorganisms to produce tumour necrosis factor, to scale-up production, and to support clinical trials, and Suntory will have exclusive marketing rights in Japan and Taiwan.

—*Teijin, Ltd* (Japan) has a licence to develop and market Biogen's Factor VIII in Japan, South Korea, Taiwan, Australia, and New Zealand.

Calgene:

—*Allied Chemical Corp* has a contract with Calgene under which Calgene will do research in nutrient efficiency in plants.

Cambridge Bioscience:

—*Virbac*, a French animal health care company, has a contract with Cambridge Bioscience under which Cambridge Bioscience will develop feline leukemia virus vaccine.

Centocor:

—*FMC Corp* has 50/50 joint venture to develop human-derived monoclonal antibodies (MAbs).

—*Toray/Fujizoki* (Japan) have signed an agreement to manufacture and market Centocor's hepatitis diagnostic in Japan.

Damon Biotech:

—*Hoffman-La Roche* (Switz) has contracted Damon to apply its microencapsulation system to the production of MAbs. Hoffmann-La Roche will retain the marketing rights to the interferon produced by this process.

Enzo Biochem:

—*Meiji Seika Kaisha* (Japan) obtained worldwide marketing rights to products based on Enzo's hybridoma technology, including a newly developed pregnancy test.

Genentech:

—*Monsanto* is testing Genentech's bovine and porcine growth hormones. Commercialization and production will be joint effort.

—Genentech has a joint development contract with *Hoffmann-La Roche* for the production of leukocyte and fibroblast interferons. Hoffmann-La Roche will conduct testing to determine its effectiveness. Genentech will supply part of Roche's requirements and receive royalties on sales.

—*KabiVitrum* (Sweden) has worldwide (except in the United States) marketing rights for Genentech's human growth hormone.

—*Fluor* will develop commercial production operations for Genentech to scale-up new biotechnology products.

(*Source*: Part of table 14, p104, OTA, 1984)

biotechnological R&D, has played a crucial initiating role. NTBFs, by themselves, are no panacea for rapid growth and economic recovery. The vigorous innovatory efforts of many NTBFs in parallel with, and in many cases coupled to, the efforts of established major corporations, however, will, together, greatly increase the possibility of the world economy innovating itself into the recovery phase of the fifth Kondratiev. Both are desirable; both are essential.

Turning briefly to Japan, a handful of dominant Japanese corporations have demonstrated great corporate flexibility and technological adaptiveness during the past thirty or so years. Even here, however, small firms have played a key role by providing the major corporations with an effective source of low-cost labour, the ability to specialize in the capital-intensive final phases of production, great employment flexibility and financing flexibility (Twaalfhoven and Hattori, 1982). Indeed, in Japan in 1978, small businesses (employment below 300) accounted for 53 per cent of the value of all manufacturing shipments. More recently, MITI has shown an interest in stimulating the creation of independent new enterprises and in 1982 announced plans to increase the availability of venture capital. While this move owes much to growing concern over employment loss in dependent subcontractors, it also owes something to a growing desire in Japan to increase the national capacity for creativity and innovativeness. In other words, the potential of independent small enterprises for technological entrepreneurship is now gaining increased recognition in Japan at a time, significantly, when major corporations, for a variety of reasons, are showing increasing pessimism concerning the future and increased caution over investments in potential new technological-market combinations (Yanauchi, 1983).

Finally, we turn to Table 6.7, which outlines briefly the patterns of development of the semiconductor industry in the USA, Europe and Japan. (We do not attempt here to discuss the different institutional, political, economic and cultural factors prevailing in these countries that contributed to determining the different evolutionary patterns; these are covered in some detail by Dosi (1984). Suffice it to say that the size and nature of military procurement, the size and nature of governmental R&D funding, the availability of risk capital, cultural tendencies towards spin-off and job-hopping, the relationship between the semiconductor industry and the home computer industry – and the size and vigour of the latter – and the nature of large R&D-performing bridging institutions, were markedly different in the US and Europe). The patterns shown in the table suggest that access to leading edge R&D, coupled to vigorous spin-off entrepreneurship and the creation of many dynamic, new but fast-growing firms is a system well adapted to the creation of new technological and market paradigms.

A system of large corporations capable of R&D and having coordinated, long-term, explicit strategies towards technology acquisition – as

Table 6:7   Patterns of Evolution of the Semiconductor Industry in the US, Europe and Japan

UNITED STATES

Leading-edge R&D in major companies.
Invention and innovation geared mainly towards own use.
High rate of spin-off and vigorous entrepreneurship.
Entry barriers initially relatively low.
Rapid market diffusion and the emergence of new techno-market paradigms.
Rapid growth of NTBFs.
Technological and market leadership.

EUROPE

Technologically laggard behaviour by major companies.
Inadequate attempts at inhouse catching-up.
Late market entry, at which time there are few possibilities for NTBF formation because entry barriers are now too high.
Technological and market backwardness.

JAPAN

National policies for technology acquisition.
High degree of coordination and cooperation.
Existence of large R&D-capable companies.
Technology acquired for whole industries and not individual companies.
Long-term development strategies at company, industry and national levels.
Emphasis on quality control and production efficiency.
Rapid catching-up in determinate (well-specified) markets and technologies.

for Japan – is a system well adapted to rapid catching up within established technological and market paradigms. A system in which neither leading-edge R&D activity – at least on an appreciable scale – nor coordinated national policies towards technology acquisition exist, seems doomed to a regime of technological and market backwardness within existing paradigms.

We turn finally to the issue of public policy towards small firms. While in this chapter we have dealt largely with NTBFs, we can at this point briefly summarize the public policy implications of the foregoing discussions for SMFs generally (for a detailed discussion of this issue, see Rothwell and Zegveld, 1982). For the purposes of policy, we can divide SMEs into three broad categories: SMFs in traditional industries; modern, niche-strategy SMFs; new technology based firms.

SMFs in Traditional Industries

These are firms operating in areas such as textiles, footwear, woodworking and metalworking. Often they will have been established for many years. They will increasingly be facing competition from the low- labour-cost less-developed countries. They need access mainly to existing technology to upgrade the quality of the products they produce and to improve the efficiency of their production sequences. Microelectronics devices can offer them many opportunities both in quality control and productivity improvement (increased numerical control and greater production flexibility).

Such firms also often need access to management expertise; how to control and organize the production sequence better; better purchasing and stock control procedures, and so on. The various schemes offered by the Department of Trade and Industry in the UK (manufacturing advisory scheme; design advisory service) appear to combine both technical and managerial aspects which together fulfill rather well the requirements of SMFs in this category. In short, schemes designed to link traditional SMFs to the existing collective industrial research infrastructure, and which subsidize the initial cost, are probably the most appropriate. Such schemes should also contain a strong element of technical training to enable the firms better to adopt and adapt new generations of numerical controlled production equipment. For further discussion of this issue see also Chapter 7.

Modern, Niche-Strategy SMFs

These are typically companies in the scientific instruments, electronics subsystem, specialist machinery and equipment areas and, as we have seen, in the CAD industry. They utilize up-to-date technology to supply often custom-built products to specialist market niches. Their needs are mainly access to R&D expertise, access to funds for major new developments, assistance with patenting and, perhaps, access to public sector markets, such as hospitals, schools, universities and offices. Because of purchasing procedures (cheapest buy given a minimum performance level) in some areas, supply is often dominated by large firms. Innovation-oriented public purchasing, especially at the local level, could provide niche-strategy SMFs with many new opportunities (Rothwell, 1983).

New Technology Based Firms

NTBFs are in a special class and, as we have seen, appear to play an important role in the diffusion of new technolgies. This, however, appears mainly to have been the case in the USA, their role in Europe during the past thirty years or so having been modest by comparison (Little, 1977). Important factors in the formation and rapid growth of NTBFs are:

- a cultural climate favouring entrepreneurship;
- access to state-of-the-art technology;
- the ability to spin-off from centres of state-of-the-art expertise, mainly existing large R&D-performing companies and universities;

- availability of venture capital (see Chapter 5);
- the presence of risk-accepting markets.

In the case of the semiconductor and CAD industries in the USA, all the above conditions were fulfilled. While in both cases the state-of-the-art technology was contained initially within the R&D laboratories of major established companies it was, as we have shown, via the vehicle of spin-off NTBFs that the rapid market diffusion of semiconductor and CAD devices occurred. In both instances, Europe entered the race at a later date, by which time entry barriers were too high for NTBF participation on a significant scale.

Clearly governments can play an important role in establishing a set of conditions favourable to NTBF formation by:

- the direct provision of venture capital or through loan guarantees to private venture capital institutions;
- the establishment of state-of-the-art centres of R&D with easy access by private companies;
- the adoption of risk-accepting public purchasing practices or underwriting the initial adoption by private industry of innovative new products;
- attempting positively to influence the national propensity towards entrepreneurial activity, by, for example, establishing innovation centres at universities and technical colleges;
- increasing personal mobility through modifying pension schemes that 'tie' potential entrepreneurs to their existing employment;
- linking together NTBFs with existing corporations in order to capitalize on potential technological and market complementarities.

It should also be noted that NTBF formation appears to be significantly 'locational' in nature, ie there is a geographical clustering effect. The implication of this for regional innovation policies is discussed in Chapter 7.

Of course, no single one of these measures will be sufficient, and governments will need to implement a coherent set of measures on the supply side, the demand side and with respect to the general fiscal and legal environments in which industry is obliged to operate (Rothwell and Zegveld, 1982, Chapter 9). In addition, the cultural climate, both in companies and in society at large, should not be forgotten; in other words the cultural propensity towards entrepreneurship should, where possible, be enhanced. Changing culture is, of course, no simple matter and is unlikely to be achieved quickly. While governments might succeed in establishing an appropriate set of enabling conditions for entrepreneurship to occur, whether it does or not will depend largely on the 'animal spirits' of managers and researchers. Thus, assisting to establish a cultural propensity towards entrepreneurship is an essential task for governments.

REFERENCES

Arnold E 1982 Competition and Policy in a Knowledge-Intensive Industry: CAD Equipment Supply in the UK. (Mimeo) SPRU, Sussex, July

Dosi G 1981 Institutions and Markets in High Technology Industries! As Assessment of Government Intervention in European Microelectronics. In Carter C F (ed) *Industrial Policies and Innovation*. Heinemann

Dosi G 1984 *Technical Change and Industrial Transformation: The Theory and Application to the Semiconductor Industry*. MacMillan

Freeman C Clark J and Soete L 1982 *Unemployment and Technical Innovation*. Frances Pinter

Kaplinsky R 1981 Firm Size and Technical Change in a Dynamic Context. (Mimeo) Institute of Development Studies, Sussex, August. Forthcoming, *Journal of Industrial Economics*

Kaplinsky R 1982 *The Impact of Technical Change on the International Division of Labour: The Illustrative Case of CAD*. Frances Pinter

Mason D 1979 *Factors Affecting the Successful Development and Marketing of Innovative Semiconductor Devices*. Unpublished Ph D Thesis, June (PCL, London; SPRU, Sussex) CNAA

van der Meer J D and van Tilburg J J 1983 *Spin-offs uit technisch kommerciële infrastrukturen*. Van der Meer and Van Tilburg, Enschede

OTA 1984 Commercial Biotechnology Office For Technology Assessment Washington DC 20510

Overmeer W and Prakke F 1980 *Software houses in de administratieve sector*. Staffgroup Strategic Research TNO, Delft

Rothwell R 1983 Firm Size and Innovation: A Case of Dynamic Complementarity. *Journal of General Management* Spring Issue

Rothwell R and Zegveld W 1981 *Industrial Innovation and Public Policy*. Frances Pinter

Rothwell R and Zegveld W 1982 *Innovation and the Small and Medium Sized Firm* Frances Pinter

Rothwell R 1983 Creating a Regional Innovation Infrastructure: The Role of Public Procurement. International Conference on Public Procurement and Regional Policy, University of Neuchatel, Switzerland, 31 October–1 November, 1983. To be published in conference proceedings.

Schumpeter J A 1939 *Business Cycles*. McGraw-Hill, New York and London

Sciberras E 1977 *Multinational Electronic Companies and National Economic Policies*. JAI Press, Greenwich, Conn.

Townsend J Henwood F Thomas G Pavitt K and Wyatt S 1981 *Innovations in Britain Since 1945*. Science Policy Research Unit, Sussex University (Occasional Paper Series No. 16, December)

Twaalfhoven F and Hatteri T 1982 *The Supporting Role of the Small Japanese Enterprise*. Indivers Research, Netherlands

Utterback J M 1982 *Technology and Industrial Innovation in Sweden; A Study of New Technology-Based Firms*. Center for Policy Alternatives, Massachusetts Institute of Technology, Cambridge, USA

Wissema J G and Laman N R et al 1982 *Mogelijkheden voor de audiovisuele software-sector in Nederland*. Bakkenist, Spits & Co, Organisatie Adviseurs, Amsterdam

Wyatt S 1982 The Role of Small Firms in Innovative Activity: Some New Evidence. (Mimeo) Science Policy Research Unit, Sussex University

Yanauchi I 1983 Long-Range Planning in Japanese R&D. Paper presented at the International Seminar on Innovation, Design and Long Cycles in Economic Development, Royal College of Art, London 14–15 April

CHAPTER SEVEN

Technology Policy and Regional Regeneration

In the advanced market economies regional disparities in economic prosperity and growth have existed throughout the postwar era. As a result, governments have initiated policies designed to redress regional economic imbalances based largely on the importation to the less-developed regions of branch plants from the prosperous regions. This created many (mainly low level) new jobs in the development regions and alleviated employment bottlenecks in the prosperous regions. Since the onset of the current recession, however, regional economic disparities have once again grown rapidly and levels of unemployment in a number of the development regions are now often twice the national average. This has led to a great deal of concern on the part of central governments and in some cases to social unrest.

As a consequence of these factors, governments have begun to rethink their regional policies since it is evident that, in the longer term, traditional measures have largely failed. In keeping with the theme of reindustrialization, ie inducing structural industrial shifts, we make a case for the adoption of 'endogenous' regional policies based on increasing the indigenous innovation potential of the development regions and on stimulating the growth there of new technology-based firms. In other words, we emphasize policies geared towards the creation of new techno-economic combinations within the regions rather than the importation of mature combinations from outside.

REGIONAL TECHNOLOGY POLICY

An important theory regarding spatial distribution of economic activities is the growth pole theory, and in a number of countries this theory has played an important role in the development of regional economic policy. A useful definition of a growth pole has been provided by O. Vanneste (as quoted in Klaassen & Vanhove, 1980 p 144): 'A

TECHNOLOGY POLICY AND REGIONAL REGENERATION

growth pole can be defined as a set of economic elements concentrated in a geographical space, among which certain links exists which sustain growth.' This definition contains a functional as well as a geographical dimension of the growth pole concept: 'a set of economic elements' being the functional element, the reference to a geographical space being the geographical element.

What makes the growth pole function as it does, is called the 'propulsive unit', a leading economic activity which generates or initiates the links to the other economic elements of the growth pole. This propulsive unit can have different forms: it may be an industrial sector, an industrial firm or even an infrastructural element such as a highway, port, airport, university, etc. (Klaassen & Venhove, 1980). Depending on the nature of the relationship between the propulsive unit and the other economic elements in a region, we can distinguish different kinds of 'polarization' (Klaassen & Vanhove, 1980). In the first place, if the links are of a technical character we speak of 'technical polarization'. The subject links may exist between a firm or an industry as the propulsive unit and other firms or industries functioning as suppliers or customers. The renumeration of production factors and the spending of this income-flow form the second set of links, and in this case we talk of 'income polarization'. In the third kind of polarization, 'psychological polarization', the nature of the linkages is based on psychological effects. Lastly, if the links are based directly on the forming of growth centres, then we can talk of 'geographical polarization'.

In the 1950s, the implementation of regional economic policies in a number of European countries was based largely on social considerations. Later on, in the early 1960s, economic grounds became the most important motivation for regional policy. In practice, governments of these countries tried to attain their objectives by the attraction of branch manufacturing plants of larger companies to the so-called development regions or industrialization areas.

The provision of different kinds of incentives (property and financial) and rapid industrial expansion contributed to this development. The high rates of industrial expansion involved the danger of production bottlenecks due to labour shortages in the more prosperous regions and the accompanying threat of inflationary pressure (Rothwell, 1983). In this respect, many authors have emphasized that persistent inequalities in the labour market between different regions were the core of the regional problems, especially in the UK (Klaassen & Vanhove, 1980 p 269; Marquand, 1981 p 9).

The resulting pattern of establishment of industries has important consequences with respect to both the structure of the labour market and the technological potential of the development regions. The location of branch manufacturing plants in development regions attracted mainly unskilled jobs to these regions as a result of the low level of decision-making authority and the absence of activities in

223

branch plants other than those concerned with the production function. Certainly branch plants rarely perform R&D on a significant level. According to Oakey (1979), this is consistent with product life cycle theory: parent plants in the well-developed regions tend to concentrate on the production of products in the early phases of the product life cycle, following R&D performed earlier in these establishments; more mature products, requiring little or no R&D input, are considered more suitable for production in branch manufacturing plants in development regions. It should be noted, however, that for some high-technology goods (eg pocket calculators), the product life cycle is so short that the production of these products can remain in the parent plant for the complete cycle and thus never travel to the regions. According to Marquand (1981), while product innovations seldom occur in branch manufacturing plants, process innovations are adopted there rapidly (this conclusion was based on the work of Thwaites: see, for example, Thwaites, 1982).

In other words, product innovations diffuse relatively slowly to the regions while process innovations diffuse readily to the regions. This accords well with our discussion of the technology-specific product life cycle model of Abernathy and Utterback presented in Chapter 1 (see Fig. 1.7).

The relatively poor industrial innovation potential of development regions is exacerbated by regional inequities in the distribution of research establishments and research employment. Surveys concerning the distribution of research establishments exist for France (drawn up by DATAR) and the United Kingdom. With respect to the UK, Marquand (1981) concluded that research institutions and research employment both private and public are concentrated in the core (mainly south eastern) regions, the development regions being deficient in these respects.

In the early 1970s, the symptoms of the severe postwar crisis became apparent. Regional unemployment rates rose quickly as companies began to rationalize and reduce both the number and size of their branch plants in the development regions. Many postwar industries entered the maturity phase of their product life cycles following saturating and declining market demand, a development accompanied with loss of jobs particularly in the development regions. At the same time, and especially for mature products, international competition became more severe, and companies experienced increasing competition in such products from the newly industrialized countries. Further, as we suggested in Chapter 1, the role of technology as a determinant of trade competitiveness in the Western industrialized countries, became more important. These factors, together, resulted in a dramatic deterioration in the economic position of the development regions.

We are thus left with a situation in which the characteristics of industrial production are markedly regional in nature. The more prosperous regions generally are characterized by a concentration of modern, R&D performing industries with high innovation potential. In contrast, the development regions generally contain centres of production based on traditional industries and the non-R&D performing branch plants of the modern industries, and possess a relatively low innovation potential.

It is certain, moreover, that if the development regions are to undergo a structural shift to higher value added, more technology-intensive production, means must be found greatly to increase their indigenous innovation potential. It is only through such a process of reindustrialization that the disadvantaged regions can regenerate their productive base to achieve long-term economic prosperity, or at least a 'fairer' share of the national 'economic cake' in conditions of reduced economic growth. The question is, of course, how to go about creating a regional innovation infrastructure conducive to such a structural industrial transformation.

Because traditional regional economic policy has tended to be less effective during periods of economic recession, and in the light of our technology-related interpretation of long-term economic development, the question can be posed whether the time is now ripe for a different approach to regional economic policy. As we have shown, traditional regional policy placed emphasis on the attraction of a 'propulsive unit' to the development region (an 'exogenous' strategy); we believe a new regional policy should start with the existing potential of a region (an 'endogenous' strategy). Below we outline a number of the essential elements of such an endogenous regional policy.

In the framework of the developments pictured above, we will now focus on the issue of the position of the smaller firm in the development regions (a regionally endogenous resource). As we have seen in Chapter 6, in some sectors small firms have considerable innovation potential. The technological performance of these firms is, however, to a large extent dependent on the technological requirements of local markets (Rothwell & Zegveld, 1982) to which small firms, especially new small firms, can be strongly bound. Johnson & Cathcart (1980) for example, compared the markets of new local firms in the northern region of the UK with those of established plants; they showed that in contrast to established firms, the new small firms concentrated to a great extent on local markets. Table 6.1 showed that lack of external communication with sources of scientific and technological knowledge, as well as with geographically distant markets, can be major disadvantages to smaller firms. The needs of small firms' customers, (other firms, public institutions or individuals) as we have suggested above, determine to a large extent their technological position (level of technological demand). In the development regions, the nature of demand can be deficient in this respect; it is often characterized by demand for conventional, low-technology goods requiring little real technological innovation. Where smaller firms are dependent on a few larger local firms as suppliers or especially as customers, and where these customers are technologically non-demanding – more often than not the case in development regions – they can become 'locked-in' to a local regime greatly deficient in terms both of the supply of, and demand for, technology-embodying goods and components.

Because of the problems of external communication experienced by many small firms, and as a result of the mostly traditional nature of demand, two important elements of a new regional policy should be: a) the improvement of small firms' access to sources of scientific and technological expertise; and b) an improvement in the quality of smaller firms' demand. We shall return to these points later.

Rothwell and Zegveld (1982) have argued elsewhere that governments would do better to support local small firms because of their more even balance between direct and indirect labour as opposed to branch plants, their less sharp fluctuations in employment over time and their firmer commitment to local interest. New technology-based firms in particular have great potential for the creation of new jobs. Small firms thus offer greater possibilities for more balanced growth in the range of local skills. Further Johnson and Cathcart (1980), utilizing data from the northern region of the UK, have indicated that this can also influence regional 'fertility', that is, the propensity of local firms to spin-off new local small firms. None of the founders of their study of sixty new firms had been unskilled workers in their previous employment and, significantly, none came from immigrant (branch plant) industry. In view of the structure of labour markets in development regions described earlier, these are important points.

Taking as a starting point the important role small firms can play in innovation and thereby in regional technological and economic development, as an important 'indigenous' element, the following components of a regional policy for the medium to long term can be suggested.

– Higher eduction and scientific and technological research institutions: what is, or should be, their role in the enhancement of the regional potential as a part of an endogenous strategy?
– Regional initiatives in the financing of economic and innovative structure-improving activities, especially in young firms.
– Innovation-oriented procurement policy on the part of (local) government to promote regional technological potential via demand.
– Promotion of 'regional networks'. Especially to smaller firms, an adequate network of external relationships is of crucial importance. We may think here of relationships with other companies, banks, (regional) government agencies and elements of the technological and scientific infrastructure.

In terms of the growth pole theory, a university or an important scientific or technological research institution may function as the 'propulsive unit' of a development region. Stankiewicz (1982) distinguishes two kinds of contribution from universities to the technological potential of a region: indirect and direct. The indirect contribution consists of the training and education of the next generation of R&D workers and of the advancement of technology in general. The presence of high-grade labour as a result of the presence of a university makes the region more attractive as a location for innovative firms. The most effective and direct way in promoting the innovative potential of a region, however, is the establishment of direct relationships between university and industry. (Universities can also be an extremely important component of 'local' innovation-orientated demand.) The rise of small firms based on new technology in development regions involves the existence of entrepreneurs with capabilities in not just technical, but also commercial, financial and managerial matters. In the Greater Boston area of the US for example, where many high-technology companies arose as spin-offs from universities and from existing high-technology companies or government institutions, special evening courses for spin-off entrepreneurs were organized in order to reduce the onesidedness of their skills.

The direct interactions between university and industry can have the following forms, although there exists no sharp borderlines between them (Stankiewicz, 1982):

- Direct knowledge transfer. We may think here of consultancy work, special courses for industrial R&D workers, etc. The existence of a network of both personal and institutional contacts should be considered as essential to an effective transfer of knowledge. This network can be established by means of intermediate organizations, such as information centres and science parks. Their main task is to facilitate the exchange of knowledge. In these science parks, (new) technology-based firms or their R&D laboratories are situated in or near the university.

- Technical assistance to companies. Compared with the previous point the participation of the university staff is more active and extends over longer periods. Suitable intermediaries to facilitate this kind of interactions are innovation centres or applied research institutes. Innovation centres are useful in providing appropriate physical facilities and the assistance of academic researchers especially to new firms. For existing companies, cooperation with universities in applied research institutes is an effective form of technical assistance.

- Universities in the role of sources of inventions and technical entrepreneurship. Universities and industry can cooperate in the translation of technological knowledge and inventions into marketable goods and services. We may think here of the stimulation of spin-offs from the university laboratories or supporting scientists to become 'internal entrepreneurs' in an already existing firm.

227

The core of the problems concerning university–industry relations is that, using Stankiewicz' (1982) words, these relations 'should be viewed as interactions between different social institutions characterized by strongly diverging value systems, norms, functions and working styles.' De Jong (1983), in his discussion of the regional conditions which favoured the flourishing of high-technology firms in the Greater Boston area, remarks that one of the factors behind the success of spin-offs from universities in this region is the organization of the activities in US universities. These activities resemble those of smaller firms: the academic research units often are more or less autonomous with a more firmlike working style. In order to reduce the tensions between university and industry, Stankiewicz proposes a 'planned diversity' of the academic world. While a number of universities should retain their traditional educational and research task, others should concentrate on the mobilization and (industrial) application of scientific and technological knowledge and function as an intermediate between the traditional university and industry. In addition to this kind of diversity, he sees a role for existing intermediaries such as science parks, innovation centres, etc. (See Rothwell, 1982).

Several authors, examining the role which universities played in the technological and economic development of a region, have stressed that the presence of a university is only one factor, though an important one, behind the development of the region in question. In many cases, a cumulation of factors makes a region into what it is. Structures grown to successes in this respect (see De Jong, 1983) are the Greater Boston area and (Segal, 1983) the university-related formation of new firms in Cambridge (UK).

A second important element of a regional policy for the medium to long term is the presence of an adequate regional financing system (see also Chapter 5). The scope for direct financial assistance on the part of regional and local government differs from country to country, but in general it is quite modest. At the same time the question can be posed whether a reorientation of (regional) government expenditures in the Western industrialized countries from more 'consumptive' to more 'productive' objectives is required. In other words much more attention is required for the productive system. In a number of countries, (regional) governments participate in so-called regional development companies (RDCs). Generally, their task is to improve the regional economic structure including the advancement of employment opportunities and innovation potential. Examples of RDCs can be found in a number of countries including the UK, the Netherlands and Sweden. The instruments of the Dutch regional development companies (Regionale Ontwikkelings Maatschappijen) consist of the provision of coordination, consultancy and information and of (minority) equity participation. The shares of the Dutch RDCs are held by the central and/or regional governments and in some cases by unions or state-owned companies.

Experience of the practical functioning of the Swedish regional development companies shows that their links to political bodies have resulted in too much emphasis being placed on 'rescue operations' for companies facing bankruptcy which are important for short-term regional employment. In the Netherlands, too, examples can be found where, as a consequence of political pressure, regional development companies were forced to help firms facing bankruptcy. This old defensive strategy is contrary to the proposed 'endogenous' strategy, in which regional development companies should concentrate on the more aggressive task of stimulating new activities to improve the economic structure. A second problem of many of the Swedish regional development companies pointed to by Olofsson (1981) is a lack of natural relationships with potentially supportive, commercially experienced partners. One remark should be made on the risk-taking financing of young high-technology firms in Greater Boston (see De Jong, 1983). In the US, the market for 'venture capital' is decentralized: Massachusetts being one of some fifty centres. This regional capital market is especially useful to local start-up firms, because of the desire for intensive contacts between capital-provider and capital-demander in the early phases of a firms' life. This capital–market structure forms perhaps the argument for Utterback's (1982) statement, that firms in the US are much better funded in general than those in Sweden. In his study, Utterback (1982) compared new firms within the computer and computer-related products sector in Sweden and Massachusetts. Good contacts between local banks and small technology-based companies including start-up, which have grown over time (an important learning process on the part of bankers) have also been important to the establishment of a concentration of technology-based small firms in the Cambridge area.

Earlier in this chapter, we remarked that the number and nature of innovations in small independent firms in development regions will depend to a large extent on the technological requirements of local markets. Where the quality of demand in terms of technology is deficient, two main options are obvious (Rothwell & Zegveld, 1981; Rothwell, 1983): attracting large established technology-based firms to the region while at the same time encouraging the growth in the number of small local suppliers as a part of an endogenous strategy and/or initiating innovation oriented public procurement procedures.

In Chapter 4, we described 'public procurement' as a direct and important instrument to influence technical innovation. The market-position of the government is important in this respect. In the case of the structure of the regional market for technology-based products, it seems useful to promote cooperation between municipalities and/or other regional government bodies in order to establish or strengthen their (near) monopsonistic market position.

It should be noted that infrastructural concerns – railways, ports, roads, airports, etc – are still important for regional development.

However, developments in information technology might greatly increase regional – and small firm – ability to plug into large, centralized data bases. Rothwell (1983) has summarized a number of the essential conditions for the implementation of a regional or local system of innovation-oriented procurement.

Technological innovation inevitably involves risk both to the producer and to the user. If they are to stimulate supplier innovations, public purchasing authorities must learn to accept the necessary level of risk. At the same time innovation-oriented procurement – the clear articulation of a felt need on the part of public authorities requiring technical development activity for its satisfaction – might be seen by potential suppliers as reducing the risks involved in innovating, notably in market entry. Public purchasing procedures should be insulated from political considerations which, inevitably, are of short-term perspective and averse to risk.

Taken together with a system of innovation-oriented procurement, regulations might be employed to stimulate supplier innovations. In this respect, performance specifications are more likely to induce supplier innovations than rigid design standards. Performance specifications should be such that they shift designs closer to the state of the art along certain preferred parameters that increase utility to the user.

Innovation-oriented procurement might be used to maximum effect in the case of wholly new products, at least in terms of stimulating major technological changes. In the case of mature products, innovation-oriented procurement can be used to stimulate mainly incremental innovations.

Provided the perceived benefits to the supplier are sufficiently great, the use of value incentive clauses in procurement contracts might considerably improve the performance of products. Similarly the adoption of the concept of total life cycle costs in purchasing decisions should result in improvements in product performance. Regulations should not be promulgated that force purchasing authorities to opt for the cheapest buy given a certain minimum standard of performance. This is in the main an anti-innovative procedure, at least as far as product innovation is concerned.

Purchasing authorities will need to acquire – or at least have access to – considerable technical expertise if they are to establish innovation-inducing performance specifications. The same holds true for the establishment of stringent evaluation procedures. At the same time, the technical strengths of suppliers, especially small and new suppliers, might require enhancement. This might involve establishing common R&D facilities or a collective industrial research centre.

There is a clear need for establishing direct links between the producer and the public user organization in order to provide feedback to suppliers concerning product performance and changes in the nature of demand as well as to enable suppliers to inform users of technical developments that might be of benefit to them. Distributors and agents must not be allowed to isolate the user from the producer.

Finally, there might be a need for discriminatory purchasing by local authorities to stimulate the growth of local suppliers. In the short term this might involve underwriting the costs of purchase.

It should be clear from the above that initiating a successful system of innovation-oriented public purchasing by regional authorities is no simple matter. It seems equally clear that the majority of problems can be overcome. This is not, however, likely to be a costless process and the public purse must bear the greatest part of the cost. Nor is it likely to be a short-term process, and local authorities and policy makers will need a great deal of patience and perseverance to see it through. It should, moreover, be a joint learning-by-doing process between suppliers and users, each working to complement the efforts of the other to their mutual benefit.

Finally, innovation-oriented public purchasing, by itself, is likely to be insufficient; it should be utilized in conjunction with a coherent set of instruments on the supply side and concerning the general environment. In short, it should be seen as one element of a local innovation-oriented infrastructure. If, however, the many empirical studies of innovation are correct, which all emphasize the crucial role of demand factors in success, innovation-oriented procurement is perhaps potentially the most powerful element of all. What is indeed surprising is its lack of application in the past.

The previously mentioned policy elements involve interactions between companies on the one side and universities and regional government agencies on the other. In general, a network of interactions between the regional actors is of great importance to all of them. Because of their disadvantages in external communication, small firms should pay special attention to the building of an adequate network of external relations. The provision of premises suited to start-ups and very small firms combined with the provision of certain common services to these firms form a useful contribution in the completion of a network of interactions. In these projects, start-up firms having many problems in common can find support among themselves.

Without giving a complete blueprint for a regional technology policy for economic development for the 1980s, we have attempted to point to a number of important elements of such a policy. Such a policy ought to be based on the fact that innovation is to a large extent a markedly local phenomenon and should therefore have a strong regional or local content.

COLLECTIVE RESEARCH INFRASTRUCTURES

In Chapter 6 we have, for the purpose of policy, divided small and medium firms (SMFs) into three broad categories: SMFs in traditional industries, modern niche strategy SMFs and new technology based firms. Although the latter two categories of SMFs, and policies for them, have received most attention lately, it should be borne in mind that SMFs in traditional industries are of great importance in all countries with respect both to employment and to contribution to gross domestic product. Traditional small firms are also clustered largely in the so-called development regions. Furthermore, the level of technology and management in this category of firms generally will need to be brought up to a point where they are in a position to introduce modern production techniques. Given the potential of new modern production technology there will ultimately be no more traditional industries, but rather declining firms employing traditional production equipment. In view of this situation, governments have an important role in stimulating and assisting the development of SMFs in traditional industries. One of the systems aimed at increasing the level of competence in these firms, which we will describe here, has been employed in a number of countries for many decades in the agricultural sector. This is the collective research infrastructure supported through a network of transfer points to the agricultural sector. In Chapter 4, for example, we described the extent of this agricultural complex in the Netherlands. Although it is important to note at the outset that because of strong differences mainly in market conditions, industrial sectors cannot be compared directly with the agricultural sector, the latter can provide useful pointers to some of the basic elements required for success. In the USA a great many attempts have in fact been undertaken to apply the 'agricultural extension model' to other sectors by providing education, development aid and the dissemination of technical knowledge to industrial firms. All these attempts have either completely or partially failed.

Rogers et al (1976) have analysed the reasons for these failures. On the basis of his analysis eight main characteristics have been formulated with which an effective knowledge transfer system has to comply. These characteristics are as follows.

The system has to have at its disposal a 'critical' quantity of new knowledge. The quantity and level of research, together with information from international sources, represent a major source of new information of potential value to the user. Research, information supply and education have a great deal to contribute and can connect firms with new developments.

Part of the system is oriented towards application and implementation. Through the activities of regional research centres and experimental application stations, an important part of agricultural research is oriented towards the direct application of research results. The relatively far reaching agricultural extension service assists implementation in the (individual) enterprise. Most of the researchers and the extension personnel have a strong orientation towards practice. A factor to be taken into account here is that they often have an agricultural background.

Users of research results have a substantial influence on the research and on information services. It is essential that research and information-service activities are adjusted to the wishes, the needs and the possibilities of the users. In the agricultural sector this is the case, at least in policy development and in the formulation of a wide range of activity programmes. The attitude of workers in research, in information and in education is such that they actively list the wishes and needs of enterprises.

Structural coupling mechanisms exist between the different components of the overall system. Relationships between the several components of the system are close. An important factor here is the 'stepwise' construction of research, information services and education; the presence of a single government department for the agricultural sector; and the organizational structure of the agricultural industry in the form of cooperatives, etc. The structural coupling mechanisms are also being made possible by existing informal networks. Agriculturalists exchange experiences easily, all parties involved speak the same 'language', pursue the same objectives and have similar ideas about the role and the importance of 'their' system of knowledge-development and knowledge-transfer.

There is frequent contact between the information service agent and the user. The frequency is high because each information agent has about 300 enterprises in his area. An important factor is that the target group is relatively homogeneous.

The social distance between suppliers and users of information can be bridged. In the agricultural sector this is certainly the case. Through the 'stepwise' construction this holds within the system as it does in the relationship between the information agent and the agriculturalist. Next to the level of education, experience, specialization, geographical distance and frequency of contacts, it is the attitude of the people concerned that plays a major role. An essential element is that the agricultural sector is very 'open', caused presumably by the absence of competition (although income levels vary considerably) and the 'visible' production processes.

Research, information services and education are treated as a single system. The 'troika' of the agricultural sector has evolved from one 'cell' to an organic composition of activities. It is of importance that the activities are coordinated by one government department.

The system has an important influence on the environment. This influence is shown in political and economic power (the so-called green lobby) and in the legitimacy of the system. As such the nature of reactions to external changes need not be passive.

Does the above mean that the experience obtained with the knowledge infrastructure in the agricultural sector can play a role in the (re)thinking of knowledge infrastructures in industrial sectors? We think that this is clearly the case. It is also clear, however, that the organization of the agricultural sector offers no panacea, nor does it offer ready-made solutions. The value of the model by Rogers lies in the philosophy behind it, clearly laid out in its eight main characteristics. In other words, the agricultural sector does offer a very interesting model for (re)thinking the process of the development, transfer and application of knowledge to traditional SMFs at the regional level.

DEVELOPMENTS IN THE INDUSTRIAL SECTOR

In addition to knowledge infrastructural systems in operation in a number of countries in the agricultural sector, there are signals that, confronted with the urgent need to upgrade the operations of traditional SMFs, systems containing the basic concept described above are now being introduced, albeit slowly and piecemeal, in other sectors of the economy. In Belgium, the basic concept as described by Rogers' eight points is being operated through the Scientific and Technical Centre for the building and contruction sector. In the German Federal Republic, a number of pilot projects have recently been executed from which it has been confirmed that such structures lead to good, positive results (ISI, 1981). In the Netherlands, in close cooperation with all parties concerned, it has recently been demonstrated how, starting from the present situation and given the eight points by Rogers, the knowledge infrastructure of the wood and furniture industry can be improved (TNO, 1983). Indeed, the Technology Policy Report published in the Netherlands in early 1984 explicitly calls for restructuring the knowledge infrastructure mainly in the traditional sectors of industry. To quote from this report:

Information supply to enterprises, specifically SMF's, can only be solved effectively on the basis of a system that complies with the main characteristics of coupling mechanisms between information supply, research and education and a large degree of co-responsibility of the subject enterprises. Optimalisation of parts of the present system will not lead to the desired results. The creation of a knowledge infrastructural system will take several years but has, in the opinion of the writers of the technology policy report, is to be taken as a basis. It is considered that for the targetted knowledge infrastructures elements can be found in the present fragmented system (Ministry of Economic Affairs, 1984).

Given the problems that SMEs in traditional sectors are faced with, and given the pressing requirement to advance their level of technical knowledge and their ability to adopt modern production technology, action to devise effective knowledge transfer systems is an absolute policy requirement. While in most countries steps have been taken to improve the utility of collective industrial research to SMFs in traditional sectors (Rothwell, 1980; Rothwell and Zegveld, 1981), in almost all cases this has not gone far enough. In particular, the degree of integration between education, collective industrial research and the user firms or sectors, is still far below that achieved in the agricultural sector. In this respect, much more effective linkage mechanisms are required and the role of 'brokers' in the agricultural sector provides a useful example of an effective linkage mechanism between at least two elements in the system: research and the user.

NTBFs AS A REGIONAL PHENOMENON

In the previous section we discussed small firms in traditional sectors. Below we shall discuss small firms at the opposite end of the technology spectrum – new technology based firms (NTBF) – and suggest that their formation is very much a 'local' or regional phenomenon. Moreover, NTBFs as a 'small firm' phenomenon are largely transitory, since it is precisely firms in this category that have potential for rapid and substantial growth.

In Chapter 6 we identified a number of primary factors associated with NTBF formation, and we shall deal with several of these below. (The importance of risk-accepting markets was discussed earlier.) The first of these factors is access to state-of-the-art technology, which we shall deal with in association with the ability to spin-off from centres of state-of-the-art expertise. In the case of the semiconductor industry in the United States, it was undoubtedly the spin-off by Shockley from Bell Laboratories to form Shockley Transistor in Palo Alto in 1955 that began the phenomenon subsequently known as Silicon Valley. In 1957 eight Shockley scientists broke away to form Fairchild Semiconductor, and by 1965 there were ten Fairchild semiconductor firm spin-offs in Santa Clara County. According to Saxenian (1983), between 1959 and 1979, there were fifty new companies in the area that had spun-off from Fairchild Semiconductor alone. The point is, it was the ability of individuals to leave the centres of expertise (in the first instance Bell Laboratories) taking with them scarce and specific knowledge that was a major enabling condition of NTBF growth.

Similarly on Route 128 linking Boston to Cambridge in the United States, an area in which there has been a proliferation of NTBFs, spin-offs from MIT research laboratories and from existing R&D performing electronics companies played the key initiating role. Finally, in the UK there has been a significant growth in new high-technology firms in the Cambridge area (there are currently about 400 electronics companies, including ten minicomputer manufacturers). Spin-offs from Pye a large local electronics company, from the government-sponsored CAD centre which is associated with the University, and from the University's mathematics department, have played a key role in this marked concentration of high-technology-based firm start-ups.

Turning now to biotechnology, we can again see the importance of spin-offs from centres of state-of-the-art research. In this instance, however, the state-of-the-art is vested in universities:

The potential industrial applications of biotechnology . . . have emerged directly from publicly funded academic biomedical research. As biotechnology has been moving to the market, universities have been buffers in commercialising the fruits of public funding, because they are virtually the *sole source* of basic know-how. Many of the new firms in the field of biotechnology have sprung out of academia, whereas in the semiconductor field, ample D & D procurement helped to create *industrial* know-how and encouraged *industrial* spin-off. In the area of biotechnology, the traditionally distinct roles of university as a source of research and training and of industry as a source of commercialisation are blurred (OTA, 1984, p415 and 416).

As a consequence, 50 per cent of all US biotechnology firms are located in California or Massachusetts, that is in proximity to university research centres performing rDNA research (Feldman, 1983). In the UK, where the number of biotechnology firms is considerably smaller, and where clustering has not yet taken place, universities have also played the key initiating role for those few firms that do exist.

In terms of the regional policy implications of the importance of spin-offs from state-of-the-art centres of expertise, it is important to note that in most countries the development regions generally contain relatively few large R&D performing advanced technology companies of the type that were important on Route 128 in the United States and in the Cambridge area in the UK. Production in these areas generally is traditional in nature, and even the regionally located branch plants of large modern firms perform relatively little or no R&D and manufacture rather mature products (Oakey et al, 1982). These branch plants thus employ few high-level technical and managerial skills. It is, perhaps, for these reasons that Johnson and Cathcart (1980) found that the 'fertility' (the propensity of firms to spin-off new local small firms) of branch plants in the northern region of the UK was relatively low: none of the founders in their study (of sixty new firms) had been unskilled in their previous employment and more come from immigrant (branch plant) industry.

In contrast to the northern region, the south-east region of the UK is relatively rich in high-technology, R&D performing companies. As a result, there has been significant spin-off activity in the south-east region. A recent study by the Department of Industry, for example, found that 49 per cent of 130 new (established between 1970 and 1980) high-technology firms manufacturing electronics components, and 61 per cent of 100 new high-technology firms manufacturing electronic equipment, were established in the south-east; 60 per cent of the founders spun off from large multi-plant companies and 18 per cent spun-off from small electronics companies employing below 200 (DTI, 1982).

Turning to universities as sources of spin-off entrepreneurs, a notable recent trend has been the establishment of formal transfer mechanisms (science parks, innovation centres) (Rothwell, 1982; NSF, 1982). It appears, however, that cultural factors are more important than institutional arrangements in the encouragement of spin-off activity, and spin-off often occurs following an extended period of consulting and research contracting for industry. One of the reasons for the high fertility enjoyed by Stanford University and MIT is the favourable attitude towards university/industry interaction adopted by the top-level administrators in these institutions. Finally, universities also have a key role to place in providing highly skilled scientists and technologists, and in this respect the universities of Stanford, Berkeley and California responded well to the needs of the burgeoning semiconductor industry not only through consultancy and research contracting arrangements, but also through establishing and rapidly expanding courses in electronics and semiconductor physics.

Moving now to venture capital, as we saw in Chapter 6, the US venture capital industry grew up alongside the burgeoning centres of entrepreneurial activity in California and Massachusetts. Thus, in this respect, US venture capital has a strong regional flavour, which undoubtedly assisted the more recent emergence of new small biotechnology companies in the above two areas. In the case of Route 128, the Boston Capital Corporation, which can grant loans only to small businesses, was an important factor in NTBF formation (Goodeve, 1967). In Philadelphia, in contrast to Boston, the banks generally were unsympathetic to small-firm entrepreneurs and, despite other favourable factors, relatively few NTBFs were established. In Britain where, as we have suggested earlier, the banks generally have funded few NTBF start-ups, banks in the Cambridge locality adopted a much more positive attitude towards funding young firms. This was the result of sustained knowledge accumulation of the type described by Bullock (1983) in the California and Massachusetts area of the United States.

In the depressed, or development regions, industry rarely creates the internal wealth from industrial growth that facilitates the emergence of local venture capitalists with industrial experience who are willing to fund high-technology start-ups. Governments might assist in plugging this venture capital gap by providing investment capital directly aimed at research and development. According to Oakey (1984), the US private venture capital experience is centrally important because the behaviour of venture capitalists in funding small high-technology firms points to many lessons that might be learned by institutional funders in both the public and private sectors. First, the rapidity with which capital is advanced or refused by venture capitalists is significant. Because of the short product life cycles common in high-technology industry, it is essential that decisions on loans be made in a 'next week or not at all' spirit.

While this is a high-risk situation, the risk is spread over a portfolio of companies thus enabling failures to be accommodated. Risks are further reduced by the personal experience of the venture capitalist, who is frequently an ex-manufacturer with considerable business and technical acumen.

Oakey and Rothwell (1984) have suggested that much of this behaviour could be replicated by public and private European institutions in their efforts to provide investment capital for new technology-based firms. Moreover, an agency might be established in a depressed area with the sole remit of providing venture capital for high-technology small firms. The agency could be established with finance from national or local government, or from combined public and private sources, and would be empowered to invest the money in suitable firms, taking an equity stake option in return for funds. To some extent the British Technology Group currently performs this function in the UK. The agency might also develop technical and business back-up services which would assist the evaluation of initial investment in suitable firms, and aid their subsequent growth.

Further advantages of such an agency would be the protection of the young firms from the asset-stripping acquisition behaviour of larger firms from outside the region (Smith, 1979) and its implicit commitment to medium-term funding of firms demonstrating growth potential. In this respect, the advantage of equity participation over a bank loan is that the venture capital agency, as in the case of the private venture capitalists in Silicon Valley, would have a continuing interest in supporting the company.

Finally, we would like to emphasize once again our plea for a technology-based endogenous regional innovation policy for the structural renewal of the depressed regions in the advanced market economies; and there is evidence which suggests that indigenously led regional renewal can occur. Howell (1982) has described the dramatic turnaround that occurred in the New England economy following a severe recession in 1974–5, which was the culmination of a long period of economic decline beginning with the demise of traditional industries in the 1930s. Between 1968 and 1975, the manufacturing sector in New England lost 252 000 jobs, roughly 20 per cent of total manufacturing employment.

Since 1975 there has been a significant growth in new, high-technology industries in New England and a total employment growth from 1975 to 1980 of 17.5 per cent, with a growth in manufacturing employment of 4.4 per cent. A significant factor in this economic turnabout is the large number of higher education establishments in New England providing it with a significant indigenous intellectual and technological resource. Also of significance was a network of financial institutions offering venture capital, and the formation in Massachusetts of Commercial Area Revitalization Districts in older cities in which special financial packages were provided by the Massachusetts Industrial Finance Agency and the Massachusetts Capital Resource Corporation. Similar initiatives were undertaken in Connecticut.

Thus technological adaptability, the availability of venture and growth capital, a significant educational resource and concerted action by local authorities, have all played a significant role in the reindustrialization of New England. Policies designed to capitalize on the indigenous resources of declining regions in other countries, involving the creation of an imaginative partnership between the business community and central and local government, stand a good chance of initiating regional economic renewal. Such policies are worth attempting; the traditional exogenous regional policies have failed.

REFERENCES

Bullock M 1983 Academic Enterprise, Industrial Innovation, and the Development of High Technology Financing in the United States. Brand Brothers and Co

DTI 1982 The Location, Mobility and Finance of New High Technology Companies in the UK Electronics Industry. Department of Trade and Industry, Research and Planning Unit for South East England (Unpublished mimeo)

Feldman M M A 1983 Biotechnology and Local Economic Growth; the American Pattern. *Built Environment* 9(1)

Fraunhofer Institut fur Systemtechnik und Innovationsforschung 1981 Darstellung, Bewerbung und Perspektiven offentlich gerfurderter Pilotvorhaben zur Innovationsleistung – eind Zwischen-balanz, Karlsruhe, West Germany

Goodeve C 1967 A Route 128 for Britain. *New Scientist* (33):346–8

Howell J M 1982 States as Economic Laboratories. (Rebuilding America) *Society* 19(5) July/August

Johnson P and Cathcart G 1980 Manufacturing Firms and Regional Development: Some Evidence from the Northern Region. *Policy Issues in Small Business Research*. Saxon House

de Jong M W 1983 Regionale condities voor nieuwe hoogwaardige bedrijvigheid. (Regional conditions for new high-graded activities): Industriele vernieuwing in Greater Boston. *Economisch Statistische Berichten* (68):3431, 1059–1063

Klaassen L H and Vanhove N 1980 *Regional Policy: A European Approach*. Saxon House

Marquand J 1981 Regional Innovation Policies in the United Kingdom. Six Countries Programme Workshop on Regional Innovation Policy, Sophia Antipolis, France

Ministry of Economic Affairs 1984 Towards a Market Sector Oriented Technology Policy. Project Group Technology Policy, The Hague, February

NSF 1982 *University-Industry Relationships: Myths, Realities and Potentials.* Fourteenth Annual Report to the National Science Board, National Science Foundation, Washington DC 20402

Oakey R P 1979 Distribution of Significant British Innovation. University of Newcastle, CURDS, Department of Geography, Discussion Paper No. 25

Oakey R P 1984 *High Technology Small Firms: Innovation and Regional Development in Britain and the United States.* Frances Pinter

Oakey R P and Rothrwell R 1984 High technology Small Firms and Regional Industrial Growth. Paper presented to CURDS/SSRC Workshop on Technological Change, Industrial Restructuring and Regional Development, CURDS, Department of Georgraphy, University of Newcastle, 28–30 March

Oakey R P Thwaites A T and Nash P A 1982 Technological Change and Regional Development: Some Evidence on Regional Variations in Product and Process Innovation. *Environment and Planning* 14:1073–86

Olofsson C 1981 Regional Development Companies in Sweden. Six Countries Programme Workshop on Regional Innovation Policy, Sophia Antipolis, France

OTA 1984 *Commercial Biotechnology.* Office of Technology Assessment, Washington DC 20510, January

Rogers E M Eveland J P and Bean A S 1976 *Extending the Agricultural Extension Model.* Stanford University, Institute for Communication Research

Rothwell R 1982 The Commercialisation of University Research. *Physics in Technology* 13 November

Rothwell R 1983 Creating a Regional Innovation-Oriented Infrastructure: The Role of Public Procurement. Conference on Public Procurement and Regional Policy, University of Neuchatel, Switzerland

Rothwell R and Zegveld W 1982 *Innovation and the Small and Medium Sized Firm.* Frances Pinter

Saxenian A 1983 The Genesis of Silicon Valley. *Built Environment* 9(1)

Segal N S 1983 Universities and Advanced Technology New Firms in Great Britain. International Workshop on the Future of Industrial Liaison, Berlin

Smith I J 1979 The Effect of External Takeovers on Manufacturing Employment Change in the Northern Region Between 1963 and 1973. *Regional Studies* 13

Stankiewicz R 1982 Industry–University Relations. Six Countries Workshop on Industry–University Relations, Stockholm

Thwaites A T 1982 Evidence of Product Innovation in the Economic Planning Regions of Great Britain. In Maillet D (ed) *Technology: A Key Factor for Regional Development.* Georgi Publishing Company, Saint-Saphoria

TNO 1983 De kennisinfrastructuur in de hout – en meubelindustries. Delft, The Netherlands

Utterback J M 1982 Technology and Industrial Innovation in Sweden: A Study of New Technology-Based Films. Massachusetts Institute of Technology, CPA, Cambridge, USA

CHAPTER EIGHT

Technology, Employment and Work[*]

In Europe, as well as throughout the world, there is a growing interest in problems of structural and technological change in relation to employment. It is increasingly being suggested that new features in the world economic situation and in world technology mean that the employment problems of the 1980s and 1990s will differ significantly from those encountered in the 1960s. It is also being suggested that the present high unemployment cannot be written off as due to a pattern of demand deficiency – a purely temporary aberration from a steady long-term growth pattern – but must be regarded as marking a transition to a rather different relationship between output and employment.

An argument for a more 'structuralist' interpretation of the contemporary unemployment problem will be presented below. Although aggregate demand is extremely important to maintaining manufacturing employment, by itself it cannot explain current trends; the rate and direction of technical change are among the central issues involved. No analysis of 'Keynesian' or 'monetarist' economics and their relationship with employment will be given but rather we shall focus on structural factors emerging from our discussion on technological and economic cycles in Chapter 1. The limitation above should not be taken to suggest that demand is unimportant. Indeed, during the past few years, employment increased in the United States as the result of expansionary policies. During the late 1970s this was accompanied by a rise in inflation, which appears to be the major barrier to the adoption of such policies in other countries during a period of slow productivity growth. More recent increases in mainly service sector employment in the US have been attained with low inflation but high budget deficits.

We presented evidence in Chapter 1 which suggested that structural changes in the relationship between manufacturing output and employment occured before the 1973–4 oil crisis, and certainly before

---

[*] This chapter is based largely on: W. Zegfeld (1984), Technology, Employment and Work, International Symposium on Perspectives of Science and Technology Policy, Guanajuato, Mexico, February.

Figure 8.1   Manufacturing output and employment in EEC-9 and the US.

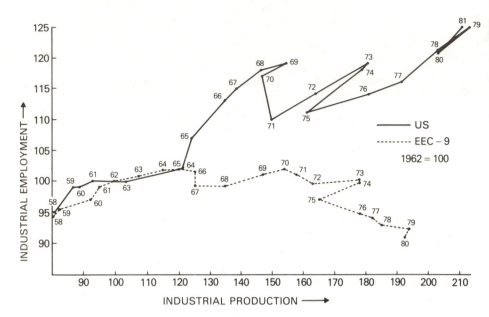

the period when the discussion on the relationship between new technologies and employment began to take on international importances.

New technologies will most probably accelerate existing trends thereby necessitating the search for new balances in the relations between technology, employment and work. Successful development of these new balances will, in an era of increasing international competition, provide countries with new comparative advantages.

SHIFTS IN POSTWAR PATTERNS OF EMPLOYMENT

During the postwar era there have been a number of marked intersectoral shifts in labour in all the established industrialized economies. It is an established fact that there has been a steady decline of employment in the primary sectors (agriculture and mining) between 1950 and 1980. The decline in agricultural employment has, moreover, been accompanied by a marked rise in agricultural output. Hence, a pattern of 'jobless' growth of output has been well established in a major sector of the economy for a considerable period. The pattern of employment change in manufacturing is not as clearcut or as consistent as in the primary sector. There are variations between countries and peculiarities in the direction and rate of change of employment growth over time. Nevertheless, one generalization can be made; the rate of increase in manufacturing employment had already slowed down markedly

Figure 8.2   Employment in high- and low-technology manufacturing, 1968–90

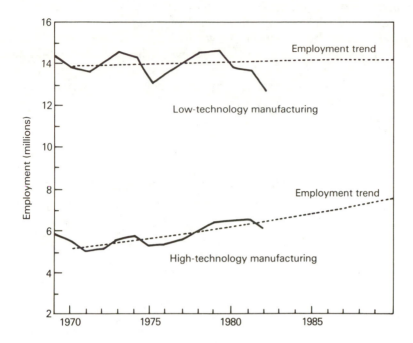

(*Sources*: U.S. Bureau of Labour Statistics, *Employment and Earnings* historical data tape: and Board of Governors of the Federal Reserve System, data series on capacity utilization in manufacturing.

a. Industries are divided into high and low technology at their three-digit Standard Industrial Classification level based on the "product-cycle" division in Robert M. Stern and Keith E. Maskus. "Determinants of the Structure of U.S. Foreign Trade: 1958–76," *Journal of International Economics*, vol 11 (May 1981), pp 207–24. I make one addition to high technology: SIC 3761, guided missiles and space vehicles. To estimate employment trends, I first regressed the log of employment against a time trend and capacity utilization in manufacturing for 1970–80. Then, in the resulting equation, I replaced capacity utilization with the average capacity utilization for 1970–80 to derive trend employment for 1970–90. Taken from: Lawrence, 1983)

in almost all mature industrialized countries well before 1973. This raises the question of whether the phenomenon of jobless growth has now become established in the secondary sector in the advanced economies as well. The data in Figure 1.9, suggests the answer is a definite 'yes'.

Figure 8.1 shows the relationship between manufacturing output and employment in the European Community and the USA over the period 1958–80 (Rothwell and Zegveld, 1982).

The differences indicated in the output/employment relationship between the USA and the nine EEC countries, can be explained on three counts: first, the higher rates of increase in productivity in the traditional sectors in Europe over those in the USA; secondly, the establishment of a bunch of new technology based firms in the USA from the 1950s onward, contributing substantially to manufacturing employment; and thirdly, the social system in the USA which leads to large labour market flexibility often at the expense of great personal suffering.

Figure 8.2 (Lawrence, 1983) shows for the USA, employment in high- and low-technology manufacturing for the period 1968–90 and Table 8.1 (Lawrence, 1983) shows shares of value added and employment in US manufacturing by production characteristics of industries for the period 1960–1980.

Table 8.1   Shares of value added and employment in US manufacturing, by production characteristics of industries, selected years, 1960–80

Per Cent

Item	1960	1970	1972	1973	1980
value added[a]					
High-technology	27	31	31	32	38
Capital-intensive	32	30	31	32	27
Labour-intensive	13	13	14	13	12
Resource-intensive	28	25	24	23	23
Employment[b]					
High-technology	27	30	28	29	33
Capital-intensive	29	29	30	30	28
Labour-intensive	21	20	21	21	19
Resource-intensive	23	21	21	20	20

a. Value added computed for each input-output (1–0) industry by multiplying gross output in 1972 dollars by the ratio of value added to output in the 1972 1–0 table.
b. Employment is derived from the Bureau of Labour Statistics series on employment and earnings. The series have been aggregated to the two-digit 1–0 industry and then to the process categories.

(Taken from: Lawrence, 1983)

Conclusions to be drawn from Figure 8.2 and from Table 8.1 are that in the USA high-technology production has a more positive effect on employment than does low-technology production.

A feature common to all advanced Western economies is the steady postwar growth in employment in the tertiary sector (the service sector), both public and private. For most, if not all, of these countries, the tertiary sector now employs more than either the primary or the secondary sectors. Notable characteristics of the tertiary sector are that labour productivity and capital intensity are both relatively low.

Now, while it is generally recognized that the marked shift of employment to the service sector is related to the increase in demand for commercial and public services by consumers and businesses, nevertheless the slow growth of labour productivity in this sector contributed to this shift. As Gershuny (1979) has put it:

One condition for maintenance of full employment in an economy (holding relative wages constant) must be that the total product rises at the same rate as does the manpower productivity across the economy. Over the past two decades, throughout OECD, manpower productivity in manufacturing industry has risen faster than GNP. Employment can only be maintained under such conditions by passing labour into the relatively low productivity growth, service sector (Gershuny, 1979).

Thus, an important question to ask here is whether there are developments in technology which are liable to cause a dramatic increase in labour productivity in the service sector, with its consequences for employment in this sector. The current debate concerning microelectronics very much revolves around this question.

THEORIES OF MANUFACTURING
EMPLOYMENT/UNEMPLOYMENT

Aggregate demand theory

As we described in Chapter 1, the relationship between industrial output and employment over the period 1950–80, in the EEC member countries, shows three distinct periods:

- the period 1950–65, characterized by high growth in industrial output (7 per cent annual average rate) accompanied by an important creation of employment (1 per cent annual average growth rate);
- the period 1965–73, characterized by high growth in industrial output (6 per cent annual average rate) and employment stagnation;
- the period 1973–80, characterized by low and stagnant growth in industrial output (1 per cent annual average rate) accompanied by 'deployment' (2 per cent annual average rate).

Thus, while the aggregate demand theory of industrial employment would appear to have been somewhat valid between 1950 and 1965, its validity for the period 1965–80 is highly questionable, at least for the members of the EEC. Under these circumstances demand stimulation measures aimed at generating employment through growth in industrial output would seem to stand little chance of more than limited success. This is not to suggest that levels of aggregate demand are unimportant, but rather that prescriptions and explanations solely in traditional terms of aggregate demand are insufficient, since underlying rationalization effects are outweighing the employment creating effects of output growth (see Figure 1.10). In this respect, in the UK in 1960, it required a growth in output of only about 2 per cent to maintain current level of manufacturing employment; by 1980 this had grown to about 4 per cent.

International comparative advantage theory

According to the theory of international comparative advantage structural unemployment in the advanced economies is primarily due to shifts in stagnant labour-intensive industries from developed countries with high-labour costs to less developed countries (LDCs) where labour costs are much lower. At the same time labour in the developed world shifts to capital-intensive sectors with potential for growth. The final result of this process is one of national specializaion in relative factor-abundant industries or products, and all countries end up being better off. According to this interpretation, unemployment in the developed world is only temporary and is due to past unwillingness to adjust under trade liberalization. If a significant percentage of employment in the labour-intensive industries in the Western economies has moved to low-wage-cost countries (LDCs), then this might then be expected to be reflected in a significant level of imports from LDCs to the developed nations.

Further, if this factor has grown in importance, and is making a major contribution to recent high levels of unemployment, then the percentage of imports from the LDCs would be expected to be significantly higher today than one or two decades ago. Thus, by separating imports originating from LDCs from those originating from the advanced economies, it should be possible to separate international competition based largely on comparative advantage (that is, low-wage competition) and competition based largely on non-price factors (that is technical change).

Analysis here shows that (Rothwell and Zegveld, 1979) in most industries foreign penetration of Western domestic markets is relatively high, and in the first place the result of competition from developed countries; and, further, that in terms of 'low-wage' competition, market penetration is weak in all but a limited number of industrial sectors such as clothing. The natural conclusion to draw from this analysis is that, contrary to 'pure' trade theory and the concept of the international division of labour, low-wage-cost foreign competition has, directly, played only a relatively minor role in the structural employment crisis in the Western economies. It might be, however, that competition from low-wage-cost countries has accelerated the scrapping of old vintages, and also resulted in product and process innovation, thereby having an indirect effect on structural change.

The technology gap and theories on rationalization and technical change

According to the technology-gap theory jobs can be lost because of lack of competitiveness in the face of technically advanced imports. In the second place, jobs are lost through rationalization by the home industry in attempting to increase its production efficiency to match that in major competitor countries, as well as attempting to overcome the price advantage enjoyed by traditional goods produced in the LDCs.

As we illustrated in Chapter 1, one way of approaching the relationship between technology and economic performance is to look at the differences between a number of economic blocs, such as the United States, Japan and Western Europe. As far as the introduction of new technologies is concerned, the impression is that Japan and the United States are quicker to make use of advanced production methods and that new leading sectors, mainly in advanced industries, come into existence sooner in the US and grow more rapidly in Japan following a vigorous 'catching-up' process.

In Western European industry the strategy mostly seems to be one of 'follower'. As we further saw in Chapter 1, a number of economic and technological indicators are available to illustrate the difference between these blocs, which confirm Europe's position behind the US and Japan. These indicators dealt with international trade, particularly in the area of high technology, and differences in technological potential including the balance of payments on patents and related items. Distinction was made in this respect to technology in its relationship to the business cycle, to the product life cycle and to the Kondratiev long wave.

Japanese and US experience confirm that, contrary to superficial appearance, it is easier to maintain full employment with a higher rate of technical change rather than vice-versa. It would be difficult for other countries, however, to imitate those features of Japanese and US society which depend on very strong cultural traditions and behaviour patterns. Japan certainly cannot offer complete solutions to the fundamental problems confronting all industrial economies including those of Western Europe in the last part of this century. Nevertheless, Japanese and US experiences do offer useful pointers on how to achieve high rates of growth and high levels of employment, even in adverse world economic conditions as well as how to attain a favourable position from which to lead the longer-term economic upswing.

REVITALIZING THE EUROPEAN PRODUCTIVE SYSTEM; A MAJOR POLICY-LINE TOWARDS THE TECHNOLOGY, WORK AND EMPLOYMENT ISSUE

In this book we have, we believe, provided ample evidence that revitalization of our productive system – reindustrialization and subsequent economic growth – are in some way linked to the emergence of new technological possibilities: that existing industries can in some way be regenerated through radical technological change and new industries be created that way. Revitalization of the European productive system has to take into account three major, and interrelated elements: technological opportunities; industrial structure; and size of the market and its structure. (These are discussed in greater detail in the final chapter).

Technological opportunities

With respect to technological opportunities three major areas are of prime importance namely the educational system and its coupling mechanisms with industry; volume, structure and financing of industrial R&D, and industrial licensing activities.

Industrial structure

In the past attention has mainly been focused on the structure of traditional branches of industry. Less attention has been paid to cooperation between complementary firms and to structural arrangements that would enhance such cooperation.

Examples of the latter are the conglomerates led by financial institutions in Japan and Sweden. New starters can also be regarded to be of great importance to the industrial structure as also is the role of the banks, of professional organizations and of norms and standards.

The size of the market and its structure

The size of the market and its structure are of overwhelming importance in the process of revitalizing the productive system. It is also the factor where the European Community has its most important role to play. Real internal European competition, sophistication of markets, the concept of leading markets, permeability of markets – including the availability of standards and buying behaviour – are of importance here. The potential role of the public sector as a leading market for innovative products is still much underestimated.

Policies aimed at letting technological opportunities play a major role in revitalizing the productive system, in close relationship with the industrial structure and size and structure of markets, will require a vector of macroeconomic policy creating a favourable climate for industry to operate in. As we point out elsewhere in this book science and technology policies and innovation policies can be no substitute for macroeconomic policy; the two lines of policy need to be integrated and should be in support of each other.

NEW BALANCE IN THE RELATION BETWEEN TECHNOLOGY, EMPLOYMENT AND WORK

In the preceding paragraphs ample attention has been paid to the issue of revitalization of the productive system by two tracks of policy; namely science and technology policy (in relation to policies towards the industrial structure and to markets) and macroeconomic policy. To these two tracks of policy a third track ought to be added: a policy which brings about new balances in the relation between technology, employment and work. This 'third track' policy can be divided into the following areas:
– policies towards activities on the front of the product life cycle;
– policies towards activities on the end of the product life cycle;
– policies towards the distribution of work and/or employment.

Policies towards activities at the front of the product life cycle

New technologies offer great potential for new products and services. In order to reap the benefits of new technology in this sense, three factors are of major importance: entrepreneurship and management, public acceptance and risk taking. With respect to entrepreneurship and management US experience has shown a very substantial increase in employment in small new technology based firms (NTBFs). The industrial structure including the venture capital system and the cultural climate have made this development much more possible than has been the case in Europe and Japan (see Chapter 5).

Public acceptance of new technology is a complicated matter. Understanding the extent of new employment opportunity would certainly help to break down barriers to change. A major complication is the often dual role of people; the one as worker and the one as consumer. In this respect it is interesting to note that compared with the reputation, justified or not, which British industry has gained for its slowness in accepting new technologies, the British private consumer shows a remarkable appetite for new products. The proportion of British households owning computers and radio cassette recorders is higher than in any other country. The key to this success may well have been the BBC's programme, broadcasted in prime time, on computer literacy. The technology is perceived as friendly, perhaps because it is under control in the home. A hands-on policy may be the best way to remove barriers.

Policies towards activities at the end of the product life cycle

Here we have to face further automation and robotization of the production process and an increase in the capital intensity of the service sector. International competition is the major external fact in these processes. Key elements here are labour relations and management capabilities from a stand point of both a techno-organizational and a socio-organizational standpoint. The role of the labour unions is crucial; in a number of countries this has led to so called technology agreements. Major problems are the participation at an early stage of the workers involved, the structural changes of work and the absolute necessity for solutions in the face of international competition.

Policies towards the distribution of work and of (un)employment

Our civilization has turned labour into the foremost societal dimension, and access to employment into a major right, since it is by employment that the door is opened to the social security system and to the goods and services essential for life in a developed society (the right to borrow, obtain credit, rent accommodation, etc) (EC, 1984).

Today 11 per cent of the potential working population in the European Community cannot find a job, and this proportion appears likely to increase at least in the near future. In the Netherlands this percentage currently stands at 18. On the basis of demographic trends alone, two million additional jobs will have to be created by 1985 just to hold unemployment down to its present level (1983), and one million new jobs created each year between 1980 and 1995 in order to reduce the unemployment rate to 2 per cent by 1995. The fact that European Community countries were able to create no more than 250 000 jobs a year on average during the 'golden sixties' is a clear reminder of the limits to what can still be done.

The evolution of relations between man and his work is a vital aspect of the transformation of industrial societies, and the relation between technology and employment/work is only one dimension. The problem is not to force the economy or science and technology to restore the full employment of the 1960s (98 per cent of the working population employed for 40 hours a week) because that is not possible – at least not in Europe if Europe will, contrary to the USA and Japan, maintain its single wage structure.

The problem for Europe is to organize the breaking down of barriers between traditional wage-earning employment and work in the widest sense of the term. Such work can provide income but also offers a social role, contacts with others, an opportunity for creation or enterprise. It must not be proposed in a single, rigid setting identical for all, but must be flexible enough to meet the wide variety of demands and to respond to freely expressed choices. Instead of offering everyone a problematical fulltime job, the aim is to allow everyone to find and choose a job in which working hours, levels of pay and social security coverage are no longer predetermined and closely linked, but can be adapted, above an indispensable minimum, to the wishes of the individual.

This strategy could greatly help to resolve the crisis of work and employment. It presupposes a close link between technological and social innovation, allowing greater flexibility in the organization of production, the use of plant and its continuous adaptation to market trends and requirements, without neglecting an adequate level of protection for everyone. This seems to be one of the essential preconditions for Europe if it is to launch itself irrevocably on the road to the 'new growth'.

CONCLUSION

Technology, unemployment and work issues placed in the context of objective social-economic analysis are calling, especially in Europe, for nontraditional policy measures at least for a medium-term period. Such policy measures will not constitute an alternative for macroeconomic policy, nor do they for industrial policy. It is an aggressive policy-mix that is required, consisting of the three tracks of policy in an interrelated manner: namely macroeconomic policy, industrial and science and technology policy and policies regarding the distribution of work.

REFERENCES

FAST II Workprogramme 1984. EEC, Brussels 1984

Lawrence Z 1983 Is Trade Re-industrializing America? A Medium-Term Perspective. Brookings Institution, Brookings Papers on Economic Activity

Rothwell R and Zegveld W 1979 Technical Change and Employment. Frances Pinter

Rothwell R and Zegveld W 1981 Industrial Innovation and Public Policy. Frances Pinter

Rothwell R and Zegveld W 1982 Innovation and the Small and Medium Sized Firm. Frances Pinter

CHAPTER NINE

Towards a Coherent Reindustrialization and Technology Policy

During the past three decades, macroeconomic policy in the Western world has concentrated mainly on the maintenance of full employment largely through the control of financial flows and through demand management. Postwar economic development up to about 1973 can be characterized as an era of continuous economic growth accompanied by some minor fluctuations about this growth path. Around 1970, the relationship between production and employment in many industrialized countries changed (see Figure 1.9) and the effects of underlying structural charges became manifest.

In Chapter 1 we stressed the importance of the structural character of the present economic crisis. In the late 1960s, a large number of postwar industries entered simultaneously the maturity and market saturation phase of their life cycles. A Dutch study by Geldens published in 1979 showed, for example, that no less than 75 per cent of Dutch industrial value-added was realized in industries in the saturation and declining phase of the industry cycle. In this phase, keywords are: rationalization and growing automaticity, growing manufacturing unemployment and price competition. Under these conditions, innovation is necessary in order to initiate new products and to enable industries to enter the first phase of a next generation of growth cycles.

The implication of this structural interpretation of the present crisis is that it should not be tackled by traditional demand management policies, but by a different kind of policy: reindustrialization and technology policy. While an adequate traditional macroeconomic stabilization policy is indeed necessary to create a favourable climate for innovation and reindustrialization, it is, by itself, not a sufficient condition to induce the necessary radical innovative activity.

Certainly poor macroeconomic conditions are not favourable to radical innovation and weak aggregate demand and uncertainties about the future both have their negative repercussions on investment behaviour in general, and on investment in new product and process technologies in particular.

Any reduction in manufacturing profitability will affect the size of future innovative efforts: the subsequent reduction in real company R&D outlays diminishes the sources of future innovations and hence the opportunities for future economic growth. Uncertainty concerning future economic developments may give rise to risk-averting behaviour, consisting of a shift to less radical projects with a short payback period, thus influencing the nature of the innovative efforts. In other words, there will be a tendency towards incremental innovation to the detriment of radical technological change.

Mc.Cracken (OECD 1977) ascribed the economic problems of the decade up to about 1975 to a combination of exogenous disturbances (such as the oil crisis, the sharp rise of prices of food and raw materials, the breakdown of the exchange-rate system and the coincidence of elections in a number of major countries in 1972) and some avoidable errors in economic policy. Although we do not altogether agree with this analysis (Rothwell & Zegveld (1981) we support Mc.Cracken's statement that an important task of government's macroeconomic policy should be 'the stabilization of expectations and the rebuilding of confidence'.

A balanced and integrated reindustrialization and technology policy contains three principal and interrelated elements determining innovative performance. As noted in Chapter 8 these three elements are:
- technical opportunity including the structure of the technical and scientific infrastructure;
- the structure of the industrial sector; and
- size and structure of market demand.

It is apparent that in an approach towards reindustrialization defined as 'the structural transformation of industry into higher added value, more knowledge-intensive sectors and product groups, and the creation of major new technology-based industries serving new markets', science and technology are the necessary, although not sufficient elements: in other words they are primary enabling factors. On the supply side, the technical and scientific infrastructure should obviously be aligned with the industrial sector and its structure. This means that not only is the structure of the industrial sector itself of great importance to reindustrialization, but also its coupling with the infrastructure.

Markets are obviously of the foremost importance to the industrial sector and to its structure. In this respect markets should be looked at not only from a more traditional standpoint of size and tariff barriers, but also from a more dynamic and cultural technology-led viewpoint which includes the concepts of 'leading markets' and 'public acceptance' of new technology. The latter issue in turn is strongly interrelated with an important element of the technical and scientific infrastructure, namely education.

We will now discuss the three elements of reindustrialization policy in more detail.

TECHNICAL OPPORTUNITY AND THE STRUCTURE OF THE TECHNICAL AND SCIENTIFIC INFRASTRUCTURE

An important factor in reindustrialization and technology policy is the transfer of scientific and technological knowledge to the market sector. 'Knowledge' as an input-factor is transferred to industry in two main ways. First, knowledge is incorporated in the labour supply to industry via the labour market. The currently perceived importance of education and training can well be illustrated – and measured – by the considerable allocation of financial resources to this area, which represent a significant share of overall government budgets. At the same time, little attention has been paid to the development of coupling mechanisms between the educational system and its 'clients', an important client being industry. These relationships clearly require considerable reinforcement.

The second priority transfer path consists of the direct transfer of knowledge and hardware to industry from the technical and scientific infrastructure, wholly or partially publicly funded R&D institutions including universities and collective industrial research institutes. Reindustrialization and technology policy should pay considerably greater attention to industry–infrastructure links. Empirical research shows, for example, that links between industry and the scientific and technological infrastructure are substantially stronger in countries with high innovation performance (Ergas, 1983).

As we have shown, the present depression can be understood in terms of a simultaneous saturation of many postwar industries, the upswing requiring the establishment of a new generation of techno-economic combinations. Now both (new) small and large established firms have their role to play in the industrial dynamic associated with the emergence of new combinations. In the earlier stages of the industry cycle smaller firms have several advantages over their larger counterparts because of their greater potential internal flexibility and responsiveness, and simpler communication patterns (see Table 6.1).

On the other hand smaller firms, unlike their larger counterparts, often suffer from a lack of scientific and technological expertise and experience difficulties in linking to sources of specialized technical knowledge. For new technology based firms (NTBFs) operating in new fields of activity, it is obvious that the efficiency of the links between them and the technical and scientific infrastructure deserve attention. The nature of the coupling mechanisms depends largely on the kind of research undertaken; whereas for fundamental research regular inter-personal contacts would probably suffice, the major coupling mechanism for applied research would be the more formal contract mechanism.

Within the framework of reindustrialization and technology policy, it is clearly important to restructure the pattern of allocation of public funds, skilled manpower supply and public R&D facilities in such a way that they match better the requirements of the market sector. To achieve this, of course, it is equally clear that industry needs to establish, as precisely as possible, its perceived set of current needs for future research.

Incentives should thus be provided to the scientific and technical infrastructure to promote a stronger orientation of its resources to answering the pressing scientific and technical requirements of the market sector. Perhaps this stronger orientation to the problems of the market sector may best be achieved by changes in the methods of funding infastructural research.

In a number of OECD countries, such as the UK and the Netherlands, there has, for example, been a recent tendency to finance research in public R&D laboratories through the customer–contractor mechanism, whereby public bodies act as a proxy for the 'customer' in the market sector. While this has aligned research more closely to industrial needs, it appears to have resulted in overemphasis on shorter-term research questions.

STRUCTURE AND DYNAMICS OF THE INDUSTRIAL SECTOR

In our model of postwar industrial evolution in Chapter 1 we described the changes in industrial structure associated with the maturization of a set of new techno-economic considerations, and in Chapter 6 we described the role of NTBFs in the emergence of the semiconductor and CAD industries in the United States. These descriptions suggest that the emergence of new techno-economic combinations is associated with the innovative and/or funding endeavours of large corporations coupled to the vigorous entrepreneurial activities of NTBFs. More recently the emergence of the new wave biotechnology industry – begun by spin-off entrepreneurs from universities – again illustrates the importance of NTBFs during the early phases of industrial evolution; in addition it demonstrates the increasing complementarities between small and large firms taking place in the infant biotechnology industry. The above suggests that an important feature of the emergence of new combinations is the system of dynamic complementarity established between small (new) and large (established) firms (Rothwell, 1983). Thus an important feature of reindustrialization policy lies in stimulating the appropriate complementary dynamic between large and small firms.

Complementarity and collaboration can, of course, exist throughout the industry life cycle: for example, between 'colleague' suppliers operating in the same market, the form of collaboration varying from joint development to joint production and sales. Complementarity may also take the form of contacts between manufacturer and user or between manufacturer and supplier(s). It is clear, moreover, that these contacts should be stronger the more technically sophisticated and complex is the product involved.

Establishing complementarities between small and large firms is, of course, not always easy. Small and large firms tend to operate in different cultures and have different perspectives regarding time. Because of these differences it is necessary to establish at least a minimum level of trust and mutual understanding during collaboration. It may well be that the financial systems in, for example, Japan, Sweden and West Germany, which take an active role in industrial development, help to provide a basis for achieving interfirm collaboration.

In Japan, in contrast to the United States, the role of NTBFs in the remarkable structural transformation that has taken place since 1945 has been very small. Large, conglomerate corporations have demonstrated remarkable corporate flexibility and dynamism during the rapid technological catching up (and subsequent overtaking in some industries) achieved by Japanese industry. Even here, however, a system of very many 'tied' subcontractors, has provided the industrial giants with a great deal of their flexibility in certain aspects of their operations (Twaalfhoven and Hattori, 1982).

While the Japanese system has shown itself well adapted to rapid catching up, it has yet to prove itself capable of initiating major new combinations. It is for this reason that MITI has recently taken steps to increase the flow of venture capital in Japan. Whether Japanese culture proves capable of adapting to an entrepreneurial industrial mode, however, remains to be seen.

In Europe, industry has generally proved itself less capable of initiating new paradigms than US industry, and less adept at 'catching up' and achieving highly efficient, high-quality production than Japanese industry. Although scientifically strong, European industry has often lacked commercial dynamism, the ability to capitalize on its great scientific creativity. European firms generally are smaller than their giant US counterparts (as well as operating in more fragmented, technically less-demanding markets) and relatively few NTBFs have been created in Europe for a variety of cultural and financial reasons. Reindustrialization policy must therefore concern itself with establishing the appropriate industry structure and set up interfirm and intersector relationships appropriate to the exploitation of new techno-economic combinations and the renewal of existing sectors.

In addition to the importance of the size of a firm and structures of cooperation between firms as supply-side factors determining innovative performance, Ergas (1983) mentions the intensity of competition among firms operating in the same market as an additional factor. He states that generally industries are characterized by a spectrum of innovation possibilities of varying complexity and cost. So there is room for a broad set of concurrent innovation efforts maximizing 'the rate of innovation, that is the rate at which technical opportunity is realized' (Ergas, 1983, p 11). Especially in new promising fields of activity, competition may be expected from start-up NTBFs.

SIZE AND STRUCTURE OF DEMAND

The size and structure of the demand side clearly are key elements in determining innovative performance. Consideration of market structures and dynamics is thus an important element in reindustrialization and technology policy. Compared with Europe, the USA and Japan both have large internal markets, and ones which adapt easily to, and indeed help to create, a technically sophisticated supply. From the standpoint of achieving international competitiveness, firms in these countries have first to compete successfully in their national markets because of the severe levels of internal competition existing there. In the effectively fragmented markets in Europe, fierce competition on more than a national basis is often lacking, largely because of the existance of many non-tariff barriers. Even within the EEC, many obstacles prevent the functioning of one 'common' market; technical and administrative barriers to trade and subsidies to industrial and agricultural firms all distort competition in the internal market. Trade liberalization, including the harmonization of standards within Europe, by doing away with non-tarrif barriers, is a major avenue for European reindustrialization policy and would provide a sensible framework for achieving greater competitiveness in world markets.

In Chapter 7, we discussed the significance of the size and structure of 'local' demand in determining the innovative performance of a particular region. In development regions, firms are confronted with a mostly traditional demand structure, which in a number of cases is exerted by a small number of buyers. Policies aimed at an improvement of the indigenous technological potential of a region should make development regions less vulnerable to the consequences of their currently onesided and mostly traditional production structure, and may in turn generate a qualitatively higher demand in terms of technology. An important element of such policies is the creation of an innovation-oriented regional procurement system.

For a large variety of products, governments provide substantial markets and are hence in a position to exercise their market power in influencing the direction of supply towards higher value added, technologically more innovative products. Thus public procurement policy can be considered to be an effective instrument to promote innovations and as a consequence effectively to generate new employment.

In the defence sector where governments enjoy a dominant market position, procurement policies are well established and in some cases have been successful in stimulating civilian innovations. Certainly defence procurement has been highly successful in stimulating very many highly sophisticated innovations in weapon systems. Extending the procedures in this sector to other public sectors such as healthcare and telecommunications, if operated successfully, would open up technologically more demanding markets for industry. (For a detailed discussion of innovation-oriented procurement, see Chapter 4.)

Procurement policy fits well with our description of the present economic situation. One of the primary aims of reindustrialization policy must be the identification, stimulation and diffusion into use of new technologies on which future economic growth can be based, and in Chapter 1, we listed a number of developments in technology, or areas of techno-economic activity, which might between them form the basis of a next upswing. The more traditional public policies of support, encouragement, experiment and adoption of new technologies, should be complemented by more ambitious long-term procurement strategies for stimulating technology. It is, however, clear that there is a great deal of tension between the requirements of innovation-oriented procurement strategies and the current policies of many Western countries which are primarily directed at reducing government deficits, and so reducing the market role of governments.

The success of reindustrialization and technology policy depends to a large extent on the acceptance of new products and services by society at large. Information and awareness programmes for different target groups, including the general public, should be strongly considered here. In this respect there is an obvious link with the educational system.

Finally, there exist strong interrelationships between the demand side on the one hand, and the scientific and technological infrastructure on the other. Existing needs in society may influence or even force the scientific and technological research institutions to try to pave the way (in scientific or technological terms) to the fulfilment of these needs, ie existing needs may establish the research agenda. On the other hand, it may be that the market becomes aware of previously unspecified needs as the result of the emergence of new technological opportunities and technological opportunity will determine the nature of a new set of market needs. Taking these interactions into account, the main factors determining innovative performance can be summarized in the following model (Fig. 9.1).

Clearly reindustrialization policy must simultaneously tackle all three of the above model elements. In addition, governments must provide a suitable regulatory framework in which all three elements can develop effectively. The four main government policy instruments – procurement, regulation, finance and technical infrastructure – should be directed at the elements of the model in a balanced way.

Figure 9.1

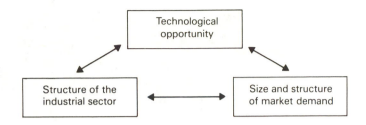

Finance, is an integral element of reindustrialization policy since it can greatly influence all other main elements. For example, public finance can significantly influence the rate and direction of infrastructural (and firm based) technological change; financial systems (including grants for equipment, innovations etc) can influence the structure and operations of the industrial sector; and the size and structure of market demand is to an extent influenced by capital availability and public policies affecting interest rates, tax levels, public sector expenditures, and so on. In this respect it is perhaps government financial strategies that act as the main link between technology and reindustrialization policies and macroeconomic policies.

Thus, in the *generic* area of finance, we see three broad levels of policy.

– Finance for R&D: this includes orienting finance of infrastructurally based R&D towards stimulating developments in main priority areas and in facilitating transfers to industry. It includes also utilizing government grants to orienting industrial R&D towards reindustrialization projects and achieving complementarity between the industrial and infrastructural streams of technological development.

– Finance and industrial structure: this involves influencing financing systems (both public and private) towards achieving the appropriate industrial structural dynamic. In general, it means increasing the availability of 'patient' money for long-term restructuring programmes in firms and of venture capital for new technology based start-ups.

– Overall fiscal climate: this involves establishing an overall climate conducive to private investment in reindustrialization projects by favourable tax regimes, directed public expenditures, moderate interest rates, and so on.

It should be a major aim of reindustrialization policy to ensure that financial policies at all three levels complement each other. Perhaps the most useful example in this respect, of overall policy coherence, can be found in Japan. Below is presented an extended model (Fig. 9.2) that includes government regulations and financial policies and structures.

Figure 9.2

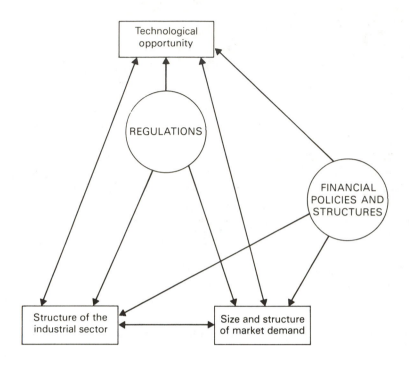

NATIONAL TECHNOLOGY PROGRAMMES

Earlier in this book we have discussed a number of specific policy areas and have emphasized the need for effective linkage mechanisms, both vertical and horizontal, in order both to achieve complementarities and avoid duplication and inconsistency within, and between, the various policy measures taken. In this section we shall describe briefly the use of major national programmes of technological development since we consider such programmes to be essentially a linkage or integrating mechanism, linking publicly funded and/or infrastructionally performed R&D to industrial companies and/or linking together different industrial companies. We shall consider two major programmes as exemplars: one that has proved its effectiveness (NASA's development of satellite communications in the US), and one that is in the very early stages of implementation (the Alvey Programme for the development of advanced information technology in the UK).

The role of NASA in the creation of a US civilian satellite communications industry

Teubal and Steinmuller (1983), in their evaluation of the role of NASA in the creation of a civilian satellite communications industry in the US, began by emphasizing that one of the major justifications of the public funding of R&D is that it may induce the private sector to undertake radical innovations which might otherwise not be undertaken, or whose introduction might be seriously delayed. The potential reduction in both technological and market risk in innovations arising as the result of major public R&D programmes may assist in overcoming the resistance which sometimes exists in private companies towards following revolutionary (as opposed to evolutionary) paths of technological development. In other words, they may assist to overcome managerial and institutional resistances to radical change and encourage the emergence of new techno-economic combinations.

NASA's involvement in the development of the US civilian satellite communications industry achieved the above justification. It is a prime example of effective linkage between a government R&D agency and private companies which led to the emergence of a new industry. It demonstrates also the effectiveness of public procurement of radically innovative new equipment.

The ECHO Programme NASA's ECHO programme was based on the principle of 'passive' satellite communication which involved 'bouncing' signals over the horizon. It demonstrated that the passive satellite approach resulted in unacceptably high signal power losses (only one part in 10^{18} of the transmitted power was returned to the receiving antenna).

The RELAY Programme It was not until NASA reached agreement with the Department of Defence that it was able to begin work on an active satellite design. (This agreement was later modified to allow NASA to engage in research on geosynchronous satellites.) This was an important step since, while the Department of Defence's interests might have prohibited private developments due to disclosure problems of sensitive information, NASA's disclosure requirements were such as to allow any firm access to its technological data base.

Thus we see that NASA became a crucial linkage mechanism for the transfer of technology into commercial use that might otherwise have become 'locked in' to the military system. Without this linkage, civilian development of active systems would probably have been seriously delayed.

The RELAY I programme for the development of a nonsynchronous active satellite accomplished its technological requirements. It represented a basic design solution that paved the way for incremental improvement and commercial adaptation. It created a large technological data base (included accumulated learning in the supplier companies) which allowed a variety of civilian and military engineering designs to be developed at less cost and with enhanced probability of technical success.

The SYNCOM Programme A critical limitation of nonsynchronous satellites such as RELAY I, was the requirement for tracking (moveable) antennas. Each of these tracking stations was extremely costly to build and, if continuous communications was required, necessitated the building of a series of satellites such that at least one would be above the required receiving area at any given time.

Despite some industrial resistance to the idea of a geosynchronous satellite, NASA supported research in this area which led to the development of the SYNCOM I satellite jointly with Hughes. While a nitrogen tank explosion on launch destroyed the communications capability of SYNCOM I, nevertheless the basic problem of orbital placement was solved. NASA soon followed up with the launch of SYNCOM II, which successfully established the viability of synchronous satellites, and all civilian communications satellites have subsequently been of the synchronous design.

SYNCOM I cost $20 million to develop and launch, and its failure to fulfil its communications role would have represented a severe setback to a private commercial company, which might have severely delayed further developments in this field. NASA, not being constrained by the requirement of profitability, was able to proceed rapidly with the launch of the highly successful SYNCOM II, thus demonstrating complete technological feasibility.

The ATS Programme The ATS programme was designed to explore a broad range of uses of satellite communications. As part of the programme, NASA developed a series of radically new ideas, thus effectively underwriting risks across a very broad range of innovations. ATS succeeded in making a number of notable technological contributions to satellite communications.

Teubal and Steinmuller have estimated that, without NASA involvement, the commercial satellite communications industry in the US would have emerged in 1970 at the earliest, rather than in 1965, at which date (1965) satellite communications were more efficient than alternative cable systems. By 1970, however, improvements in cable technology were such that cable systems would have been more efficient than the newly emerging (effectively 1965 vintage) satellite systems which would have been introduced, in the absence of NASA participation, by the later emerging industry. Given this factor, and given the considerable technical and financial risks involved in developing active geosynchronous satellite systems, the US civilian satellite communications industry – and in turn the industries in other countries – might have experienced further considerable delays in development.

Teubal and Steinmuller have divided NASA's contribution into three stages: invention; demonstration of feasibility; commercial development. The invention stage included a series of critical experiments which determined that no physical barriers existed to orbital transmission and reception. The demonstration of feasibility included the testing of a wide variety of system designs which by creating skill and knowledge had crucial implications for emerging supplier companies. Commercial development came about following the establishment by NASA of two quasi-private companies, COMSAT and INTELSAT, when commercial users began to undertake the contracting of commercial satellite communications systems and ground station installations. Thus we see a good example of a major national R&D that was effective throughout all the innovation stages (from invention, through production learning, to commercialization) and which utilized both supply factors (R&D funding, information transfer) and demand (public purchasing). The crucial role of NASA as the major coordinating mechanism (between innovation stages and between supply and demand) is obvious.

The Alvey programme for advanced information technology in the UK

The report of the Alvey Committee on 'A Programme for Advanced Information Technology' (Department of Industry, 1982) was the outcome of an initiative by Kenneth Baker, the Minister for Information Technology:

The catalyst to the formation of the Committee was the unveiling last October of Japan's Fifth Generation Computer Programme [ICOT, 1983], and Japan's invitation to other countries, including the UK, to discuss participation in the programme. The UK delegation to the conference in Tokyo at which the Programme was announced reported back to a conferenced in London in January, which was attended by a representative cross-section of industrialists and other experts. The scale and cohesiveness of this and other Japanese programmes . . . was seen by this conference as a major competitive threat . . . In the light of these factors the conference called for an urgent study into the scope for collaboration in the UK, geared to our particular strengths and requirements (DoI, 1982, p5).

One of the prime tasks of the Alvey Committee lay in identifying specific targeted priority areas in which the UK should build up technological strengths as a basis for commercial exploitation:

We see these priority areas as basic enabling technologies. We have had little difficulty in identifying them or the associated infrastructure and systems which link them . . . Necessary for any electronic based activity is secure access to world class software tools and technology together with the design tools and technology for Very Large Scale Integration (VLSI). Also essential for IT [information technology] is a leading edge knowledge of handling information – especially what is now developing as Intelligent Knowledge Base Systems (IKBS) – and of the interaction of man with machines (MMI) (DoI, 1982, p15).

The Committee acknowledged the strategic nature of developments in the four enabling technologies and emphasized increasing market restriction in these areas and a growing tendency for 'national appropriability' in the leading technological activity countries. In such circumstances, the importation of state-of-the-art knowhow and devices may become increasingly problematic. Thus :

The only option is to have a domestic capability in the enabling technologies. To achieve this a coherent programme is necessary. This must be a national effort based upon colloboration. Collaboration is essential for several reasons. First, as stated, the technology is intrinsically difficult and complex. No single organisation has the know-how to make sufficient progress on its own. Secondly, no one organisation has sufficient spare resources either in money or in particular in skilled manpower to tackle independently the high risk and long lead time type of projects which are involved. Thirdly, there are sufficient technical strengths in the UK to pursue these technologies successfully. However, these strengths are widely scattered in industry, the academic sector and research organisations. Compared with our competitors our overall research effort is badly fragmented. The interface between the research community is nowhere near as productive as it is in the US, for example. And our industry does not collaborate on basic research to the same extent as in Japan. The technical assets which we possess are not well mobilized as they need to be if we are to match the competition. A collaborative effort can help achieve this . . . As many of the technical areas need to be tackled simultaneously from more than one angle; the best line of approach will often not be known in advance. The form of co-operative working depends upon the sharing of information and results, the existence of confidence and trust between the rival schemes. This is possible only within a collaborative framework (DoI, 1982, p16 and 17).

While the Alvey Programme will facilitate collaboration at the research stage, commercial exploitation will be the responsibility of individual companies operating in wholly competitive conditions, although it is hoped that firms will capitalize on potential complementarities between their operations where these exist. In this respect, an important aspect of the Alvey Programme is its recommendation that collaboration be encouraged between small and large firms. To facilitate technological diffusion, in those areas where government bears the greatest proportion of the research costs the results will be seen as public property, and will be available for exploitation by any British company. Where individual companies bear most of the research costs, they will retain intellectual property rights.

In order to facilitate coordination between institutions and measures, Alvey recommended the establishment of a new directorate within the Department of Industry:

to provide a direct line of financial accountability and also to harmonise the programme with other DoI programmes for IT. The Directorate must be dedicated to the implementation of the programme and must have the resources to achieve this. . . . Inherent in our concept of the Directorate is the conviction that the programme cannot be implemented effectively unless one man is held ultimately responsible for its management ... To provide accountability he should report to a Board, which would serve as a Steering Committee, and which would supervise the overall strategy and management of the programme.

The Alvey Programme will cost £350 million over five years, of which the government will contribute two-thirds and industry will supply the remainder. Some £57 million will go to support research and training in academe, which will be 100 per cent publicly funded. As regards the rest of the programme, which will be carried out in industry, government funds will cover 90 per cent of the costs of projects in which wide and open dissemination of research results is required, and 50 per cent of the cost of other projects. This funding is, of course, for research only, and the costs of development, prototype testing, manufacturing and marketing will be carried wholly by industry. However, some £58 million has been earmarked for demonstrator projects linked to particular advanced applications of information technology.

It was recognized that the long-term implementation of the Alvey Programme would require an increase in the supply of graduates with high level skills in information technology. Accordingly, the University Grants Committee has agreed to increase the number of posts in information technology, both for teaching and for research. This initiative, it is hoped, will result in an extra 600 or so graduates annually. At the same time the Science and Engineering Research Council is to fund forty-five additional Research Fellowships in the areas covered by Alvey.

In summary we can see that Alvey is a programme based on the choice of certain fundamental enabling technologies, the core feature of the programme being one of coordination based on establishing efficient linkages between the different actors and institutions which constitute a currently fragmented, but in total considerable, national research base. In order to facilitate coordination and to maintain flexibility in the programme, a new institutional mechanism – the Alvey Directorate – has been established within the Department of Industry (now the Department of Trade and Industry).

While it is much too early to pass judgement on the effectiveness of the Alvey Programme, Land (1983) has made a number of interesting criticisms. One of these is essentially that the programme is one of 'technology push':

All but one of the non-civil service members of the committee represented suppliers or research interests. All members of the working groups represented the same interests. Of the 115 organisations which are listed as having provided substantive inputs to the committee only three can be said to represent the user rather than the supply or research side of the industry. The three were ICI, the CEGB and the Hospital for Nervous Diseases. The outcome of this selection is bound to be a one-sided viewpoint of the problems, and a set of proposals which favour certain kinds of solution over others (Land, 1983).

To set against this, Land applauds the recommendation of the Committee for bringing the user into the research programme in the area of intelligent knowledge base systems (IKBS).

A second major criticism levelled by Land is the omission from the list of enabling technologies of communication technology.

Communication technology, such as fibre optics, satellite communications, communication protocols, public and private networks, have a central role in the computer systems of the future. The communication industry is an important national resource. All the other technologies selected by Alvey interact with communication technology (Land, 1983).

It is interesting in this respect that the French appear to be tying their initiatives on information technology closely to the communications industry. In other words, communications appears to be the 'carrier' for a range of related developments in information technology in France.

Finally, it is worth adding that each of the projects associated with Alvey will be independently monitored for progress. Inbuilt evaluation, as we suggested in Chapter 3, should enable the Directorate continually to adapt the programme in the light of feedback from the evaluator groups and to take new initiatives where necessary.

TECHNOLOGY CHOICE

In Chapter 1 we presented a list of technologies that, it is being mooted, will contribute, to a greater or lesser extent, to the next economic (Kondratiev) upswing. Some of these technologies will make their major contribution in the renewal of existing sectors (robotics, flexible manufacturing systems.); others will largely generate new techo-economic combinations (biotechnology). It is unlikely, of course, that any one country will become world leader across the board, which implies the need for governments to select certain technologies and techo-economic combinations and to identify main priority areas. It is clear, for example, that in the UK information technology and its applications define a main priority area on which considerable national resources will be focused in a coordinated manner. (Main priority areas identified in France and Japan were shown in Tables 3.3 and 3.4).

The rational, systematic choice of national technological priorities is by no means a simple task, and procedures and institutional arrangements to this end vary considerably from country to country. (For procedures utilized in Japan, see Dore, 1983, and for an overview of procedures in a number of countries, see Irvine and Martin, 1983). Here we shall simply offer a set of questions that governments intent on technology choice might sensibly seek to answer.

- What is the long-term market potential of each techno-economic combination?

- Can public markets influence the rate and direction of development?
- To what extent do we bias resource allocation in favour of the limited set of technologies chosen from the broader range of alternatives?
- Is it possible to back fully a limited number of primary selections, while at the same time offering limited support (ie maintaining a limited capability) over a broader range of technologies?
- To what extent will the ensuing pattern of resource allocation – 'locked' largely into a handful of primary technologies – effectively reduce our national technological flexibility and hence our ability to respond to new techno-economic threats and opportunities as they arise?
- Are some technologies inherently more expensive or more difficult to develop than others? If so to what extent should this influence our primary selection?
- How does each technology match with our national stock of 'human capital' and with our identified set of comparative national technical, industrial and market strengths and weaknesses?
- How 'appropriable' to the nation are the benefits to be derived from each particular stream of technology?
- How can we achieve a reasonable balance between the resources devoted to industrial renewal and those devoted to the creation of new combinations?
- To what extent will each combination be subjected to especially stringent and difficult regulatory requirements in other countries?
- At what stage in the chain of technological development can we even begin to make rational choices between a variety of emerging techno-economic options?
- How 'broad' is each technological stream in terms of its range of potential techno-economic alternatives and combinations?
- Which actors and institutions should be involved in the selection process?
- To what extent are there interdependencies between the different technological streams?
- To what extent are we able to capitalize on potential synergies between the chosen streams of technology?
- Which institutions will play the major role in developing each of the chosen fields and/or which phase of development will they each concentrate on?
- Who will play the major coordinating role?
- How far should government involvement go, from the choice of broad technologies to the choice of individual products?
- At what stage will government's role begin to diminish in each area as private industry begins increasingly to dominate R&D activity?

– How do we allocate resources between (vertical) policies of technology choice and more general (horizontal) policies of support for innovation?

FEATURES OF A COHERENT POLICY

As we saw in Chapter 3, there are considerable differences between the innovation policies adopted by different countries. Some countries opt largely for rather general policies designed to create the right environment for innovation. Other countries intervene more directly in the innovation process, promulgating some combination of technologically or industrially nonselective (horizontal) measures and (vertical) measures of technology/industrial selection. More recently, there has been a general trend towards the increasing adoption of policies involving the selection and support of main priority areas. Whatever type or combinations of policies are adopted, we can say with confidence that they should contain at least the following features (the list is by no means exlcusive).

Coherence
The actions of the various institutions involved in policy formulation and implementation should be coordinated in order to avoid the promulgation of contradictory measures, especially between innovation and other policies. More positively, potential synergies must be sought and capitalized upon. Innovation policies and general macroeconomic policies must pull together.

Consistency
Innovation policies must be insulated from the dictates of the short-term political cycle. While this might not be too difficult to achieve with horizontal policies, it might be more difficult with vertical policies involving major programmes of restructuring. Innovation policy should not be the creature of party dogma.

Flexibility
While innovation policies should be consistent, they should not at the same time be inflexible. Policies must be capable of responding to changing industrial needs, threats and opportunities. Greater inherent flexibility might be achieved if the policy initiative has inbuilt 'learning by doing'. In other words, policy measures should incorporate continuous evaluation, with positive feedback to the policy system in order continuously to improve policy effectiveness.

Complementarity

Policies should not only complement each other, but they should complement also the strategic interests of domestic companies. This means that policy makers should be aware of the long-term strategic thinking within major national companies.

Realism

Policy makers must recognize the inherent limitations of public policy and accept them. Overoptimistic expectations, unmet, might result in disillusionment and the termination of promising initiatives. Policies should thus be based on a realistic assessment of industrial potential. Public policy makers should also recognize their own limitations: while, in consultation with industry, public bodies might be involved in the selection of rather broad areas of techno-economic activity, the choice of individual projects is probably best left in the hands of industrial managers.

We would like to emphasize once again that technological innovation policies, by themselves, are not enough; they must go hand in hand with the appropriate general economic and social policies. Governments must strive to create a favourable overall economic climate (low interest rates, moderate corporation tax regimes), a favourable social climate (stimulate the social acceptance of new technology and help overcome social and institutional rigidities and resistances to change), a relatively stable political climate (dramatic political swings create uncertainty) and avoid rapid policy changes (stop–go policies can deter the adoption by firms of the necessary long-term development strategies). In other words, reindustrialization can only occur effectively when government achieves overall policy coherence. Well thought out and implemented technological innovation policies are a necessary but not sufficient condition for successful reindustrialization.

Finally, throughout the book we have pointed to the structural nature of the current economic crisis and have emphasized the central role of technology in the structural changes we have described. In seeking solutions to the structural crises it is therefore obvious that technology cannot be regarded as a residual factor, nor can it be treated in isolation. We have taken the position that social, economic, industrial and technology policies must go hand in hand. From the policy standpoint, this has profound implications since, as pointed out above, it calls for an integration of technology policy into industrial, social and economic policies. This in turn has implications for the institutions involved in policy formulation and implementation. It implies an integration of the aims and means of a wide range of – usually independent – policy bodies. We consider technology as an effective integrative element in the broader policy area; we consider a suitable integrative mechanism to be reindustrialization policy.

REFERENCES

Department of Industry 1982 *A Programme for Advanced Information Technology.* HMSO

Dore R 1983 *A Case Study of Technology Forecasting in Japan: The Next Generation Base Technologies development Programme.* Technical Change Centre

Ergas H 1983 Innovation, More of Less. (Mimeo) OECD, Paris

Geldens J 1979 Een profielschets van Nederland. In Orde van Organizatieadviseurs *De Vennootschop Nederland.* Deventer

ICOT 1983 *Research Report on Fifth Generation Computer Systems Project.* Institute for New Generation Computer Technology, Tokyo, Japan

Irvine J and Martin B R 1983 *Project Foresight: An Assessment of Approaches to Identifying Promising New Areas of Science.* (Mimeo) University of Sussex, Science Policy Research Unit

Land F 1983 Information Technology: the Alvey Report and Government Strategy. (Mimeo) London School of Economics

OECD 1977 *Towards Full Employment and Price Stability* (McCrakken Report) Paris.

Rothwell R 1983 Firm Size and Innovation: A case of dynamic complementarity. *Journal of General Management.* Spring issue

Rothwell R and Zegveld W 1981 *Industrial Innovation and Public Policy.* Frances Pinter

Teubal M and Steinmuller E 1983 *Government Policy and Economic Growth.* Research Paper 153, *The Maurice Falk Institute for Economic Research in Israel*, Mount Scopus, Jerusalem

Twaalfhoven F and Hattori T 1982 *The Supporting Role of Small Japanese Enterprises.* Indivers Research, Schiphol, Netherlands

Index

271